JOHN MILTON,
ENGLISHMAN

JOHN MILTON,
ENGLISHMAN

by

JAMES HOLLY HANFORD

LONDON
VICTOR GOLLANCZ LTD
1950

Printed in Great Britain by
The Camelot Press Ltd., London and Southampton

TO
HIRAM HAYDN
BEST OF PUPILS, EDITORS, AND FRIENDS

CONTENTS

INTRODUCTION

THE OBJECT OF THIS BOOK is to describe the individual,
John Milton, in those aspects of his personality which relate most
closely to his function as an English poet. Nothing we know
about him or the times in which he lived is really irrelevant to
modern interest, and the most accidental details of his personal
and literary career are worth the pains which an army of
investigators has taken to assemble them. There are, however,
central issues which must determine a selection amid a body of
material so vast. These issues inevitably reflect a contemporary
sense of value.

Actually, Milton's fame, which is said always to have been
more or less a matter of politics, is as much so to-day as it ever
was. If seventeenth century Puritanism and the English Civil
War seem more remote to us than they did to Johnson or
Macaulay, it is only that the debate has been transferred to a
larger and more philosophic stage. There are three reasons for
Milton's remaining a controversial figure: He gave such
eloquent answers to questions that still divide mankind. He
made his own character an issue in the public causes for which
he fought. And as a poet he did not detach himself from his
imaginative creation. The present writer is less interested in
evaluating Milton as an artist, a thinker, or a man than he is in
explaining the processes of a creative personality, but he does
not expect or particularly wish to escape what others have
failed to escape: the betrayal of an attitude. As an American,
familiar with England and English tradition chiefly through
books, he sees Milton with a difference. As an observer of the
current world of revolution and reaction, peace and war, he
interprets the great protagonist of the struggles of another age
in the light of behaviour he has observed.

The emphasis implied in the title is one which Milton himself
suggests. On his way home from a year of foreign travel he
signed himself in a friend's autograph book in Geneva, Johannes
Miltonius, Anglus, adding an ethical couplet from his own
writings and the motto: "*Coelum non animum muto dum trans mare
curro*"—"I change my sky but not my mind when I cross the
seas." The mind which he did not change was the mind of a
man of virtue and an English patriot. Milton inherited the

emotions and the ideology of a great nationalistic movement which had identified itself with the cause of religious reformation and has appropriated the cultural and intellectual energies of the revival of ancient learning. He aspired in youth to celebrate his country's glories, beautifying old tradition as Spenser had done before him, and rivalling in his mother tongue the greatest achievements of other lands. In manhood his devotion was to what he believed to be the peculiar purposes for which God had elected England among the nations. He regarded himself as uniquely endowed to understand and interpret these purposes. When he saw them politically defeated, he assumed the role of a poet-prophet, proclaiming divine truth to after-times in a form that men would not willingly let die.

There is much in our own epoch to make us apprehend Milton vividly. We are as familiar as he was with the ardours of revolutionary hope, with the anxieties of an armed conflict on which the whole future of mankind seems to depend, with the passing heroic exultation of victory, with disappointment and frustration in the results of war, with deadly fear of ultimate disaster. We are familiar also with the problem of the man of higher sensitiveness and intelligence who undertakes to play a part in practical affairs, but, finding that events will not obey his will, takes refuge in a symbolic world, whether of religion or philosophy or art. Similar situations are always recurring in the world's history, and the way different individuals react to them in various times and places and under diverse systems of belief is as interesting a matter as any which the mind can contemplate. Such a concern, in the case of a great genius like Milton, leads to the desire to understand more deeply the inner workings of human nature, the interplay of emotion and idea, the relative weight of personal and social forces, the real springs of action.

The difficulty of doing so with a figure of the past is, of course, immense, and Milton's own articulateness is something which hinders as well as helps the process. For the autobiographic portrait which he gives us and on which our interpretation must mainly rest, is itself a figment of the mind. His personality as a poet and even as an apologist in prose is something other than the real man, as he lived, a fellow creature with ourselves. Yet the two bear a relation to each other, and we are not without means of tracing the lineaments behind the mask. In any case the pattern of Milton's life as he conceived it, the image of himself that he elaborated before the world, is a fascinating thing. Its essential feature was the doctrine of his own special calling and direct inspiration from on high. The idea was Hebrew and Hellenic as well as Christian in its origin, and it suited well both with the larger Puritan thesis of a British Israel and with the great tradition of poetic eloquence to which the nobler spirits of the age were drawn. How Milton came by and developed it, what kind of privileges and obligations it imposed on him, what consequences it had in his life and art will concern us throughout the ensuing narrative.

I have not been able in this study to give adequate discussion to many intricate questions of fact and interpretation which still tantalise inquiry, but have had simply to declare the conclusions which seem to me most consistent with general probability. The researches of E. M. W. Tillyard, W. R. Parker, J. M. French, the editors of the Columbia Milton and many others have been passed over with little or no mention. To deliberate their validity and relevance would be to construct another and more monumental Masson. I am indebted to the Trustees of Western Reserve University for the academic liberality which has given me leisure to write this book.

JAMES HOLLY HANFORD.

YELLOW SPRINGS, OHIO.
April, 1949.

CHAPTER ONE

CHRIST AMONG THE DOCTORS
1608–25

WHEN JOHN MILTON WAS BORN, on December 9th, 1608, England was post-Elizabethan. The great Queen had died five years before, capping a glorious career with tragic utterances worthy of herself:

> I saw one night my own body, exceedingly lean and fearful, in a light of fire. Are you wont to see such sights in the night? . . . All the fabric of my reign, little by little, is beginning to fall.

James the Scot ruled at Whitehall, with caution instead of statesmanship for his staff of office. He had suffered from being brought up an object of contention in a distracted court, where the best efforts of humanistic education were bound to be but little to the purpose.

"I have spanked his bottom," said his tutor, old George Buchanan, to a court lady who had reproached him for laying a hand on God's anointed, "and your ladyship may kiss it if you choose."

It added nothing to his real prestige that he had declared the theory of sovereignty in one pamphlet and the rules of poetry in another, or that he had philosophised about witchcraft and blasted tobacco in works better calculated to attain the status of best sellers than to do the public good. The crown of England was his by default, and he entered without security into a heritage which neither he nor his immediate forebears had done anything to create. He was to be Milton's sovereign, claiming a reverent loyalty, for a matter of seventeen years. And when he yielded the crown, it was to be to a king even more handicapped by circumstances and equally incapable of adapting himself to the necessities of the time.

Admittedly the difficulties for any monarch were great, if not insuperable. The Commons were restive even before the Queen was dead. As Elizabeth's grip weakened and her sturdier ministers left the scene, the voices of protest in Parliament took on a bolder tone. The monopolies wherewith her favourites had been rewarded were an easy object of attack by the increasingly aggressive merchant class. The rebellion of Essex had left its scar. A scramble of parvenus for James's favour shook the structure of government by talent, and the tradition of Elizabethan statecraft gave way to opportunism and unpatriotic intrigue. James had dismissed most of the old councillors and was surrounding himself with men he did not fear. Sir Walter Raleigh, chief foe of Spain, was in the Tower. Sir Francis Bacon, distrusted by Elizabeth and Burleigh, but now employable as an instrument of the royal prerogative against the Parliamentary movement, rose to the office of Lord Chancellor. George Villiers, first Duke of Buckingham, was shortly to insinuate himself as court favourite and manipulator of royal policy. Both were doomed to fall, victims to the people's hate.

The ecclesiastical establishment, so carefully maintained by Tudor power and policy, though its deep foundations were in the long run to prove secure enough, showed signs of cracking in its superstructure. Church questions were inevitably the ones which aroused the loudest clamour in those times. It is not that they were all important in the homes of individual Englishmen or in the daily communications of the market place. Then, as always, the primary elements of the good life —economic and personal security, freedom to come and go at will, choose one's sexual partner, beget and nourish children, work and find congenial recreation after work was done— were the engrossing objects of concern. But these freedoms were involved with others. And in the pursuit of them men were as yet relatively inarticulate. While the institutions which secured the secular rights of men were gradually coming to understand themselves, the Church, which had aspired to order the whole of life, and had formulated its programmes of old time, spoke fully and intelligibly. Religious issues were made to seem the test and touchstone of all others. As we look back on it, a great transfer of attention had been brought about in the desires and interests of humanity. Only a few persons tried to explain its workings. Henry Robinson might insist that the wars of religion were really struggles for economic and political power, but the world was largely convinced by its own rationalisations and saw in the conflict of rival causes a continuation of the battle between good and evil which had begun before the foundations of the world.

In England, by 1608, James had already held argument about the liturgy with the Puritan divines and found them proof against the less than angelic wisdom even of a defender of the faith. When Milton was eight, the King attempted in the Declaration of Sports to protect the easy pagan way of serving God by having a good time on holy days, and met with widespread opposition. When he was eleven, the Pilgrims took off from Plymouth to their refuge in New England, leaving their brother Puritans, of similar conviction but less tender conscience, to till the soil of popular unrest at home. It was not long before the bishops would have to look out, not only for their spiritual authority, inherited with an unfortunate flaw in the title from St. Peter, but for their emoluments and for their very lives.

For all these signs of weakening in the political and ecclesiastical structure which the Tudors had built up, the land was at peace, and much that was basic in English sentiment and habit remained unchanged. If patriotism no longer attached itself to the sovereign and his court as staunchly as it had done in the years following the defeat of the Armada in 1588, the tradition of those times was still remembered and its energies only awaited new leadership and a new interpretation of the English cause. Culturally the nation was still enjoying the fruits of a creative epoch. Shakespeare had not yet quite finished his work, and he had eight years more to live. Jonson, Drayton, Beaumont and Fletcher, Webster, Bacon and Donne were in the midst of their careers. The public theatre had but lately reached the highest point of its social and artistic significance. English music was pre-eminent in Europe. Elizabethan pageantry was crystallising itself in the court masque. The tournament was still in vogue as a chivalric pastime embodying the fictions of medieval chivalry. Popular amusements, though beginning to feel the hand of local law, stubbornly resisted advancing Puritanism and continued to reflect the heartiness of Merry England.

The life and traditions of the business and professional classes showed no less stability. English sobriety and civic consciousness had always characterised the thought and behaviour of the middle class, and it was among them that Puritanism had the strongest hold. But this Puritanism was fanatical only in spots. It did not in general preclude modest luxury and even culture. The legal profession was well organised

and strong. Medicine was rising gradually. It was possible
for merchants, yeomen, and professional men to achieve the
status of gentlemen, and the steady push of groups and individuals for power and dignity went on without conscious
revolutionary implications. If religious controversy was beginning to become too exciting, religion itself, for those not yet
immediately involved, remained a matter of placid interest
and deep satisfaction. The average Englishman was a connoisseur of sermons, a maintainer of domestic piety. He was
traditionally concerned over the danger of Romanism, and his
alarm had been made acute by the Gunpowder Plot. Consequently, he responded naturally to pressure for simplification
of the ritual and the completion of the "godly, thorough work
of reformation" begun by Luther. Both economic and spiritual
interests led the nation to friendliness with the Protestant
governments of northern Europe and hostility toward the
declining but still powerful imperialism of Catholic Spain.
The higher ecclesiastics had always been suspect. But so long
as the main body of the clergy were not too eloquent in disloyalty, the people continued to revere these surpliced gentry,
as they did the secular nobility itself.

In such an England, Milton was born and grew to manhood.
The deepest influences in shaping his personality are to be
found in his family tradition and domestic environments, but
this environment itself reflected the larger setting of the times.
His father, John Milton, Senior, was a self-made man of good
but not aristocratic background. He was the son of a Roman
Catholic yeoman, Richard Milton, of Stanton St. John in
Oxfordshire, a man whose conversion or sturdy adherence to
the proscribed religion had doubtless injured both his social
and his economic position. We know little of this Elizabethan
grandfather of the poet, but a record of 1601 shows him heavily
fined for non-attendance at the parish church. The father was
"brought up" at Christ Church, meaning probably that he
was educated as a chorister there. Manuscripts of musical compositions written by him have survived in the college library.
Family tradition declared that his father discovered him to be a
Protestant and disinherited him, whereupon John Milton,
Senior, went to London to seek his fortune at about the time
that Shakespeare did and at about the same age. Like Shakespeare, also, he found a friend, one eminent as a scrivener, by
whose advice and assistance Milton entered that profession.

The effects of this history on the sentiments and motivations of the Miltons it is tempting to conjecture. Added to the normal drive of the middle classes of those times to rise above their station would be, in the elder Milton's case, the need of recovering something which was his right. More obviously the tradition of loyalty to Protestantism might have derived intensity from the idea that the family was paying for a sacrifice which had been made for the faith.

The occupation of scrivener implied no training at the Inns of Court and classed its members rather with the merchant than with the professional group. The scriveners were legal stationers, notaries, law writers, and collectors. They might become moneylenders and brokers, in which capacity they had acquired a rather bad name in song and story. Their business was regulated and protected by a guild organisation, the Scriveners' Company. Milton was admitted to the freedom of this company in 1600 as an employee or apprentice of James Colebrun. By 1603 he had his own establishment at the sign of the Spread Eagle in Bread Street, the poet's birthplace.

There is every evidence that the elder Milton rose rapidly to such professional dignity as was compatible with his occupation and to an unusual degree of prosperity. He had four apprentices in 1621. In 1622 we find him enrolled as an assistant among the officers of the company; in 1625 he was chosen steward; in 1634 he was offered the mastership, but declined. During this period and later, court records show him to have been a party in several complicated lawsuits growing out of his activity as broker and trustee. Then in 1637 he was sued by Sir Thomas Cotton for the recovery of divers sums of money given to Milton and his partner, Bower, to be lent at interest and alleged to have been collusively misappropriated. By that time he had retired.

The total impression gained by reading the record of these actions is that the elder Milton may have taken advantage of his position in unethical if not illegal ways, but there is really no telling at this distance of time. We do know that he became rich. There are records of considerable investments in London real estate and of mortgage loans. As John Milton, Junior, grew up he became, as we shall see, more or less a participant in these business activities. It is possible that the father originally intended him, as eldest son, to become a partner. If so, the processes of his disillusionment are an unwritten but essential portion of the history of the Milton family and the making of a poet. We may note in this connection that the younger son, Christopher, who represented his father in the 1637 action, did follow the legal profession and, ascending beyond his father's sphere, became a member of the Inns of Court, a leading barrister, and finally a judge. John Milton the poet expresses a decided animus against the law and lawyers. Yet he was ready enough to engage in litigation on his own behalf.

Milton's mother, Sarah Jeffrey, was the daughter of a merchant tailor. There is no evidence that she had either dower or inheritance. Her sister, Margaret, is said to have been up to the time of her marriage in 1602 a servant at Newton Hall, a fact which is indicative of not necessarily menial position, but certainly a relatively humble family background. Of the mother's personality we learn only that she was a woman of "incomparable virtue and goodness," and, from Milton himself, that she was known throughout the parish for her charities. This sort of thing is often said by sons of mothers, and it is often true. We may suspect that she was a strong and religious-minded woman. Milton had an elder sister, Anne, who married when he was nearly fifteen. The younger brother was born, after the deaths of two earlier children, in 1615.

The early biographers are eloquent in their description of the atmosphere of the Milton home, with emphasis on the cultural interests and the paternal generosity and foresight of John Milton, Senior. The elder Milton evidently combined business astuteness and ambition with the literary and artistic enthusiasm which by this time had become the portion of a considerable number of prosperous members of the upper middle class in London. We may compare him with his contemporary, Thomas Campion, physician by profession, who carried his avocation of poetry and music far beyond the point of ordinary amateurism, or with the later Izaak Walton, whose distinguished role as essayist and biographer has obscured the fact that he was a hard-working and successful merchant. Milton's father was himself, like Campion, a composer of distinction, and at least a dabbler in verse. He contributed a madrigal to one of the most famous collections of the day, *The Triumphs of Oriana*, a collaborative enterprise in honour of Elizabeth.

The names here associated with his are those of composers of high standing at a period when English music, in happy association with poetry, was of an excellence unsurpassed in later times. Thomas Morley, the editor, who had been a pupil of William Byrd and organist of St. Paul's, is still remembered as author of the best book of Elizabethan musical theory and the composer of many exquisite airs and madrigals. John Wilbye and Thomas Weelkes, fellow contributors with the elder Milton, were equally distinguished. The mention of these names suggests the associations of Milton's childhood. It is not surprising that we find him later in intimate acquaintance with one of the chief successors of this Elizabethan professional group. Other compositions of the elder Milton are recorded and preserved, notably settings of four psalm tunes in the widely used Protestant hymn-book of Ravenscroft. His virtuosity was put to the test in a prodigious vocal work of symphonic proportions, now lost—"an *In Nomine* of forty parts," for which, according to Phillips, he was rewarded with a gold medal and chain by a Polish prince to whom he presented it. These facts are not the less important because they have come down to us bare of personal detail. It is evident that Milton's father was an accomplished artist, if not a genius. His son was later to say to him in Latin verse, "We share the muse between us."

The social and personal implications of the elder Milton's musical career are no less relevant than the artistic. The point is that he had been and might have continued to be a professional, but made a choice which, while moving him only from one questionable status to another, gave a better chance of economic security and ultimately a greater dignity. Aubrey, and he alone of the biographers, says that Milton "gained a plentiful estate by music and left it off many years before he died." The son inherited music only as an amateur accomplishment consistent with gentility, but he inherited also some of the traditions of a family which had an artistic commodity to market under the patronage system with all its human complications.

Something may be added as evidence that John Milton's boyhood environment was literary as well as musical. There exists in manuscript a number of poems by one John Lane, among them a continuation of Lydgate's metrical romance, *Guy, Earl of Warwick*, in twenty-six cantos, dated 1617, for which "Johannas Milton, Londoniensis civis," has written a complimentary sonnet. Lane has himself introduced into another poem a passage in praise of the elder Milton's music.

Among Lane's published works are a poem denouncing the
vices of Elizabethan England, and an elegy on the death of the
Queen. He was no great luminary, but he may nevertheless
have played his part in determining the interests and ambitions
of his friend's son.

Encouragement in literary and intellectual ambition Milton
certainly received from older persons at an early age.

> My father [he says in the *Second Defense of the English People*]
> destined me while yet a little boy for the study of humane
> letters, which I seized with such eagerness that from the
> twelfth year of my age I scarcely ever went from my lessons
> to bed before midnight; which, indeed, was the first cause
> of injury to my eyes, to whose natural weakness there were
> also added frequent headaches. All which not retarding my
> impetuosity in learning, he caused me to be daily instructed
> both at the grammar school and by other masters at home;
> and then, when I had acquired various tongues and also
> some not insignificant taste for the sweetness of philosophy,
> he sent me to Cambridge, one of our two national universities.

This clear testimony, written in long retrospect, is confirmed by
an earlier utterance in a Latin poem addressed to his father
when Milton was enjoying the fruits of literary leisure at
Horton.

> You did not command me, Father, to go where the way lies
> open broad and there is freer field for earning lucre; where
> the hope of gain shines golden and sure. Nor did you drag
> me to the bar, to grope among the nation's ill-guarded laws,
> nor damn my ears to the insipid clamour of pleaders. . . . When
> at your cost, dear Father, I had mastered the tongue of
> Romulus and seen all the graces of it, and had learned the
> noble idiom of the magniloquent Greeks, fit for the mouth of
> Jove himself, you persuaded me to add to these the flowers
> which France boasts; and the speech which the modern
> Italian pours from his degenerate lips, bearing witness in
> every accent of the barbarian tumults; and the language in
> which the singers of Palestine speak their mysteries.

Elsewhere in the same poem Milton claims his father as an
older companion and fellow worker in the arts.

> If it has been your fate to beget me a poet, why do you
> think it strange if, being so closely united by the precious

tie of blood, we pursue kindred arts and related interests: Phœbus himself in his desire to divide himself between two persons, gave one half to me and the other half to my sire, and thus we, father and son, possess the divided deity.

Finally, in *The Reason of Church Government*, written in 1641, Milton attributes his conviction that he might become a great writer to the praises given by others to his early efforts.

After I had for my first years, by the ceaseless diligence and care of my father (whom God recompense!) been exercised to the tongues, and some sciences, as my age would suffer, by sundry masters and teachers, both at home and at the schools, it was found that whether aught was imposed me by them that had the overlooking, or betaken to of mine own choice in English, or other tongue, prosing or versing, but chiefly by this latter, the style, by certain vital signs it had, was likely to live.

Though he was here referring to a later period and rather to the encouragement of his teachers than of the members of his family or their friends, it seems reasonable to suppose that his father was the first of those who noticed the evidences of his genius.

A further indication of parental interest and pride is the fact that, at the age of ten, Milton sat before a distinguished artist for his portrait. The canvas survives in all its original beauty, and serves better than any verbal record could do to bring before us the boyhood charm of one who retained, through all the passionate and violent experiences of his life, a winsomeness which drew toward him both men and women and sorted well with the sweeter aspects of his genius. The picture is the work of Cornelius Janssen, a predecessor of Van Dyck, or of his more famous teacher, Marcus Gheerhaerts, the younger, who had flourished at the court of Queen Elizabeth and was now "picture-drawer to his Majesty," James I. It shows the boy in a stiff, brocaded doublet, not unlike that of the Droeshout Shakespeare, but richer and with a delicate lace collar setting off the finely moulded head. The cheeks have a ruddy glow. The hair is auburn. Lips and chin are sensitive and of a singular loveliness. But for the inscription, we might fancy the portrait to belong to a still earlier period in Milton's childhood, yet there is maturity of intelligence in the clear and steady eyes, confirming in every way our impression of Milton as a boy of high and acknowledged promise, the natural object of stimulating attention from adults.

The biographer, John Aubrey, says that Milton was already a poet when this portrait was painted. He himself, as we have seen, dates the beginning of his severe study from his twelfth year. By that time he was already at St. Paul's School, and the lineaments of his boyhood personality would seem to be clearly before us. Some important questions nevertheless remain unanswered. The early biographers repeat Milton's statements and give the name of his tutor as Thomas Young, a Puritan divine, friend of the minister of the Miltons' parish church. Aubrey, quoting the authority of the younger brother, Christopher, adds the detail that his father ordered the maid to sit up with him at his studies till twelve or one o'clock. Young, we know, could have been Milton's tutor in London only between the years 1618 and 1620. Was he kept out of school a year or more at this time? Or had there been earlier tutors and was he only then entering St. Paul's? And what of the headaches and eyestrain and the fact that Milton was older than most boys when he finished school?

The biographers conjecture this and that according to their general idea of Milton's personality. I venture to add that his later illnesses suggest a nervous origin the nature of which would be clearly revealed in his childhood patterning if we had the facts. His later insistence on the idea that thoroughness of preparation is more important than speed of progress sounds to me like a rationalisation of events injurious to his self-confidence in early life, though successfully compensated by intellectual achievement. The problem is posed again by complaints about the slowness of his maturation ("I do notice a certain belatedness in me") considered against the fact, which he also recognised, of his superior capacity ("abilities haply not the worst for two and fifty degrees of northern latitude"). It is a question, also, whether his relations with his wonderful father were exactly as he and his biographers interpreted them, and whether his expressions of sympathy with his sister, Anne, and his willingness to all but adopt her children may not have involved emotional dynamics which were concealed from him as they are from us. The reader may pass judgment on these matters as the narrative goes on, but the burden of proof is in any case on those who insist on seeing Milton merely as a healthy, happy little pigeon of St. Paul's, with extraordinary advantages and aptitudes, and no personal or family liabilities other than the fact that his eyesight would not stand the strain to which his passion for study tended to put it.

The latest and best student of Milton's school life, Professor D. L. Clark, raises the question whether the poet may not have projected his later illnesses and eye trouble back on the memory of his childhood. He points out that in the autobiographical passages written before his blindness Milton recalls only the hard work, the high ambition, and the delight which he took in literature, particularly poetry. It is in a defence of his personality against an attack which had made his blindness a visitation of God that he first generalises his physical fragility. "Devoted even from a boy to the study of humane letters and always stronger in mind than in body, I set an inferior value upon the service of the camp, in which I might have been easily surpassed by an ordinary man of a more robust make." The idea that he injured his eyes by overwork in childhood is an extension of the thought that he lost them finally in a deliberate martyrdom, "overplied in liberty's defence." Clark reminds us that all the traditions of controversy required a speaker to present himself in as favourable a light as possible, that the best rebuttal to an accusation which, though meaningless to us, would then have carried weight would be that his blindness had been coming on from childhood.

I interpret Milton's defences more inwardly than Clark, but I find his conclusions as to the facts of Milton's schooling quite consistent with the ideas I have put forth. The poet, it is conjectured, entered school at the normal age of seven, but eye trouble (not necessarily persistent or acute), combined with the overload of extra-curricular studies, retarded him so that he entered college a few years later than he ordinarily would. He may have stayed out between 1618 and 1620 while Young coached him in the regular studies of the fourth or fifth form, but more probably Young gave him special instruction to supplement the school work. The essential fact here is that Milton, though brilliant, was retarded. The traumatic effects of this might easily last a lifetime, however it may have been explained to him. Something of this sort—and not albinism, congenital syphilis, or other extraordinary and sensational impairment—is, in my opinion, the "secret of John Milton."

Milton's entry into the school, whether in the first form at the age of seven or a few years later, brought him the experience of one of the great educational agencies of his time, the foundation on which the Oxford reformers, Colet and Erasmus, had staked their hopes of a truly Christian humanism for England. The old ordinance written by Colet quaintly set forth its combined scholarly and religious aims.

> I would they were taught all way in good literature, both Latin and Greek, and such as have the very Roman eloquence joined with wisdom, especially Christian authors that wrote their wisdom with clean and chaste Latin, either in verse or in prose, for my intent is by this school especially to increase knowledge and worshipping of God and our Lord Jesus Christ and good Christian life and manners in the children.

The original curriculum, with its preference for Christian writers, had changed by Milton's time, but the ideals of sound learning, pure Latinity, and pure religion were still its guiding principles. The discipline was in our eyes incredibly Spartan. Boys assembled at seven from their London homes, for there were day scholars only; they sat on backless benches without desks, all eight forms in a single room, till eleven and again from one to five. Rewards, in the form of honours and money prizes, and punishments, including whipping, were freely administered. Latin began in the first form, Greek in the fifth, with memorisation of the rules. The authors read included the major classics in both languages, including some of the maturest and most difficult. Hebrew grammar and the Psalms were studied in the last year.

Much was made of the rhetorical analysis of the ancient classics and their imitation in prose and verse, the object being mastery of the very eloquence of the originals in their own tongue. The exercises were those of the Roman schools, and the motivation similar, except, of course, for the more exotic character of a discipline so far removed from its original setting. Milton's reaction to it was acceptance, but with reservations. When he comes to construct his own model school, it is, as we shall see, a restoration of what he believed to have been the institutes on which the Renaissance grammar schools were actually founded. But he implies that the actual practices come far short of that. He is sure that Latin can be learned much faster than it is; he wants more substance to the curriculum; he denounces the "preposterous exaction of forcing the empty wits of children to compose themes, verses, and orations which are the acts of ripest judgment and the final work of a head filled by long reading and observation." These are later, professional reflections. They throw no light on the question whether Milton thought he himself had been well or ill treated educationally by the regular discipline at St. Paul's, for he may have escaped its limitations either by not being there in the first years or by the work with tutors.

The critical attitude was a habitual one with him and doubtless goes well back into his school life, but he was convinced that his own basic training, however acquired, was sound and right.

> For this good hap I had from a careful education to be inured and seasoned betimes with the best and elegantest authors of the learned tongues, and thereto brought an ear that could measure a just cadence, and scan without articulating: rather nice and humorous in what was tolerable, than patient to read every drawling versifier.

A clearer reflection of his temper as a student and of his responsiveness to the literary curriculum is in the following:

> I had my time Readers, as other have, who have good learning bestow'd upon them, to be sent to those places, where the opinion was it might be soonest attain'd: and as the manner is, was not studied in those authors which are most commended; whereof some were grave Orators & Historians; whose matter me thought I lov'd indeed, but as my age then was, so I understood them; others were the smooth Elegiack Poets, whereof the Schooles are not scarce. Whom both for the pleasing sound of their numerous writing, which in imitation I found most easy; and most agreeable to nature's part in me, and for their matter which what it is, there be few who know not, I was so allur'd to read, that no recreation came to me better welcome.

Milton is here giving an account of his developing ethical idealism and the main relevance of the passage is, I think, to his writing of erotic Latin elegiac verse in college, but the mild reaction to the grave historians and orators, the eager one to poetry, sounds authentic for St. Paul's. Milton half confesses sharing in his tender years the characteristics of a type which he later describes as "of soft and delicious temper, who will not so much look upon truth herself, unless they see her elegantly dressed." For such a person, granted competent Latinity, the processes of verbal and æsthetic instruction would not seem dull under a good teacher. He would read, analyse, paraphrase, and imitate, without rebellion and with an increasingly creative sense. Certainly the effects of his classical rhetorical training are evident in all his work, and the ideals which animated it in no small measure determined his career. English, on which education would now rely for a comparable result, was not included in the formal curriculum at St. Paul's, but Milton must have picked up, even from his academic masters, many valuable suggestions regarding the language and literature of his mother tongue. The Headmaster, Alexander Gill, had ideas on the subject, having written a book on English spelling, etymology, prosody, etc., with many references to and quotations from the English poets.

Of other but equally deep significance for the moulding of Milton's personality and the focusing of his purposes is the fact that the school was dedicated to the Boy Jesus. There stood in Colet's time, though not in Milton's, over the Headmaster's chair a beautifully wrought figure of the divine Child seated in the attitude of one teaching, which all the flock as they entered and left school saluted with a hymn. The prayer for Monday afternoon was designed to impress on the students the episode of Christ in the Temple.

> Our Lord and Master, Sweetest Jesus, who while yet a boy of twelve years, disputed in such manner among those doctors in the temple at Jerusalem that all were amazed at thy most excellent wisdom, we ask thee that in this thy school, of which thou art head and patron, we may daily learn that learning and that wisdom, whereby first we may know thee, Jesus, who art the true wisdom, then out of that knowledge worship and be like thee, and in this short life walk in the way of thy teaching, so following thy steps that, as thou thyself hast attained, we descending out of this light, may also blessedly attain some portion of His glory through thy grace.

The founders knew what they were doing when they devised this ritual. No teacher of those times would question the wisdom of encouraging intense identification with Christ, and one imagines that the exemplum would often have been found to produce dramatic results on the behaviour of sensitive and able children like Milton. It may, of course, be argued again that Milton's specification of his twelfth year as the beginning of a new seriousness in work is a matter of later interpretation. My own opinion is that he experienced at school the kind of childish conversion which the pious Colet had anticipated. The pattern, as we shall see, is a recurrent one.

> The childhood shows the man,
> As morning shows the day. Be famous then
> By wisdom;

he was afterwards to make Satan say to Christ. It is not inconsistent with what we know of pre-adolescent adaptation to think that the fantasy and the resolve could have operated powerfully in him at that time.

Of Milton's personal relations in the St. Paul's period we have some important information. Here obviously was to be his problem. His protected childhood had presumably failed to prepare him for the ordinary associations of life, and it is fairly evident that his progress toward independence was slow. That he was only a day student was probably fortunate. The rough give and take of a boarding school might well have been for him, as it was for Shelley, a violent experience. At St. Paul's it was possible to profit by the day's instruction, shine in the master's eyes, and return at night to nourish dreams of greatness. But Milton was lovable and he had a need of friendship. It is interesting, therefore, to look as closely as the evidence permits at the two associations of personal character which we know him to have formed at St. Paul's.

The first is the memorable friendship with Charles Diodati, which was to continue till the poet's manhood. Diodati was of exactly Milton's age, but two years ahead of him in school. As a boy of foreign ancestry, though thoroughly Anglicised, Diodati must have shown some differences in appearance and culture from his fellows. Later evidence proves him to have been an outgoing personality. Mature, social, not over-serious, but of sufficient intellectual and æsthetic interests, he was probably thoroughly at home in the society of St. Paul's. His family tradition would have given him a unique position in the school. His grandfather had been a Protestant exile from Italy; his father, Theodore, born at Geneva in 1573, but educated in England and at Leyden, was a physician of distinction. An uncle, Giovanni, was one of the leading Protestant theologians of the time. Milton's interest in the family was later demonstrated by his going out of his way to look up the ancestral home in Lucca and by his sojourn in the Geneva establishment of Giovanni Diodati. He may well have been a visitor in earlier years in the household of Theodore. The inference that he had special intimacy with Charles Diodati at St. Paul's rests on their later friendship, but it is natural to suppose that Milton found in him from the first a protector and an appreciative companion. Diodati's attitude toward the beautiful and sensitive spirit who so obviously belonged to another world than this was, as we shall learn from his own lips, a mixture of admiration and concern. The influence of so positive and self-possessed a personality must have been powerful in determining Milton's activity and ideals at a time when something more than the aid and counsel of his elders was sorely needed.

Milton's other St. Paul's friend was Alexander Gill, Jr., son of the Headmaster and himself usher or undermaster in the school. He was nine years Milton's senior, an exhibitioner at Trinity College, the author of a Latin elegy on Prince Henry. He was from later evidence a person capable of politically imprudent utterance in the fellowship of university wits. Milton's interest in him is known to us from two letters addressed to him in 1628 when the poet was at Cambridge and one from Horton in 1634, by which time they are fellow connoisseurs in the writing of Latin verse. It is remarkable, though not perhaps surprising, that the only two relationships which Milton seems to have carried over from his school days should have been with persons so completely unlike himself as Gill and Diodati. Evidently he admired their dash and brilliancy, and, putting forth his best effort to win attention, accepted their patronage and expanded under their appreciation of his talents. With Gill the relationship is more intellectual, with Diodati more emotional. In either case, it is Milton's first and perhaps his only experience of junior membership in a coterie of like-minded friends, banded in the enjoyment of learning and properly scornful of Philistine dullness. Even this experience was partial, and later Milton shows himself capable of rejecting the opportunity of very similar associations with disrelish and even hostility. The fact is that his memories of academic happiness in youth appear to associate themselves chiefly with St. Paul's. He never speaks ill of the school as he almost invariably does of the university. It gave him the groundwork of humanistic ideals which he was thereafter to defend against scholastic pedantry. It gave him confirmation of parental hope. Its memories enriched his later years.

When Milton paid tribute along with others to Edward King in "Lycidas" he wrote lines describing the idyllic association of students in work and play. These lines apply officially to Cambridge, and doubtless are idealisations of experiences there, but they contain also, I believe, recollections of earlier days of more consistent happiness. Milton reinforces his sentiment regarding King and his later acquaintances with the much more powerful feeling for Diodati. The rough satyrs who dance unrebuked and the genial mentor who listens with friendly ear to the fresh songs of the academic shepherds were first known to Milton, not on the reedy banks of Cam, but within the cloistered spaces of St. Paul's.

Together both, ere the high lawns appeared
Under the opening eyelids of the morn,
We drove afield, and both together heard
What time the gray-fly winds her sultry horn,
Batt'ning our flocks with the fresh dews of night,
Oft till the star that rose, at evening, bright,
Toward Heav'n's descent had sloped his west'ring wheel.
Meanwhile the rural ditties were not mute,
Tempered to the oaten flute,
Rough Satyrs danced, and fauns with cloven heel
From the glad sound would not be absent long.

Such voices of delight continued to haunt Milton throughout his life. For all this the seriousness of his early years is what he took greater pains to have the world remember and it is this, for better or worse, to which one is obliged to give the strongest accent. Students of Milton have traditionally quoted his description of Christ's boyhood in *Paradise Regained* as being essentially a transcript of his own. More recent writers tend to react against the sentimental fallacy implied in such interpretation, reminding us that the lines in question were composed by a poet aged sixty-three as a holy meditation appropriate to the Son of God at the beginning of His vigil in the wilderness. There is perhaps a balance to be struck between extremes in this, and our conclusion must be based on knowledge of the ways, not of any poet's, but of Milton's imagination. At any rate, I give the lines, feeling well assured that there is an analogy between his own boyhood resolves and the ideas which he puts into the mouth of the Saviour of mankind:

> When I was yet a child, no childish play
> To me was pleasing, all my mind was set
> Serious to learn and know, and thence to do
> What might be public good; myself I thought
> Born to that end, born to promote all truth,
> All righteous things: therefore, above my years,
> The Law of God I read, and found it sweet,
> Made it my whole delight, and in it grew
> To such perfection that, ere yet my age
> Had measured twice six years, at our great Feast
> I went into the Temple, there to hear
> The teachers of our Law, and to propose
> What might improve my knowledge or their own,
> And was admired by all; yet this not all
> To which my spirit aspired; victorious deeds
> Flamed in my heart, heroic acts; one while
> To rescue Israel from the Roman yoke,
> Then to subdue and quell o'er all the earth
> Brute violence and proud tyrannic power,
> Till truth were freed, and equity restored:
> Yet held it more humane, more heav'nly, first
> By winning words to conquer willing hearts,
> And make persuasion do the work of fear;
> At least to try, and teach the erring soul,
> Not wilfully misdoing, but unaware
> Misled; the stubborn only to subdue.
> These growing thoughts my mother soon perceiving,
> By words at times cast forth, inly rejoiced,
> And said to me apart: "High are thy thoughts,
> O Son; but nourish them, and let them soar
> To what highth sacred virtue and true worth
> Can raise them, though above example high;
> By matchless deeds express thy matchless Sire."

The effects on Milton's boyhood of the outward life of London are more difficult to measure than those of home and school. London was already a noisy and in spots a sordid place, with its narrow streets, its rioting apprentices, its busy wharves and market-places. But it was easier then for ear and eye to avoid the noise and sordidness, for the silver-streaming Thames, the white towers along its shores, the tolling bells of city churches, were not, as now, overwhelmed with the smoke and clatter of the age of industry. It was also a venerable place. Monuments of the past, in the form of ancient buildings, civic ceremonials, tournaments and pageantry were there in rich abundance. We know that Milton was keenly interested in history and romance, and these things would naturally have impressed him, as they had done Spenser before him, in his daily journeyings from Bread Street to St. Paul's. The Cathedral itself was, of course, an object of daily familiarity. The boys played in the yard and walked the studious cloister. John Donne preached there in Milton's time. The un-Puritan description in "Il Penseroso" is evidence enough that the poet received profound impressions from the building and its service.

> There let the pealing organ blow,
> To the full voiced quire below,
> In service high and anthems clear,
> As may with sweetness, through mine ear,
> Dissolve me into ecstasies,
> And bring all Heav'n before mine eyes.

The social pleasures of the town, except for those which were to be had in his father's house, presumably came later. He may well have seen and heard gossip of the great survivors of the tradition of Elizabethan letters, but one doubts if he ever had peeped behind the shutters of the Mermaid, Dog or Triple Tun, where the poets were in rousing session, with Ben Jonson at their head.

Of Milton's boyhood verse only two psalm paraphrases seemed to him, when he came to publish the first volume of his poems in 1645, of merit enough to be preserved, and he was at pains to indicate in a head note that they were "done by the Author at fifteen years old." It is not believed that they were school exercises. Milton had begun the study of Hebrew at St. Paul's but the paraphrases required would probably have been in Latin. The stylistic influence which has been pointed out as dominant in Milton's renderings is that of Sylvester's translation of the epic of creation written by the Huguenot Du Bartas. The appeal of this turgid and over-ornamented poem for Milton is hard for us to understand, but we are reminded that Dryden also admired it in adolescence, though later he thought it "abominable fustian." Milton too must have outgrown it or if he retained a fondness have judged it of no poetic worth in comparison with Spenser, for he never mentions it in paying tribute to the bards to whose lineage he belonged. It remains true, however, that this poem, with its visualisation and adornment of the scriptural story, its high literary pretension and its edifying purpose is the most obvious English counterpart of *Paradise Lost*. It was well remembered by Milton when his epic was written, and the heavenly muse, Urania, whom Sylvester elaborately invokes in a separate poem, became the symbol of his own highest inspiration.

Milton's paraphrases are not without their eloquence. There is a buoyant enthusiasm in the meter, and the style is brightly coloured, though unoriginal. The second piece, Ps. cxxxvi, still finds a well-deserved place in the hymn-books.

> Let us with a gladsome mind
> Praise the Lord, for He is kind,
>   For His mercies aye endure,
>   Ever faithful, ever sure.

The sage and serious youth was evidently already the master of his English speech. It was not, however (in spite of Aubrey's statement), until a few years later that Milton really became a poet. By that time he was already in college and his sensitive spirit had been subjected to certain shocks which, as I shall try to show in the succeeding chapter, created a new epoch in his emotional experience.

CHAPTER TWO

ACADEMIC EXERCISE

1625–32

MILTON'S NAME IS ENTERED on the registry of Christ's College, Cambridge, under the date February 12th, 1625. He actually matriculated on the ninth of April following, just before the opening of the Easter term, being then sixteen years and four months old. What he was doing in the months preceding is not known. He may have retained a connection with St. Paul's, he may have worked with a tutor, he may have studied independently. The French and Italian which he says he learned at his father's expense could have occupied him at this time. The statement that he had already got some taste of the sweetness of philosophy before he went to Cambridge suggests an exploration of books not read at school. In any case he was in the process of becoming "full ripe" for academic life.

The first recorded episode at Cambridge is some kind of quarrel with the authorities. John Aubrey, giving Christopher Milton as his source of information, reports it as follows: "His first tutor there was Mr. Chappell, from whom receiving some unkindness he was afterwards (though it seemed opposite to the rules of the college) transferred to the tuition of one Mr. Tovey." Between the lines of the manuscript Aubrey has added "whipped him," thus making the affair dramatic. This could easily be mere gossip. Corporal punishment was still in use at Cambridge for younger students, but the prælectors and deans were said to have administered it, not the tutors. Milton himself alludes in his first Latin elegy to a period of exile from the college and says he has no wish to endure longer the "threats of the stern master and other things to which my nature cannot submit." The phrase is ambiguous, but may mean whipping. The elegy is headed *anno aetatis* 17 by which Milton usually means "at the age of 17." Its setting is spring. The college records show that he was back for the Lent term of 1625-6 under a new tutor. We infer that his rustication took place about March of his second academic year.

Whatever the specific facts, it is evident that Milton's college life was not untroubled, and it is a safe conjecture that he was ill equipped to meet the attitude of persons less willing than his earlier well-wishers to accept him at his own valuation. We see him as a young idealist, learned, brilliant, full of creative energy, but open to injury and in need of wise guidance from some really mature person capable of recognising at once the strength and the weaknesses of his personality. His portrait at the age of twenty-one, cherished long after his death by his widow and considered by her to be his one authentic likeness, is almost too good, from the biographer's viewpoint, to be true. It confirms our impression of his youthful delicacy and makes his college epithet, "The Lady of Christ's," seem appropriate.

B

It may or may not suggest to the observer the determination and the intransigence which went with his gentler traits. We shall return to the incident of Milton's rustication and to the evidence that there was strain as well as stimulation in his college relationships. It is necessary meanwhile to present something of the general academic setting as background to his behaviour and his words.

It was, as Milton tells us later, his parents' intention that he should enter the Church, and many years were to elapse before he actually rejected this, to outward appearances, natural and congenial destiny. His real purposes, however, were obviously more literary than religious. He sets forth for the University with the honours of a successful scholar and poet on his head, in confident expectation of distinguishing himself before the more illustrious audience of a great intellectual centre. His life at Cambridge is to be that of a humanist in the approved tradition of the Christian Renaissance.

Unfortunately for him, the educational system was still far from humanistic. Students were assigned to tutors, whose personal interests to some extent determined the direction of their studies, but the main objective of training was fitness to perform in the scholastic exhibitions. To this end the study of logic was insisted on and must have occupied a good portion of the student's intellectual energy. Some idea of the procedure, as between teacher and pupil, may be gained from a contemporary account of Joseph Mede, the most popular and famous tutor in Milton's college.

After he had by daily lectures well grounded his pupils in Humanity, Logic, and Philosophy, and by frequent conversations understood to what particular studies their parts might be most profitably applied, he gave them his advice accordingly; and, when they were able to go alone, he chose rather to set everyone his daily task than constantly to confine himself and them to precise hours for lectures. In the evening they all came to his chambers, to satisfy himself that they had performed the task he set them. The first question which he used to propound to everyone in his order was "*Quid Dubitas?*" What questions have you met in your studies to-day? for he supposed that to doubt nothing and to understand nothing were verifiable alike. Their doubts being propounded, he resolved their *quaeres*, and so set them upon clear ground to proceed more distinctly; and then, having by prayer commended them and their studies to God's protection and blessing, he dismissed them to their lodgings.

Mede, to judge from his letters and from the stories which have come down about him, was a unique person, the talking point of the student body and one whose personality served to mitigate the boredom of instruction. One would like to think, with Marjorie Nicolson, that he is memorialised as Old Damoetas who loved to hear the shepherd pipings in "Lycidas." The poet piped for him, of course, as he did in open consistory to all. But he did not come under him as tutor, his *quaeres* being resolved, as we have seen, by less genial lips.

The day's routine of life at Cambridge has been assembled from the records by David Masson. Students flocked at 5 a.m. to the college chapel, roused from their slumbers by the ringing of the bell. The morning service of the Church might be followed on some days by a short homily from one of the Fellows. Then breakfast and the day's work. There were "college studies," including lectures, examinations, and tutorials; and there were "university exercises," when the students assembled with those of other colleges in the "public schools" of the university to hear lectures and take part in disputations. After four hours or so thus spent, the students dined together in their several college halls. After dinner more declamations and disputations either in college or the public schools, then free time, evening chapel and supper in the hall at seven. Of the three vacations which broke the year at Christmas, Easter, and through the summer months, a part was often spent in residence. Latin, Greek, or Hebrew were supposed to be used at all times except in chambers during hours of relaxation. In general the students were looked after like children, which indeed they often were. They were not to be out of the college after ten. But we hear of much infringement of the rules, of unauthorised comings and goings, of indulgence in forbidden recreation and adornment, of drunkenness. Strictness varied according to the Puritan or anti-Puritan leanings of those in power.

A quadrennium or four years' course of study was required for the B.A. degree, in the last term of which students were expected to take part in "acts" and "opponencies" in the public schools. In the "acts" the boys appeared to read a

Latin thesis on a given subject of moral or philosophical nature under the chairmanship of a master of arts and before an audience of sophisters (fourth-year students) and graduates. The opponents were called on to refute his arguments. We shall have samples of these performances from Milton's pen. There were also oral examinations both in the University and in the colleges, and a final proposing and answering of questions out of Aristotle. The M.A. was awarded after an additional three years of similar discipline, but in practice continuous residence was not required. Even for the B.A. one or two out of the theoretical twelve terms might be omitted. The whole system was slanted toward scholarship disputation, tending to make *cymini sectores* of the type deplored by Sir Francis Bacon. It was transported to America with the founders of Harvard University and bore fruit in the lucubrations of the Puritan divines. But humanistic learning was possible under it through contagion from individual to individual and at the hands of tutors who strayed beyond the system to greener fields.

The student body at Cambridge in Milton's time consisted of some three thousand individuals, distributed in over a dozen colleges. The majority were, at least in theory, destined for the ministry. Socially they were distinguished by the amount of tuition they paid in three classes, Greater Pensioners or Fellow Commoners, Lesser Pensioners (including Milton), and Sizars. It is pointed out by Masson that Milton could hardly have occupied alone the study and bedroom which are traditionally said to be his, for it was rare even for a Fellow to have a chamber by himself. The names of his room-mates or indeed of any of his close acquaintances are unrecorded. The evidence is all that he was non-gregarious though keenly aware of the personalities which surrounded him and highly critical of their behaviour.

Politically and ideologically, both Cambridge and Oxford were at this time suffering from a complication of disorders, bred partly out of their own tradition, partly out of their involvement in the manœuvrings of the opposing parties of Church and State. Cambridge had been a seat of schismatic Puritanism in Elizabeth's time. The active movement had given way to pressure, but men of nonconformist temper still survived there. The official interests of both universities dictated loyalty to the ecclesiastical establishment and to the Crown. Charles I ascended the throne at almost the exact moment of Milton's matriculation, and Oxford and Cambridge rallied to him. Parliament viewed their tendencies with an increasingly jealous eye.

In the years preceding Milton's entry ideological excitement had centred in the writings of Richard Montagu, a one-time Fellow of King's College, whose anti-Calvinistic point of view was a scandal to the rank and file of the clergy, but who had been supported by the higher ecclesiastics and by the royal favourite, Buckingham. This controversy reached its height with the publication by Montagu of a pamphlet appealing directly to the Crown in 1625, and the interference of the court party with the Parliamentary attempts to suppress him created issues which contributed powerfully to the rebellious movement then gathering head. Buckingham himself was elected to the chancellorship of Cambridge while actually under impeachment by the Commons. When Charles sustained him against the protests of Parliament, the dominant party in the academic body exulted in their victory, but there was plenty of dissent. It was into such an atmosphere of political and religious tension that Milton entered, with his own sympathies in large part predetermined. He could not possibly escape partisanship. Buckingham was assassinated in 1628. Milton's friendly tutor at St. Paul's, Alexander Gill, son of the Headmaster, drank a toast to the murderer at Oxford, uttering words of wild disloyalty. He was tried by the Court of Star Chamber and sentenced to lose his ears. On this occasion, at least, the poet, however absorbed in his own achievements, must have had the great issues of the time disturbingly thrust upon him.

Charles himself made a point of patronage of the universities, and it was possible then, as it has been in retrospect, for those who put traditional values above others to see the works of advancing democracy only as an interference with the business of scholarship and culture. How the purposes even of higher learning might nevertheless be defeated by royal concern with what went on in academic halls is illustrated by the suppression in 1628 of one Dorislaus, who had been chosen to give historical lectures on a foundation newly established in the name of Francis Bacon. This scholar gave offence, albeit his subject was the *Annals* of Tacitus, by seeming to "speak too much in defence of the liberties of the people." The matter was reported, action taken, and the Baconian Lectureship, from which so much illumination might have been expected, came to nothing.

We are not surprised to find Milton about this time proclaiming his allegiance to history and seeming to belong to an incipient party of Baconian reform.

The presence of factions in Milton's own college is well attested and might be taken for granted in any case. The members were almost equally divided in their votes for and against Buckingham as Chancellor. A later tradition punningly defined three tutorial student groupings as follows: The followers of one William Power, who were thought too loose, like their tutor, were called Poweritans; William Chappell's pupils, thought too precise, were Puritans; and Mede's, "that kept the middle between both," were Medians. Chappell, however precise in discipline, was not too much a Puritan to be patronised by Laud. He was given an Irish deanery the year after Milton's graduation and became Bishop of Cork and Ross in 1638. Power was suspected of leanings to Popery. Milton should obviously have been a Median. It is, at least, conceivable that he might have followed the peaceful academic path to be pursued by Henry More, who owed to Mede his latitudinarian position and the beginnings of his Platonism. The fellowship which Milton is said to have been denied must have come naturally to him could he have been gently led along the studious middle way. As it was, he sought compensation by the conspicuous exercise of his brilliant talents, winning admiration certainly, but not perhaps goodwill. It was at Cambridge that he became a controversialist. A poet he would have been in any case, and it is as such that we shall first consider him.

The first Latin elegy, to which allusion has been made, reveals Milton's reaction when in the spring of 1626 he found himself voluntarily or involuntarily in his father's London house while his class-mates were pursuing their accustomed studies by the Cam. We may well believe that the poem was prompted by the event, though its main concern is to describe his London satisfactions—books, Nature, the theatre, the sight of passing maidens—with an accent which makes it clear that something has happened to him emotionally of which the rebellion against authority is itself a part. The poet addresses himself to the receptive and appreciative ear of the absent Diodati, assuming an air of urbane superiority, a sort of moral and intellectual swagger, which might easily have collapsed in the actual presence of his friend. The opening lines are touched with the sentimentality of an adolescent attachment, nursed in solitude as a protection against the world:

> At length, my friend, thy far sent letters come,
> Charged with thy kindness, to their destined home;
> They come, at length, from Deva's western side,
> Wherefrom she seeks the salt Vergivian tide.
> Trust me, my joy is great that thou shoulds't be,
> Thou born of foreign race, yet born for me.

Casually he mentions the episode which is uppermost in his mind.

> I well content, where Thames with influent tide
> My native city laves, meanwhile reside.

Cambridge, his forbidden college room, the indignities of punishment are nothing in his thoughts. Here in the freedom and cultural leisure of his father's house he really lives. Would that the poet Ovid had never suffered a worse lot than such a banishment!

The recital which follows is the first full expression of Milton's sensitive æstheticism. It is a sketch for "L'Allegro" and "Il Penseroso," written before he has attained the detachment of those masterpieces. The young poet is first of all an impassioned reader. We suspect that even when he says that he is rapt away by the theatre he means simply or chiefly that he leaves heavier matters and turns to the literature of the stage. At any rate he describes comedy in Roman, tragedy in Greek terms, with a single touch which suggests the *Romeo and Juliet* of Shakespeare. "From time to time there is in my tears a sweet bitterness, as when an unfortunate lad has left his joys untasted and falls pitifully because of thwarted love." When he goes forth from the house to enjoy the springtime, walking in the groves of some city park or in the adjoining country, it is not the variety of the natural scene which he describes, but the groups of maidens who pass by, "stars breathing soft flames." These presences, though at a distance, are intensely real. He launches forth in panegyric, extolling English beauty above that of Greece and Rome, but he abounds in the recollection of classical love poetry, of which the elegy itself is obviously intended to be an echo. We recall that he had been enamoured of the "smooth elegiac poets," that "no recreation came to me better welcome." Their matter was "agreeable to nature's part in me," in those years "which are excused though they be least severe."

In this moment of his happy exile he all but makes the transition from art to life—not quite, for after the avowal of susceptibility to female charm he sets his face against it. It is high time, after all, that he should leave these allurements while the blind boy Cupid still permits it. Against the dangers of the ill-famed halls of Circe he will use the help of the divine plant moly, and go back, as it has been arranged for him to do, to the safety of Cambridge and the "raucous murmur of the schools." Thus does Milton declare himself Puritan, but most engagingly. He will return to the symbol of Circe and the protecting herb in an imaginative elaboration of the theme of chastity. This early poem is as naïvely boyish in sentiment as it is exquisite in execution. We have in it not only our best view of Milton at seventeen, but the key to his youthful personality in all its aspects. He has begun what was to be with him a life-long process of resistance and retreat. Henceforth, the world, besides being a most interesting place, is divided between friends and enemies. And subtle weapons of offensive and defensive war are in his hands.

Milton was, as I have said, back at college under a new tutor, Tovey, for the Lent term of 1626. There are no letters, poems, or other records to indicate his activity either then or in the following summer. The autumn of his third Cambridge year, on the other hand, is marked by a sudden and extraordinary outburst of Latin verse. It is as if the poet, recovering from whatever shock he had experienced as a result of his rustication, had launched forth in a deliberate effort to vindicate himself before the academic world. The series begins with Latin elegies on the deaths of four public figures: Richard Redding, University Beadle; John Gostlin, Vice-Chancellor; Launcelot Andrews, Bishop of Winchester; and Nicolas Felton, Bishop of Ely. The two last mentioned had been in times past masters of Pembroke Hall and their deaths in the autumn of 1626 would in a sense be university as well as national events. Milton is evidently seeking occasions for the exercise of his talents. But he embodies even in these pieces something of himself.

The elegy on Redding, which is little more than an epigram, portrays with affection mixed with wit the familiar figure of the old man with snowy locks marshalling the "togaed hosts" of students, and now summoned in his turn by the herald Death.

The other poems are more elaborate. The elegy on Andrews opens with a vision of the plague spreading death on European soil, "entering the marble halls of the great and fearing not to lay low the host of princes." In the lament for Ely, Milton develops more richly than hitherto the theme of immortality, a motive of much significance to his youthful imagination. He fancies himself borne like Elijah amidst the winged soldiery of the Almighty through the starry sphere up to the portals of Heaven itself, the palace of crystal, the courts paved with jasper and malachite. The images which thus present themselves to his mind and his personal participation in the celestial rapture acquire greater intensity in his later work. But here at the age of seventeen and on an occasion sufficiently remote from his immediate concern, he becomes for the moment the bard of eternity, the rapt prophet to whom has been vouchsafed by special privilege an insight into the mysteries of God. The almost equally characteristic note of youthful affection and regret, which we shall meet in more poignant form in later poems, appears fleetingly in the elegy for the Vice-Chancellor Gostlin.

These elegies, then, are something more than show pieces. Beneath the tinsel of classical allusion and Augustan phrase they reveal not only a warm experience, but a measure of poetic inspiration and an individual relationship already established between Milton and his Muse. The contemporary literature of death and the common experience of the plague are no doubt partly accountable for his inspiration.

The longest and most ambitious poem of this period, the Latin epic on the Gunpowder Plot, is less personal. It belongs, however, to the same literary moment as the others and must, like them, have been composed within a few months of Milton's return to Cambridge in the autumn of 1626. Milton is here the Protestant patriot, giving voice with others to the appropriate emotion of a national celebration, the intensity of which was determined by continued apprehension of a similar event. He is also the English humanist employing the well-worn motives of neo-Latin Christian verse. Satan, envious of the happiness of Britain under good King James, incites the triple-tyrant of Rome, appearing before him in Homeric vision, to assail his most dangerous enemy before it is too late. Virgilian rumour spreads the news in England of the Catholic designs.

The plotters are captured and dragged to torment. The nation celebrates and pours forth its gratitude to God.

There is much here to remind us of the later Milton—the violent, almost automatic anti-Catholic feeling, a fascinated preoccupation with the author of all evil, already partly sublimated into a grandiose image of malignity and power. Satan sweeps in his flight over sea and land. He breaks forth in sighs that flame Hellish fire. "His eyes blaze and the adamant row of his grinding teeth sounds like the clashing of arms." This is mere rhetoric, but it is a rhetoric which Milton is to make his own. It is amazing that he should have advanced so far, and the most plausible explanation of this sudden flowering is that Milton's experiences of the past year, fed by his wide, ranging study, had released forces which had been long maturing in him but had so far found no adequate outlet. Henceforth he is a poet, not merely in intent and expectation, but in deed. The medium will soon be his native English, but academic circumstance or some kind of hesitancy within himself delays his achievement of this new freedom.

From the autumn of 1626, the beginning of Milton's third college year, to the spring of 1627 we have no record. Then come two personal documents of significance: a verse epistle, Elegy IV, to his old preceptor, Thomas Young, written probably in March, and a prose letter which followed it a few months later. The latter is dated May 26th, 1625, in the published collection, but this has been convincingly shown by Professor Parker to be an error. Young had left England in 1620 to become minister to an English congregation in Hamburg. He has had correspondence with Milton and complains that his pupil's letters have been few and short. Milton has received from him the present of a Hebrew Bible. Now, in the spring vacation of 1627, the poet, moved by a new warmth of feeling and a new pride in his own achievement, also by news which has come to him that Hamburg is in danger of attack, summons all his eloquence to address him in gratitude and affection. The elegy is his first outpouring of friendship and sets a pattern for later expression. There is more than rhetoric in Milton's identification of himself with the object of his love. He fancies his letter finding Young sitting with his sweet wife, fondling his children, poring over Scripture or some learned volume of the Fathers. He is anxious for him and indignant with the harsh Fatherland which has compelled him to earn his bread abroad and so to expose his family to the risks of war. But he bids him feel secure. He is in his exile like Elijah, like Paul, like Jesus. God, who protected Israel against its foes, will watch also over him.

The prose letter, though it lacks this imaginative fervour, is equally revealing of the processes of Milton's mind. It is a mild assay at a Platonic rapture:

> The ardour of my regard makes me imagine that you are always present, that I hear your voice and contemplate your looks; and as thus (which is usually the case with lovers) I charm away my grief by the illusion of your presence. I was afraid when I wrote to you the idea of your distant separation should forcibly rush upon my mind; and that the pain of your absence, which was almost soothed into quiescence should revive and disperse the pleasurable dream.

Young, a solid Puritan who "cut his hair short" was doubtless less concerned than his star-led pupil with the effect of reality upon the pure idea. But Milton is about his poet's business, practising with a new experience, and elaborating the thoughts which rise out of it for future use. A year later, after Young had returned to England and invited Milton to visit him, he writes a second letter. The glow of affectionate idealisation which characterises the elegy appears again in this address, showing how symbolic a value Milton has found in the good man and how deeply his emotions are engaged in his comings and goings. Young, "with moderate means, but regal spirit," has retired to his little farm like some Serranus or Curius, to "hold triumph over riches, ambition, pomp, luxury, and whatever the herd of men admire or are amazed at." From such an attachment a whole life direction may easily be taken. But Young gave only one of the focal points of Milton's emotion in his college years. He is essentially a parental figure. It is Gill and Diodati who stand more nearly in the relationship of peers.

The moment which we have now reached in Milton's development is obviously an important one. He is undergoing an adolescent intensification and sublimation of emotion and at the same time developing a role with relation to the individuals who make up his personal environment. Unfortunately, the documents which belong to this transition and might mark its stages are not precisely datable. We must do our best with the evidence at hand. One personal event and Milton's

reaction to it we can definitely fix as belonging to the first part
of his twentieth year, i.e. between January and September,
1628, the second half of his third year at the University. His
sister Anne, married to Edward Phillips, lost her second child,
a daughter, in January, 1628. The poet's grief finds expression
in an English elegy, written perhaps in the following spring or
summer. This is a real creative outburst, comparable to the
verse epistle to Young, but discarding the artificiality of Latin
in favour of a better love, the mother tongue. The circumstance
of death, now personally brought home to him, enables him to
speak with a tenderness not present in the Latin lamentations:

> O fairest flower, no sooner blown but blasted,
> Soft silken primrose fading timelessly,
> Summer's chief honour, if thou hadst outlasted
> Bleak winter's force that made thy blossom dry.

And the theme of immortality is touched on with memorable
eloquence:

> Yet can I not persuade me thou art dead,
> Or that thy corse corrupts in earth's dark womb,
> Or that thy beauties lie in wormy bed,
> Hid from the world in a low delvèd tomb.

Characteristically, Milton contemplates "that crowned Matron,
sage, white-robed Truth" and the "golden-winged host" of
heaven. Characteristically, too, he lessons the bereaved mother
to "curb her sorrow wild" and render back God's gift in hopeful
patience. The writing of this poem engaged some of the chief
motives which were to dominate his religious verse.

The use of English is in itself momentous in a way that without sympathetic understanding of Milton's personality we shall
find it difficult to appreciate. With all his pride he is a very
timid and dependent person. He has won favour in a medium
approved by learned friends, one to which all his scholastic
effort has been directed and in which his skill has admittedly
found few competitors. To venture beyond this certainty is to
court a new and untried valuation. In the Latin, moreover, he
could rest easily in the arms of imitation. There hardly existed
a choice of styles. In English there were many strong competing
voices.

To assure himself that he will not fail he calls upon a new
defence. Did he not lisp in English numbers as a child and be

admired of all? And is he not attuned to values no less in
English than in Latin style? This calls for a proclamation, and
such a proclamation Milton makes in an English poem which
he suddenly inserts in the midst of a Latin oration delivered
before the College, most probably in the summer vacation of
1628, about the time of the elegy on his sister's child. He speaks
of the new departure as the fruit of a conviction deeply medi-
tated. He apostrophises his mother tongue as an object to which
his childhood is attached by bonds of dear affection, a *mother*
tongue indeed. Sustained by an assurance of its protectiveness
he is carried forward to the thought of accomplishments of
epic magnitude:

> I have some naked thoughts that rove about
> And loudly knock to have their passage out;
> And weary of their place do only stay
> Till thou hast decked them in thy best array;
> That so they may without suspect or fears
> Fly swiftly to this fair assembly's ears;
> Yet I had rather if I were to choose,
> Thy service in some graver subject use,
> Such as may make thee search thy coffers round,
> Before thou clothe my fancy in fit sound:
> Such where the deep transported mind may soar
> Above the wheeling poles, and at Heav'n's door
> Look in, and see each blissful deity
> How he before the thunderous throne doth lie.

This digression is not the less significant for being on the
surface a mere graceful moment in a vacation exercise. Milton
can write lightly about things that move him inwardly. The
meaningfulness of these reactions is tested by their recurrence
and by such occasional betrayals of sensitiveness as, in this
instance, the phrase "without suspect or fears." The conflict
between the Latin Milton and the English Milton is not a
conflict of speech alone, nor is it purely individual. We shall
have occasion to identify it in many forms both in his own
career and in the larger cultural pattern which this career
reflects.

Proof that the poet is by no means as bold as he sounds is to
be found in his mode of dealing with a new emotional episode
which now emerges as the successor of his moments of friendship
and of grief. John Milton, after having banished Cupid and

fled from the halls of Circe, proclaims himself at length a lover. Inevitably he is a Latin, an Ovidian lover, or, rising in the scale, a Petrarchan or a Chaucerian one. The English of his own time, even in a style "which choicest spirits and deepest wits admire," is not a safe medium for these roving thoughts, much less so the naked lover-speech of Donne. The seventh elegy, "at the age of 19," gives a light account of the unexpected wounding of his heart by Cupid. One suspects a social incident seized on with delight and magnified beyond recognition. The Italian sonnets to Diodati, which we cannot date but which fit too well with the elegy to be far distant from it, give the detail, literary or realistic, of what seems to be the same event. Three-quarters of their phrases come almost literally from Petrarch but Milton has succeeded in weaving out of them an individual sonnet story. The lady's name is Emilia. She is a type of foreign beauty, a singer, learned, and endowed with more languages than one. The poet has been long a boastful enemy of love, but now is completely entangled in its snares. "I tell it to you Diodati as a marvel." His heart in all other respects is a fortress, in one part only is it weak—against the strength of beauty's powerful glance. He writes in an exotic tongue, of his own good folk not understood, the youths and maidens who surround him laugh and ask why. And he replies: "It is love's language, of which love is boastful." The sequence is preceded by an English sonnet, with Chaucerian rather than Petrarchan echoes:

> O Nightingale, that on yon bloomy spray
> Warblest at eve, when all the woods are still, . . .
> Now timely sing, ere the rude bird of hate
> Foretell my hopeless doom in some grove nigh; . . .
> Whether the muse, or Love, call thee his mate,
> Both them I serve, and of their train am I.

A lover? Yes. But as yet perhaps only a lover of the tradition of courtly love (Italian and English) or a lover by proxy through that tradition. We have a stray bit of evidence of the range of his interest in poetry, in the survival of a copy of the works of the Italian sonneteer, Giovanni della Casa, bearing his signature on the title page, with the date, 1629. His senses, however, are awakening; and woman individual, not the maiden bands of Elegy I, exists.

Milton's declared servitude is something childish but very

natural. It is also, being highly un-Miltonic, of short duration. But before it is over there is one full moment of sensuous lyricism in the fifth Latin elegy on the coming of spring. This is "ætate 20," say in April, 1629, with Milton already a B.A. All nature is alive with passion. Earth yearns for the embraces of the sun and bares her fertile breast. His own powers of song return. His heart is afire with a mysterious impulse. His spirit is borne to the dwelling of the gods. Two lines from the English sonnet on the nightingale are deftly translated and made part of the Latin text.

> *Iam, Philomela, tua foliis adoperta novellis*
> *Instituis modulos, dum silet omne nemus.*

The two pieces have, however, a different inspiration, and it is only in the foreign medium that Milton's muse is unabashed.

To this engaging episode of lyrical love, though by no means to the sexual impulses which prompt it, Milton writes a positive finis in the Sixth Elegy, composed at the Christmas season of 1629, the year after his graduation B.A. from Cambridge, when he was just arrived at the age of twenty-one. And either at this or some later time he appends a Platonic recantation to the book of elegies. We have reached the end of an academic epoch, the beginning of a period of greater leisure for contemplation and free study, perhaps also, of more frequent residence on his father's estate at Horton. Milton was given to observing his anniversaries. His coming of age may well have seemed an appropriate moment for serious consideration of his life purposes.

The Latin poem was composed in response to a holiday greeting from Diodati. The latter has sent his poet friend an account of the holiday revelry in which he has been engaged, complaining that these distractions have left no room for poetry. Milton replies with a distinction between the two kinds of poetry, light elegy which he has himself renounced and epic which it is his purpose to begin. The former is the care of many gods. If Diodati will but listen to the Orphean lute, playing to the dances of the maidens, he may recall the creative power which his deadening indulgence has driven away. Bountiful feasts and frequent draughts of old wine are not hostile to lyric inspiration. For the poet who will sing of higher things—wars and heaven subject to mature Jove, pious heroes and leaders half divine, the sacred conferences of the high gods, the abysmal realm where barks the savage dog—for such a poet the austere living is required. He must eat sparingly like Pythagoras and water must be his only drink. His youth must be chaste, his character without a stain. Such a poet is sacred to the gods and is their priest. His inmost soul and lips breathe Jove.

Thus does Milton enunciate the full ascetic doctrine of the sacred bard. As an earnest of the rededication of his powers he tells Diodati that he is composing a Christmas ode: "I am hymning the king of heavenly lineage, prince of peace. . . . This is my gift to the birthday of Christ, the first rays of dawn brought me the theme." There is no reproach in this but an indication that he intends henceforth to be himself. The duality of his consciousness remains. But for the moment at least he is able to put the social competence and the easy hedonistic philosophy which have so fascinated him in his friend's personality in their place.

The afterpiece to the elegies puts the change in him on other grounds.

> In these verses I once with froward mind and ill directed zeal set up idle trophies of my folly. For baneful error caught and drove me thus astray, and my heedless youth was an unsound teacher; until the shade-embowered Academy offered me its Socratic rills and taught me to reject the yoke I had accepted. Straightway all flame was quenched, and from that time my breast is rigid, encased in thick ice; whence it comes that the Boy himself fears cold for his arrows and even Venus dreads a Diomedean strength.

Milton's devotion to Platonic study has doubtless been the growth of many years (we have already seen it colouring his love for Young) but he here represents it as something approximating a conversion. We shall have occasion to consider a further manifestation of it in prose of this same period.

The great Nativity Ode, which is clearly a fruit of the resolution recorded in the sixth elegy, brings us at once to a summit in Milton's early poetic achievement. Its immediate inspiration is the fervid and ornate religious verse of the Spenserian tradition, Phineas Fletcher in particular, which, we remember, was indigenous in Cambridge. As the poem progresses, the tones, if not the ideas, are Milton's own. The central image is

the Platonic music of the spheres, which the poet here equates
with the song of the heavenly host and with that which the sons
of morning sang together in the Book of Job. In the second
prolusion he had written that we if we had pure ears could
hear this music. Now he tells us that it once was heard miracu-
lously by men, their penalty of sin suspended for the moment
in honour of the Saviour's birth. Could it have continued, sin
would be no more. The golden age would have returned.
There is a conscious relationship at this point between the
Nativity Ode and Virgil's prophetic eclogue, the Fourth, to
Pollio, which is strikingly messianic in its phraseology and was
traditionally interpreted as a witness to the truth of Scripture.
Ovid has given way to a nobler muse.

The conception of Christ is severely Protestant. He is the
power of pure religion, the heroic idea of truth, combating
error, binding the old dragon in stricter limits, putting to
flight the host of multiform divinities whom man in his ignorance has created and bowed down to. The passage in which
Milton calls their hideous names is the first study for the
demonology of *Paradise Lost*:

> Peor and Baalim,
> Forsake their temples dim,
>   With that twice-battered god of Palestine;
>
> And sullen Moloch, fled,
> Hath left in shadows dread
>   His burning idol all of blackest hue;
> In vain with cymbals' ring
> They call the grisly king,
>   In dismal dance about the furnace blue.

We miss the traditional images of the manger, the sweet
simplicity of the carols or the nativity plays, the sentimental
rapture of a poet like Crashaw. Milton's devotion is of sterner
stuff. There is, on the other hand, a clear serenity, a reverent
wonder which expresses the solemnity of the moment as perhaps
no other human utterance.

In the last verses of the sixth elegy Milton speaks of other
songs "played on my native reed" which wait to be recited to
Diodati and of which he will be the judge. The phrase is
conventional. Milton calls himself a shepherd and thinks of his
verse as pastoral until he comes to be a prophet wholly inspired

by the heavenly muse. The allusion would be appropriate to minor lyrics such as the song on May morning or even to the companion pieces "L'Allegro" and "Il Penseroso" which have, because of their stylistic maturity, ordinarily been thought to belong to a later period. The important fact biographically is that Milton is interested in English poetry in his later college years, and is looking not to Young or Gill but to Diodati as a sympathetic audience for this as he had for the amatory Latin and Italian verse.

We have datable compositions from the next two or three years which show a variety of experimental styles and which associate Milton, however tentatively, with the vernacular literary community. Before discussing them, however, we must revert to the intellectual and public aspects of his university career, of which poetry was officially a minor part. The quarrel with the tutor must surely have been partly ideological. We have seen something of the general tensions in the university. The evidence that Milton became involved in them lies chiefly in his correspondence with Gill and in the required orations and exercises of the colleges and University, which he, almost alone of his contemporaries, preserved and published for the very reason that they were written in all seriousness and represented his first salvo of propaganda and personal defence. These documents, though often of doubtful date, point clearly to the fact that in the years following his quarrel with Chappell, Milton had come to grips both with the academic and the social system and had assumed a consistent role of intellectual and individual nonconformity.

The first news we have of Milton as a student careerist occurs in a letter to Alexander Gill dated July 2nd, 1628, a matter of weeks before the assassination of Buckingham and Gill's disgrace. He proudly reports to his former teacher that he is called on to do a poetic assignment for a friend, "a fellow of our house who had to act as respondent in the philosophical disputation in this commencement and who chanced to entrust to my puerility the composition of the verses according to annual custom required to be written on the questions in dispute." He then proceeds to a subject which he knows will strike an equally sympathetic chord: the state of culture in the University, the lack of scholarly thoroughness, the prevailing desire for trivial forensic skills and quick rewards, the easy substitution of verbal subtlety for knowledge which Erasmus had made ridiculous. Milton is repeating the old humanistic argument and anticipating the more modern assault on academic sterility at Cambridge which was to be made a little later under the influence both of democratic and of Baconian ideas. He speaks evidently as one who intends to enter the Church:

> Truly, amongst us here, as far as I know, there are hardly one or two here and there, who do not fly off unfeathered to theology, while all but rude and uneducated in philology as well as philosophy, content to pick up lightly as much theology as may suffice for anyhow sticking together a little sermon and stitching it over with worn rags from other quarters, insomuch that it is to be dreaded that by degrees there may spread among our clergy that priestly ignorance of a former age.

Such convictions, however adult sounding, have a very personal reference. Milton recalls his earlier constant conversations with Gill, whose company he never left without a manifest increase in learning. Finding no such associates in his studies at Cambridge, he would, he says, certainly be looking to London, were he not planning to spend the summer in deep literary repose, "hiding myself, so to speak, in the bower of the Muses." This is the regular use which Milton makes of absent friends. We need not exaggerate the depth of the reaction in order to find it an important index to his later behaviour.

In treating the Latin prose exercises, which next to the poems are our great source of knowledge of what Milton's mind and culture were really like in this epoch, we find it difficult to distinguish between his earlier and his later college years. The prolusions seem, however, to stand in the order of their composition and one of them is datable in the summer of 1628. The theme of the first—whether day or night be the more excellent—is silly enough and the argument, for the most part, mere hair-splitting. The piece becomes eloquent, however, when Milton embarks on a description of the morning and of the joy which it brings to living things. The poet's idealistic emotion has here seized upon one of its favourite themes, and we are suddenly in the atmosphere of "L'Allegro" and of *Comus*. It is well known that he was an early riser and believed with Goethe that man's best work is of the morning. Very probably the association was conscious with him from the beginning of his college days, for another prolusion on the same theme, extant in a manuscript, is pretty clearly a juvenile performance. This set of mind and habit is the earliest clear intimation of Milton's essential asceticism.

Equally consistent with what we meet elsewhere is the defensive attitude which he assumes toward his audience. He bespeaks their goodwill, but openly announces that he does not possess it:

> As many heads as I behold with my eyes in this great concourse, almost the same number do I see of visages bearing malice against me. . . . Of so much effect in producing private grudges is the rivalry even in schools of those who follow different studies or different principles in the same studies.

The fact that this is a debate is, of course, relevant, but the general evidence of Milton's sense of isolation is too strong to allow us to believe that he is not converting jest to earnest. He implies that it is the excellence of what he has to offer which predestines his words to fall, for the most part, on deaf or hostile ears. It is significant that he finds among his hearers a few who wish him well. The "fit audience" of kindred spirits is always a necessary part of his thought of himself. One suspects that the rivalries in study are a result as well as a cause of personal hostility. One suspects also that the dislike which he finds in his associates is largely a figment of his imagination. Everything indicates that Milton was a singularly winning person and that when he met opposition it was usually because he sought it. There is, of course, the matter of his intellectual arrogance which he may or may not have found it easy to conceal. We have in any case the clear outline of a role in which Milton was so often to see himself—the role of the one against the many, the chosen servant of God speaking to the unregenerate.

The later prolusions show a further development of these emotions and ideas. In the second he declares himself an adherent of the Platonic against the Aristotelian way of thought. In the third he argues in favour of the humanistic attitude in study and expresses scorn of the perpetual theological wrangling of the schools. The indication given by these pronouncements of the tenets of the philosophic party to which Milton belongs is amplified by an undated Latin poem,

"*Naturam Non Pati Senium*," "That Nature is not Subject to Old Age," which may have been written either for one of the exhibitions or as an independent contribution to the general issue. The question is the old one of the degeneracy of Nature, which had been raised anew in philosophic circles by the publication in 1627 of George Hakewill's treatise, *Apology of the Power and Providence of God—or a Censure of the Common Error Touching Nature's Perpetual and Universal Decay*. Milton takes the new progressive viewpoint which is also the Baconian against the conservative and traditional one. The physical world is not in its decline. The forces of Nature are as mighty as ever. The sun god runs his race unwearied, the elements break not their faith. God has willed that all things march on without diminution till the final conflagration destroys the world. The poem is adorned with Milton's richest eloquence. There is no philosophic subtlety and none was needed. Whether or not he is familiar with the intricacies and shadings of the theory of progress he is not wanting in enthusiasm for the idea. The poem belongs in the category of philosophical disputations, but is significantly Miltonic in point of view. If the poet accepted it as a commission it was not only because he was gratified by the recognition of his special skill, but also because his friend was on the right side of the debate. There was a parting of the ways at Cambridge; and Milton is being educated, as undergraduates always are, by the rivalries of ideological professors, who find it easier to pass on their points of view to pupils than to maintain them publicly themselves. Politics are not far in the background here. We recall the episode of Dorislaus and the professorship of history.

The fourth and fifth prolusions contain nothing of biographical interest, but the sixth is again full of his personality. It is the one which contains the verses on the English language. "At a Vacation Exercise," and if the date prefixed to this composition is to be trusted should have been written in the summer of 1628. The occasion is a sportive student dramatisation of the Aristotelian metaphysics. Milton is the master of ceremonies. He begins with a little oration of his own in defence of the thesis: "That Sportive Exercises on occasion are not Inconsistent with the Study of Philosophy." The reader may judge from the following extracts what kind of a temperament it is which thus deploys itself before its little public in these ingenious pleasantries, bearing in mind the while his own presumably

duller, certainly less learned academic youth, and remembering
that John Milton was nineteen. Throughout the defence of
relaxation which proceeds through all manner of instances and
arguments, the ground tone of the speaker's own introspective
memories and private formulations of conviction continues to
be heard.

> I shall not consider it a burden to praise according to my
> abilities, pleasantries and witty sallies, in which I acknowl-
> edge my capabilities are quite limited. . . . I am about to
> speak seriously to-day in praise of jocularity. And this is
> done not without cause indeed, for what is it that more
> quickly conciliates and retains friendships longer than a
> cheerful and agreeable disposition? And truly you will
> hardly find one is pleasing and welcome who lacks sportive
> remarks and pleasantries and elegant little witticisms.

Later in the oration, before proceeding to the horseplay,
Milton speaks seriously and with responsibility of the priority
of earnestness in the balanced life.

> But in truth, I think that he who is wont to be so moved
> with stupid jokes as openly to neglect the serious and more
> useful things for them; he, I say, would not be able to make
> much progress in the latter, nor in the former line: not
> indeed in serious matters, because if he were adapted and
> framed by nature for managing serious affairs, I believe he
> would not so easily allow himself to be led away from them;
> nor in trifling matters, because hardly anyone can crack
> jokes delightfully and charmingly unless he has also first
> learned to act seriously.

The most suggestive passage of all is one in which Milton toys
with the dramatic role he is playing as "father" of the younger
actors. The intricate jocosity and the attitude of sexual sophisti-
cation the poet here assumes betrays, in my opinion, a suppressed excitement. The reason for the traditional institution
which it is his part to represent is, he says, that "wishing to
approach as near as possible to paternity we desire to assume
under a pseudonym that which we do not even risk, except in
secret; just as girls according to their custom imagine playful
weddings and confinements, laying hold of and enjoying those
things which they pant for and eagerly desire." The annual
festivity, he goes on, has been dropped recently, because those

who were about to become "fathers" conducted themselves
so turbulently in town as to make it necessary that they be
relieved of this anxiety. Why then has *he* suddenly become a
"father." Is it that he has bargained with some God to be
changed from a woman to a man? He has been called by some
"The Lady." "Why do I seem to those fellows insufficiently
masculine?"

> Doubtless it was because I was never able to gulp down
> huge bumpers in pancratic fashion; or because my hand
> has not become calloused by holding the plow handle; or
> because I never lay down on my back under the sun at
> mid-day, like a seven year ox-driver; perhaps in fine,
> because I never proved myself a man in the same manner
> as these gluttons. But would they could as easily lay aside
> their asshood as I whatever belongs to womanhood.

The comment which suggests itself most appropriately is,
"The Lady doth protest too much." Do we exaggerate in
thinking that he is really driven to bay by an innocent cruelty
the purport of which neither he nor his fellows understand?
His answer is confused. In one breath he accepts the invitation
to coarse jesting which makes him one of the boys. In another
he retreats into his citadel of moral and even social superiority.

One further academic performance—the undated seventh
prolusion—remains to be mentioned. It is in many ways the
finest and most Miltonic of them all and suggests that he has
made his choice of attitude and is no longer to be disturbed by
the rout of Circe's swine. The oratorical effort, he declares,
is displeasing to him, partly from a sense of its high requirements. The orator must be "equipped and perfected with a
certain encompassing support of all the arts and of all science."
His age does not permit this, but he is "afire and ablaze" with
the purpose of so perfecting himself. He invokes the glades and
streams of his beloved country villa, where in the summer just
gone by he has enjoyed the fruits of literary leisure, seeming
to grow as it were in a bygone age. The probability is that he
had already retired to Horton in the first or second of his
graduate years and is now called back, really against his
inclination, to become again a showpiece in the schools. The
oration is in praise of knowledge and Milton treats the congenial subject in his loftiest Platonic vein:

I believe, my hearers, it is known and recognised by all, that the great framer of the universe, although He had founded all other things on change and decay, had intermingled in man, beyond what is mortal, a certain divine breath and as it were a part of Himself, immortal, imperishable, immune from death and destruction: after which it had sojourned spotlessly and chastely on earth for a while, a guest as it were from heaven, should wing itself upward to its destined mansion and its native land. Whence it follows that nothing can be recounted justly among the causes of our happiness, unless it in some way takes into consideration both that eternal life and this temporal life. That is the sole contemplation, according to the judgment of almost everybody, by which our mind without the aid of the body, remote and as it were wrapped up in itself, copies the eternal life of the immortal gods. This, however, without knowledge is altogether sterile and joyless. For who can contemplate and examine seriously the ideal form of things, human and divine, of which nothing surely can be known, unless he has a mind saturated and perfected by knowledge and training.

Again, and somewhat more gracefully than in the earlier prolusion, he touches on his own problem of sociality.

Many complain that the majority of the more learned class are hard to please, boorish, uncouth in manners, with no grace of speech for winning the minds of men. I acknowledge indeed that one who is commonly reclusive and withdrawn in studies is much more ready to address the gods than men. . . . But if worthy and suitable friendships have befallen none cultivates them more sacredly.

The final fruit of knowledge is the expansion of the spirit until it has filled the world itself and far beyond with a certain divine extension of magnitude. The learned man will become one whose power and authority the stars obey. He will reside in every age as if alive, to be born as though a contemporary of time itself. Ignorance, on the other hand, is veiled in darkness and benumbed. Its votaries complain that life is short, art long. Venerating the body they cast off all concern for time, character, or health by eating and drinking after the manner of sea beasts, spending their nights in gambling and debauchery. Thus weakening themselves they become eager for all kinds of turpitude and falsely and wickedly transfer the blame to Nature.

The prolusions, this last one particularly, are invaluable in helping us understand not only the processes by which Milton arrived at his security, but the entire nexus of ideas with which he supports his ambitious programme for himself. The system is complete in its essentials by the end of the University period and its expression in prose gives explicitness to the development which we have seen to be implied in the poetry. Milton disparages sophistry and mere ostentation precisely because he thinks nobly of the art of rhetoric and proposes to be an orator. As exercised by men of learning and high purpose, the eloquence of prose and poetry are one. Both have as their objects the spiritual and moral good of men, and the soul of one, as of the other, is an inspiration from on high. "Undoubtedly," Milton writes in the seventh prolusion, "one family, one man endowed with knowledge and wisdom, like a great gift of God, may be sufficient to reform a whole state."

The concept of a function which blends the roles of scholar, poet, orator, and prophet is derived jointly from the traditions of humanism and Christianity, with the Platonic philosophy mediating between them. The appeal of this philosophy to Milton's emotions becomes increasingly intense and personal. In an undated Latin poem, *"De Idea Platonica,"* he makes a hard-headed Aristotelian express disbelief in the reality of the idea and scold Plato for bringing such a fantastic notion into philosophy, then betray the truth by bidding him recall the poets whom he has banished from his Republic in order to establish it. The sceptic asks where the archetypal man is to be found. Not Tiresias the seer or the mystic Hermes ever saw it in their dreams. It is precisely this archetypal man whom Milton will himself reveal through the divine art toward the mastery of which the best effort of his youth is bent. The Platonic symbol of the music of the spheres, with its ascetic implications, gives a focal point to the whole doctrine.

> If *we* carried pure and chaste and snow-clean hearts as did Pythagoras of old, then should our ears resound and be filled with that sweetest music of the ever-wheeling stars, and all things should on the instant return as to the golden age.

The poet returns to the idea not only in the Nativity Ode, but in *Arcades* and *Comus*. His own aspiration is to be of those who hear this music and transmit it through his words to man.

It is a matter of relative indifference whether he does so in prose or verse, in the pulpit or the forum, or if necessary in a purely private capacity to whatever audience may be persuaded to attend. In any case arduous preparation and much practice are essential, and a continuous invocation of the gift.

The last English poems of the University period are for the most part of a lower inspiration than the Nativity Ode, and they reveal a literary versatility which is not to be lost sight of in our emphasis on the main line of Milton's purposes. He attempts to continue the religious vein in "The Passion," written presumably at the ensuing Easter season, 1630, but he abandons the poem in the midst of a series of forced conceits. The sacrifices of Christ awakened no authentic response in his religious nature. Two humorous pieces on the death of Hobson, the Cambridge carrier, belong in the category of student verse. They were popular in their day and appear in several anthologies. The lines to Shakespeare—written for the folio of 1632, though dated by Milton, 1630—again remind us that he was not wholly apart from the literary currents of his age. It would be interesting to know who procured them for the volume. The conceit of Shakespeare building his own monument through his imaginative creations is in an elaboration of Jonson's in the famous tribute prefixed to the folio of 1623. We have no reason to doubt the sincerity of Milton's admiration for the bard.

Contemporary with these pieces in 1631 is the lovely epitaph on the Marchioness of Winchester, second of his English elegies and a first assay in octosyllabic couplets. The spirit of the poem on a Fair Infant finds an echo in the tenderness with which Milton celebrates this young mother's death in child-bed, but there is a new refinement both of feeling and of language:

> Gentle lady, may thy grave
> Peace and quiet ever have;
> After this thy travail sore
> Sweet rest seize thee evermore.

The final lines render the theme of immortality and point forward to the apocalyptic close of *Comus* and the elaborated ecstasy of "Lycidas" and the "Epitaph of Damon." They do not, however, include the idea of the mystic marriage of the soul with God which gives heightened fervour to these later works.

There are a few further religious and didactic lyrics which may belong to the University period, notably the poem "At a Solemn Music," celebrating again the heavenly diapason to which human ears are closed by sin and praying for its renewal in our hearts:

O may we soon again renew that song,
And keep in tune with heaven, till God ere long
To His celestial consort us unite,
To live with Him, and sing in endless morn of light.

Finally, we have a deeply introspective sonnet wherein the poet distrustfully assesses his progress toward the high goals which have been set for him. The occasion is a birthday, his twenty-third, on December 9th, 1631, just before his graduation as Master of Arts, or more probably, considering Milton's common usage, his twenty-fourth, when he was domiciled at Horton. The poem is written in a different context from the Nativity Ode and substitutes a soberer religious emotion for the kind of ecstasy which naturally associates itself with the Platonic symbol. Milton confronts the fact of his immaturity, but finds, as he is often to do when similar questionings possess him, full consolation in the acceptance of God's will to which he has, even in these young years and before any real affliction, been schooled. The "timely happy spirits" with whom he compares himself unfavourably might include Diodati, now embarked on a medical career.

How soon hath Time, the subtle thief of youth,
Stolen on his wing my three and twentieth year!
My hasting days fly on with full career,
But my late spring no bud or blossom shew'th.
Perhaps my semblance might deceive the truth,
That I to manhood am arrived so near,
And inward ripeness doth much less appear,
That some more timely-happy spirits indueth.
Yet be it less or more, or soon or slow,
It shall be still in strictest measure even
To that same lot, however mean or high,
Toward which time leads me, and the will of Heaven.
All is, if I have grace to use it so,
As ever in my great Task-master's eye.

The sonnet is perfect Puritanism in its soul-searching and its resignation, equally so in its assumption that God demands of His servants strenuousness as well as worship.

It is not to be supposed that Milton would follow without remission the implications of this second earnest dedication of his powers. A mood is a mood, even for the poet whose life and literary work are so nearly of one piece. We shall find him relaxing both in speech and act and incorporating the principle of relaxation into his doctrine of the well-balanced life. Yet the impression he actually made on the friend who knew him best was that of overseriousness. There are two Greek letters addressed to Milton by Diodati which are really quite undatable though they have been assigned by Masson to his earlier years at Cambridge. When the first was written the two friends were evidently in almost daily association. They have planned a holiday together, but the weather is bad. Diodati encourages Milton to hope for sunshine and remember their agreement, fearing lest he turn his mind, as he so easily can, to other things. "For all will be fair to-morrow; and the air, and the sun, the river, and trees and birds, and earth and men will laugh and dance together with us." In the second letter Diodati is away in the country enjoying its delights, but longing for companionship. Speaking of this need, he takes upon himself to remonstrate with his friend:

> But you, extraordinary man, why do you despise the gifts of nature? Why inexcusably persist in hanging over books and studies all day and all night? Live, laugh, make the most of youth and the hours; and cease studying the zeals and recreations and indolences of the wise men of old, wearing yourself out the while. I, in all things else inferior to you, in this one thing, in knowing when to set a measure of my labours, both seem to myself, and am, your better. Farewell, and be joyous.

These engaging expressions, the only ones we have from Diodati's pen, conform Milton's own intimations of his personality and of the relationship which had traditionally existed between them. Diodati could have seen Milton only occasionally during this period. He was apparently at Oxford or Chester most of the time, and in 1630 he spent a year in theological study at Geneva. It would have been well if he could have been closer at hand to promote his friend's recreation and perhaps mitigate his asperity toward the lighter-minded among his fellow students. As it was, Milton must have missed many a good hour of social pleasure. We sadly record a remark made in one of his later pamphlets concerning the amateur dramatics at Cambridge which shows his critical instinct getting the better of his enjoyment:

> In the colleges many of the young divines, and those next in aptitude to divinity, have been seen upon the stage, writhing and unboning their clergy limbs to all the antic and dishonest gestures of Trinculoes, buffoons, and bawds; prostituting the name of that ministry, which either they had or were nigh having, to the eyes of courtiers and court ladies, with their grooms and mademoiselles. These, while they acted and overacted, among other young scholars I was a spectator; they thought themselves gallant men, and I thought them fools; they made sport and I laughed; they mispronounced and I misliked; and, to make up the atticism, they were out, and I hissed.

This statement is part of an animadversion against the earlier literary indiscretions of a prelate who had attacked Milton, and it is politically as well as personally slanted. We have, however, learned enough from the prolusions and the letters to make us sure that he had no exuberant affection for his ordinary colleagues, scorned them professionally, could not take them for what they were, was easily offended by their animality. When he parted from them it was without regret.

Of his elders, on the other hand, or at least some of them, he retained pleasant memories, as he had done of those who guided and admired him as a schoolboy. Writing ten years later in reply to the scandalous assertion that he was "vomited forth from the university," Milton takes occasion to acknowledge "the more than ordinary favour and respect I found at the hands of those courteous and learned men, the Fellows of that college wherein I spent some years." They had, he says, at his graduation signified in many ways how much better it would content them that he should stay—

> As by many letters full of kindness and loving respect, both before that time, and long after, I was assured of their singular good affection toward me.

Except for accidents like the affair with Chappell, Milton was created for the delight of teachers. He throve on their appreciation and it fortified him against the casuality of an unselected adolescent world.

CHAPTER THREE

PASTORAL INTERLUDE
1632–8

"ON MY FATHER'S ESTATE where he had determined to pass the remainder of his days, I enjoyed an interval of uninterrupted leisure, which I entirely devoted to the study of Greek and Latin authors; though I occasionally visited the metropolis either for the sake of purchasing books, or of learning something new in mathematics or in music, in which I, at that time, found a source of pleasure and amusement. In this manner I spent five years till my mother's death."

Such is Milton's own summary of his life at Horton. If he had added, "Nor did I neglect to exercise the divine art of poetry as occasion offered," the statement would have been more complete. Actually Milton's interest in English poetry reached a height in this period under the new or at least intensified stimulus of approval by men of real artistic judgment and authority. Writing in 1654, when this interest had long been in abeyance, he thinks of other occupations as constituting his main effort. We shall need, in trying to understand his development and further explore the sources of his creativeness, to concern ourselves equally with all his activities in this epoch. The records include, as before, letters, poems, his own retrospective statements, the testimony of his contemporaries. We have, in addition, two folio manuscripts in his hand, one in which he kept drafts of English poems, the other containing notes from books he was reading. There are, of course, no more orations. His book-buying can be documented from the dozen or so volumes which have come down from his library with the purchase dates. Of his study of mathematics there is no detailed evidence. The science was making great progress at this time. That he was enamoured of music and had a connoisseur's knowledge of its most modern developments we know from later references. With all this data the image of Milton in his twenties ought, one would think, even at this remove of time, to be complete and perfect. Yet our knowledge is lacking at essential points, and our interpretation of these years of literary leisure must depend on our total reading of his life history. The issue continues to be the weighing of cultural influences against characteristic manifestations of his individuality.

To what extent and with what degree of personal concern did he watch the drama of public events which was unfolding itself in these years? From 1632 to 1637 England was suffering under a determined and well-organised administrative effort to enforce authority in Church and State. The last Parliament had been "broken" in 1629, after sturdily resolving against the promotion of non-Calvinistic doctrine and against the various devices whereby Charles was trying to raise money in default of a Parliamentary grant.

> Whoever shall bring in innovation in religion, or by favour seek to introduce Popery or Arminianism, or other opinions disagreeing from the true and orthodox Church, shall be reputed a capital enemy to this kingdom and the commonwealth.

> Whoever shall counsel or advise the taking and levying of the subsidies of tonnage and poundage not being granted by Parliament, or shall be an actor or instrument therein, shall be likewise reputed an innovator in the government, and a capital enemy to this kingdom and the commonwealth.

Sir John Eliot, imprisoned as a martyr to the rights of Englishmen, died in the Tower in 1632. Religious discontent found voice in the attacks of Bastwick, Burton, and Prynne against the bishops, and a new quality of public anger was roused by the brutal punishment of these offenders. John Lilburne was shortly to stand in the pillory declaiming passionately until his mouth was stopped:

> I am the son of a gentleman and my friends are of rank and quality in the country where they live, and I am in my present condition deserted of them all, for I know not one of them dare meddle with me in my present estate . . . yet notwithstanding for the cause of Christ and to do Him service I have and do bid adieu to father, friends, and riches, pleasures, ease, contented life and blood and lay down all at the footstool of Jesus Christ . . . for in naked Christ is the quintessence of sweetness and I am so far from thinking my affliction and punishment which this day I have endured and still do endure under a disgrace, that I receive it as the

welcome cross of Christ and do think myself this day more honoured by my sufferings than if a crown of gold had been set upon my head.

Milton's retirement left him only a spectator of these issues, and there is no outward sign of an emotional involvement which would lead us to anticipate the kind of action he ultimately took. He was, however, already in sympathy with the national movement, and by the end of the Horton period, in 1637, could give voice to the indignation of the time, foretelling in his loftiest vein "the ruin of our corrupted clergy then at their height."

Blind mouths! that scarce themselves know how to hold
A sheep-hook, or have learned aught else the least
That to the faithful herdsman's art belongs! . . ,
But that two-handed engine at the door
Stands ready to smite once, and smite no more.

The passage is a poet's cry, echoing the ecclesiastical denunciations of Dante and Spenser; but it is also an echo of the conviction of his college days that the office of a pulpit demanded a spiritual sincerity and a quality of humane learning not to be observed in the majority of those who were preparing themselves for it. It is not only the bishops whom he is attacking but his own professional colleagues and their kind, in contrast to the type of true shepherd represented for him by Young.

His personal decision regarding a Church career was in process of being arrived at. There is evidence of conflict and defensiveness in this matter in a letter addressed to an unknown friend early in the Horton period and preserved in two drafts among the first entries in the manuscript of his minor poems now at Trinity College, Cambridge. Milton has been reproached for idling his time away in study. He replies, with a good deal of conscience-searching, that it is not indolence or mere love of learning, but a sense of the need of thorough preparation which keeps him at his books. He allows the assumption to remain in his critic's mind that when he is ready it will be through the ministry that he will render an account of the talent which has been entrusted to him. If, he says, he should dilate on the degree to which the great commandment to labour while it is yet day weighs upon him he would run into the contradiction of doing that which he excuses himself for not doing—"preach and not preach." But the whole tenor of the letter shows that his ambition is set toward something which the Church in its present condition cannot give. Beside the motive of providing for a wife and family, which would be itself sufficient to overcome any mere proneness to dream away his life in study, there is, he says, a more powerful persuader to action in "the desire for honour and repute and immortal fame." It is not, therefore, "endless delight in speculation" but a "sacred reverence and religious advisement" which holds him back— "not taking thought of being late, so it give advantage to be more fit."

The real purposes implied in this are the all-embracing ones suggested in the seventh prolusion, where Milton speaks of the man who has gained possession of the stronghold of wisdom as being one to whom Nature has delegated her executive power, "as if to some prefect." The eloquence by which such sway is to be exercised might under ideal conditions be that of the pulpit. But for Milton himself there is a better way. And the actual situation, as he has been observing it, gives him the excuse he needs for not entering a profession which would necessarily and in any case have clipped his wings. Later he interprets his decision as having been specifically determined by Laud's enforcement of conformity. He is speaking in *The Reason of Church Government* of the obligation which he felt to lend a hand to those who were fighting the battle against episcopacy:

It were sad for me if I should draw back, for me especially, now when all men offer their aid to help ease and lighten the difficult labours of the Church, to whose service by the intentions of my parents and friends I was destined of a child and in mine own resolutions, till coming to some maturity of years and perceiving what tyranny had invaded the Church, that he who would take orders must subscribe slave, and take an oath withal, which unless he took with a conscience that would retch, he must either straight perjure, or split his faith, I thought it better to prefer a blameless silence before the sacred office of speaking, bought and begun with servitude and forswearing. Howsoever, thus Church-outed by the Prelates, hence may appear the right I have to meddle in these matters, as before the necessity and constraint appeared.

C

It is thought by some that disappointment at not receiving a fellowship at Christ's College underlay his turning against the ministry; by others that he was actually offered a fellowship and declined it out of conviction. Possibilities abound in all directions. His friend and classmate, Edward King, whom Milton felt was the right sort of candidate for the Church, was elected Fellow by royal mandate in 1630. Milton's statement that he had letters expressing the wish of the college that he might have stayed is no evidence that he was invited. If the election was controlled and he was passed over, his admirers among the tutors might well have so expressed themselves. Such an outcome of party politics might have served to bring the true state of affairs home to him personally, and in this sense he would have been "Church-outed." But the scope of his ambition was already beyond the most spacious Puritan conception of the preacher's function. I conclude that he had the common experience of outgrowing a parental plan without knowing that he had done so.

We do not know who the friend was and cannot guess. Milton says he profited by him whenever they met and suggests that spiritual admonition from this source was not infrequent. It does not sound like Thomas Young, with whom his relationship was quite unstrained and who apparently played the role rather of a receiver than a giver of good counsel. We should look rather to some custodian of souls who had not learned that John Milton's lips were wise though young and that the only way to deal with him was to listen. The Puritan divines of those times were good and learned men, skilled in cases of conscience and wonderful exhorters. As such they held the ear of England. Milton had had opportunity in London and at Cambridge to hear them and was doubtless full of admiration. By the logic of their own doctrine, however, he looked for personal direction within himself, and an attempt to help him, while he could not resent it as officious, was likely to do nothing except increase his own disturbance. Yet it remains possible that no weighty exhortation was ever made. Milton's sensitiveness anticipated criticism and the conviction that an ununderstanding and even hostile world awaited him had already been borne in on him. Perhaps it was Young after all who for the moment replaced the student audience, though a friend. In any case the intricate apology for his "tardy moving" is obviously addressed as much to his own conscience as to

the good watchman who has admonished him and shows
how easily he falls into questionings about himself. He
concludes:

> Yet, that you may see I am something suspicious of
> myself, and do take note of a certain belatedness in me I am
> the bolder to send you some of my nightward thoughts some
> time since.

Whereupon he quotes the sonnet written on his recent birthday,
"How soon hath Time, the subtle thief of youth." This, of
course, is the real point. Milton has analysed himself in prose
to the length of showing his reader, singly, how he might deal
with a whole congregation "and spoil the patience of a parish."
In offering the sublimation of such thoughts in a poem he at
once releases himself from them and makes his most winning
appeal.

Another but more serene plea for continuance in a way of
life which shows no bud or blossom of practical accomplishment is afforded by a Latin epistle in verse addressed to the
poet's father. No date is attached to this composition. It has
been assigned to the end of the Horton period or even later,
but belongs with the *Letter to a Friend*, which is certainly early,
in its relevance to the problems of Milton's career. The absence
of any intricate or shuffling apology and the fact that he comes
before us not as a hesitating candidate for the ministry, but as a
poet with no other goal than achievement of distinction in the
literary art may suggest that his irresolution is at an end. It
need not, necessarily, for poetry is not really a profession or
inconsistent with the ministry, and the poet's father is perhaps
not the person who roused guilty feelings on this score. The
intimation is that if this parent had had his way his son would
have been a lawyer:

> You did not, Father, bid me go where a broad way lies
> open, where the opportunities for gain are easier, and the
> golden hope of amassing riches shines steadily. Nor do you
> force me to the civil code, and the ill-guarded principle of
> national justice, and thus condemn my ears to senseless
> clamour.

His defence is the defence of poetry itself, which his father, by
his devotion to the sister art of music, ought to be the first to
recognise:

Do not look down upon divine song, the poet's function, than which there is nothing that more commends his ethereal birth and heavenly ancestry. . . . The gods on high love song; and song has power to stir the trembling depths of Tartarus and to fetter the gods of the lower world. . . . Poetry used to add beauty to royal banquets, when luxury and the measureless depths of insatiable appetites were not yet known, but the feast sparkled with wine temperately enjoyed. Then as he sat at the festal board, as tradition enjoyned, the minstrel, with his unshorn locks encircled with oak leaves, would sing of the prowess of heroes and of deeds that deserve imitation, and of Chaos and of the broad based foundations of the universe.

The old conviction of the divine calling and high utility of the poet as the best kind of teacher and inspirer now serves him to good purpose in defending his favourite occupation and the way of life which it requires. He will return to the subject in more detailed analyses of the poet's function in the tradition of the great theorists from Aristotle and the Italians to his own Ben Jonson and Sir Philip Sidney. He tries not to disparage the musician's art, but cannot quite refrain from suggesting its inferiority. "Empty modulations of the voice, when devoid of words and their meaning and of rhythmical language . . . befit the choruses of the woods not Orpheus." He praises his father's own expertness, saying that he may justly be termed Arion's heir. For his sire's uneasiness the youth has words of sweetly assured reproof. If he has begotten in his son a poet he must accept a sharer in the gifts of Phœbus. Milton already feels himself one of the company of scholars, though the humblest of them all. In time to come he will take his seat in the midst of the ivy and laurel wreaths of the victor. "No longer shall I be lost in the obscurity of the stupid crowd."

Such is the Miltonic platform as framed for the ears of one who from the first encouraged him to the scholarly and the artistic life. Hostile criticism, though but surmised as lurking ready to join his own doubts to undermine him, is encountered in a different mood.

Hence, wakeful cares, hence complaints, and the glance of envy with its twisted looks askance. Savage calumny, open not your snaky jaws. Over me, loathsome crew, you have no power for ill; I come not under your jurisdiction, and safely, with breast free from care I shall walk high above your viperous stroke.

We shall see how well or ill he kept this poise when the attack did come.

Whatever the resolution of Milton's specific doubts about the ministry, the life he lived at Horton was a good and fruitful one and not more ivory-towered than that of many choice spirits of our own time, who after privileged years of self-cultivation *in der Stille* come to play their parts thereafter *in dem Strom der Welt*. Some will even have it that Milton's best and happiest work was done there. It is not possible to pass an unconditional judgment. Let us try rather to describe the occupations which enthralled him and to further define the idealistic philosophy which was henceforth to be the burden of his utterance. Freed from irrelevant academic obligations and from the irritations which he had built up for himself in his personal relationships, he was able to concentrate on a programme suited to his purposes. He was able to store up from imaginative literature and from the impressions of a beautiful and serene environment a pattern of satisfaction in the life of the senses, delicately but keenly experienced, which never wholly deserted him—remained at least as a memory and yearning in his latest days. What this was to mean to him is well expressed in the following idyllic passage from *Paradise Lost*:

> As one who long in populous city pent,
> Where houses thick and sewers annoy the air,
> Forth issuing on a summer's morn to breathe
> Among the pleasant villages and farms
> Adjoined, from each thing met conceives delight,
> The smell of grain, or tedded grass, or kine,
> Or dairy, each rural sight, each rural sound;
> If chance with nymph-like step fair virgin pass,
> What pleasing seemed, for her now pleases more,
> She most, and in her look sums all delight.

The summer's morn, the tedded grass, the nymph-like step are Horton images revived for him by smell or sound or touch amid the darkness of his latest years. For the more immediate and vivid record of his delight in the æsthetic relaxation to which he gave himself so happily we have the familiar companion pieces, "L'Allegro" and "Il Penseroso." It will be well to discuss them before the other Horton documents, for they evidently represent that first zestful enthusiasm for vacation freedom which gradually gives way to soberer and more purposeful enjoyment. It is possible, as we have seen, that they were actually written before Milton had left the University, but even so they are expressive of the mood begotten in him by the kind of escape which was afforded in his father's country home.

The poems are a comprehensive record of æsthetic pleasures. The two imaginary personalities which Milton creates for purposes of expression are in reality one. L'Allegro is Milton in his sunny waking mood; Il Penseroso is Milton dreaming. Each poem describes a full day's occupation, but both the merry and the pensive days are ideal or exceptional. "L'Allegro" and "Il Penseroso" are an extension of the holiday hours which the poet sparingly allowed himself. These hours are filled with the enjoyment of nature, of society, of books, of music. L'Allegro delights in the morning. Long before sunrise he wakens and lies dreamily listening to the pure bird notes. The lark from his high station is his watchman to warn him of approaching dawn. At length he rises and is the solitary witness of the birth of a new day:

> Straight mine eye hath caught new pleasures
> Whilst the landscape round it measures;
> Russet lawns, and fallows gray,
> Where the nibbling flocks do stray,
> Mountains, on whose barren breast
> The lab'ring clouds do often rest;
> Meadows trim with daisies pied,
> Shallow brooks, and rivers wide.
> Towers and battlements it sees
> Bosomed high in tufted trees,
> Where perhaps some beauty lies,
> The Cynosure of neighb'ring eyes.

The English countryside, its farms, its cottages, and its simple people are for Milton a poem; it is as if his own mind had created them, and he himself remains amid this beauty as the animating spirit of the whole. But he is also the man of culture, the social being, who sees the world with a fine detachment and yet can mingle with it. Sweet brier and eglantine are about him; the merry din of barnyard fowl is in his ears. He dresses and goes forth to walk straight east toward the pageant of the rising sun. As the day advances he notes with pleasure the appearance of each familiar rural sight; the whistling plough-man, the singing milkmaid, the mower—and, toward evening, the country dancing on the village green. He has an artist's eye for landscape and an English gentleman's love of it. He is present, at least in spirit, at the rural gatherings, and listens to the naïve folk stories which pass from mouth to mouth as the country ale goes round. Nor is he ill at ease in the company of his equals and amid the more sophisticated pleasures of the town. A society function pays its tribute of colourful and poetic pageantry. The stage is an endless source of imaginative and sensuous delight. Music, whether heard in masque or concert or participated in with a group of kindred enthusiasts, thrills him to the point of ecstasy. Such are the Muses' un-alloyed delights for one who, like L'Allegro, accepts them as his feastful friends.

The companion poem records the satisfactions of solitary meditation. It is not the Muses to which Milton here pays homage, but the Muse. The scene, to be sure, is largely the same; the spirit that walks among them is for the moment changed. Il Penseroso courts only those aspects of the world which create the poetic *Stimmung* and quickly lose their sub-stance to become part of the baseless fabric of a dream. The nightingale, the moon, the curfew,

> Over some wide watered shore,
> Swinging slow with sullen roar;

above all firelight and candle, the hearth cricket, and the bellman's drowsy call from out of doors. In such surroundings the mind itself has scope. Books feed it and the hours go by in the richer happiness of thought and vision. The direction of Il Penseroso's reading is clearly marked and well worth noting. Obviously it is no planned programme like that which, as we shall see, must have occupied his morning hours. He begins with Plato in the half-mystical Timæus, passes from that to the even more irresponsible vagaries of his successors: Michael Psellus perhaps, and certainly the thaumaturgic Hermes. Thence to the realm of pure poetic fiction.

Significantly Milton pauses in his literary wanderings to brood over the works of his poetic compeers of the past which are lost or were left unfinished. It is not merely romantic yearning that prompts him to wish that Orpheus might repeat

for him the hymn which half regained Eurydice, or that
Chaucer might return to finish the tale of Cambuscan. These
lacunæ are an invitation to John Milton, and his confidence is
fostered by the creative stirrings he begins to feel within him.
On such dreams and hopes he sleeps and if the morrow brings
as yet no actual achievement it advances him another step
toward his chosen goal. The day is Sunday, with rain followed
by clear weather. The poet walks again abroad and sleeps at
noon. The genius of the wood, who must be none other than
his friend the musician Lawes, awakens him with music.
There follows church service with pealing organ and clear
anthem of the full-voiced choir. The mood induced is a higher
and more solemn one than that with which "L'Allegro" closes,
portending the increase of wisdom and an attainment of that
prophetic power which was for Milton a necessary thought in
any serious hour. And so we are brought back from the world
of untroubled enjoyment to that of earnest aspiration, with its
inevitable anxiety of choice, its "intense labour, which I take
to be my portion in this life," and its vision of final ecstasy as a
reward of the ascetic life.

The serious studies of the Horton period can be reconstructed
in some detail from the notebook above mentioned, happily
discovered among the papers of a noble family by the British
Historical Manuscripts Commission in 1874. They evidently
relate to his preparation for the duty of guiding men through
eloquence and wisdom, as he had proposed that function to
himself and others in his university days. There is not the
slightest doubt that the Commonplace Book is Milton's. It
shows his handwriting in all its stages and that of several of his
known amanuenses. And every entry is characteristic. The book
is what was known in the poet's time as a "topic folio," the
seventeenth-century substitute for the card catalogue. There
are three parts, headed respectively *Index Ethicus*, *Index Politicus*,
Index Economicus. The individual pages begin each with a topic
—"*Rex*," "*Matrimonium*," "*Libertas*"—and contain extracts or
summaries of passages from Milton's reading which have struck
him as worth remembering under that head. It has proved
possible by close examination of the entries to determine
approximately the order in which the books from which they
were taken were read; and, since Milton changed his style of
penmanship during his Italian journey, to tell with certainty
which belong to the Horton period.

He began, apparently, with the records of early Christianity in Eusebius and his continuers, turning aside to study the writing of the Fathers themselves: Clement, Cyprian, Ignatius, Tertullian, Justin Martyr. The contemporary secular history of the Greek Empire was represented by Procopius and the later Byzantines, that of Rome by Sigonius and others. All this is clearly in pursuance of a plan of historical study, appropriate to one who like Milton was "industrious after wisdom" and convinced that languages are acquired as a means of coming at the "solid things in them." History as opposed to dialectic had, we recall, already been championed by him in a university oration. It was natural, therefore, that he should, when he had opportunity, turn systematically to such study as a serious preparation for the part of intellectual and spiritual leadership which, whether in sermon, book or poem, he was determined some day to play.

The evidence of the Horton entries in the Commonplace Book is confirmed and supplemented by Milton's own statements:

Some years I spent [he writes in 1642] in the stories of those Greek and Roman exploits, wherein I found many things both nobly done and worthily spoken, when coming in the method of time to that age wherein the Church had obtained a Christian emperor, I so prepared myself as being now to read examples of wisdom and goodness among those who were foremost in the Church, not elsewhere to be paralleled; but to the amazement of what I expected, Readers, I found it all quite contrary, except in some very few. Nothing but ambition, corruption, contention, combustion: in so much that I could not but love the historian Sigonius, who in the proem to his fifth book professes he was fain to intermix affairs of state, for that it would else be an annoyance to hear in a continued discourse the endless brabbles and counterplotting of the bishops.

This passage suggests that Milton's programme as set down in the Commonplace Book involved systematic study of ancient secular and ecclesiastical history, at least from Apostolic times. A letter addressed to Diodati (September 23rd, 1637) points forward to its continuance through the Middle Ages:

I carried the study of the affairs of the Greeks continuously down to the time when they ceased to deserve the name of

Greeks. I was long occupied with the obscure history of
Italy under the Lombards, Franks, and Germans to the
moment when that nation was emancipated by Rudolph,
king of Germany. Henceforth it will be best to read separately
what each city accomplished under its own military leadership. . . . Meanwhile I beg you, if you can without trouble,
to send me Giustinani's History of the Venetians.

The later entries in the Commonplace Book show that Milton
did actually proceed with the study of the city-states.

The intellectual and scholarly maturity of Milton's researches into the affairs of men is made clear enough by the
selection and ordering of the materials and by the well-defined
purpose which appears to animate them. Looking back on this
period from a later time, he speaks of "many studious and
contemplative years altogether spent in the search for religious
and civil knowledge" and he remarks more specifically in the
Second Defence: "I had in my youth studied the distinction
between civil and religious rights." Though these statements
are coloured by interests which became absorbing only in later
years, even the Horton entries show that Milton was reading
not merely for delight and ornament but for ability. They also
show that his political Puritanism, or more properly his
liberalism, was of early growth. Thus a note on Constantine's
giving the clergy immunity from civil office and one praising
the modesty of princes who refuse to meddle in matters of
religion suggest that his convictions on this subject were already
formed. Others, under the heading *Census et Vectical*, were
probably prompted by interest in the illegal exactions of
Charles. More surprising at this early date is the following:
"Sulpitius Severus declares that free peoples have ever loathed
the name of king." In his pamphlets published before the
condemnation of Charles, Milton neither says nor implies
anything against the royal prerogative. The Horton entry
shows that he was a Republican by conviction long before the
outbreak of the civil war. His earliest notes regarding marriage
tell the same story of libertarian inclinations. Though there
is nothing about divorce till later, Milton is evidently ready
to go along with those radical Protestants who held lax views
on the marriage relationship, extending even to the theoretical
countenancing of polygamy.

In all this Milton had, one may suppose, no guidance other

than the cultural tradition of his age and his own general purpose of exercising a superior kind of spiritual and moral leadership "beside the office of a pulpit." Professor Haller has pointed out to me that Thomas Young read many of the authors the poet mentions and that in general his programme of humanistic learning in the service of reformed religion parallels that which the leadership of the Puritan clergy had actually adopted. Milton undoubtedly owed much to their example. It might, however, be hard to match the competence and range of exploratory interest exhibited in his studies. Having adopted for himself the motto, "Not how soon but how fit," he must needs erect a conception of fitness difficult enough of attainment to justify his delay.

The Commonplace Book does not, of course, embody the complete record of Milton's private studies. It contains no entries from the Bible and few from the classics or from English or Continental *belles-lettres*. Musical and scientific materials are also lacking. A marginal reference to an *Index Theologicus* suggests that he may have kept several notebooks for various classes of subject matter. A part of his scholarly activity certainly went toward the textual study of the Greek poets, perhaps with a view to editing them. His copies of Pinder and Euripides bear witness to the meticulous care with which he worked at the task of comparing scholia. A marginal note in his Lycophron presumptuously suggests an emendation solely on the ground that the line would be nobler so. The new adjective has no support and does not go in the metre. In these activities Milton's habit was to work hard and continuously till a job was done. "My genius is such," he tells Diodati, "that no delay, no rest, no care or thought almost of anything, holds me aside until I reach the end I am making for, and round off, as it were, some great period of my studies."

In such moments of concentration Milton would have wanted no companionship. We can all but visualise his high abstraction from such things as a call to dinner or an invitation to a walk. But by the same token, in the intervals of relaxation he would have wanted or needed it the more. The evidence is that he had become aware of a problem of social relationship and was further elaborating a theory in support of his own withdrawal. He makes a point of non-gregariousness in the seventh prolusion. "To babble with one another stupidly" is "the friendship of ignorance, or really the ignorance of friendship."

In "L'Allegro" and "Il Penseroso" the debate should be between the truly social being and the recluse, but L'Allegro himself is a recluse. He walks among men, to be sure, but holds them at arm's length. On the other hand, Milton cherished with a romantic yearning the idea of philosophic association with the wise and good. "What," he asks, "can be imagined more delightful, what more happy than those conferences of learned and most eminent men, such as divine Plato is said to have held very frequently under that famous plane tree?"

If he pursued this ideal very exactingly, his range of companionship in the country would have been limited indeed. The real problem, of course, is his relationship with women. He should obviously have been taking advantage of the golden hours, but the chances are heavily against his having done so. When he speaks of the desire for a house and family of one's own which "about this time of a man's life solicits most," he speaks not only as one who had made a resolution against marriage, but as one who was in the process of making a substitution for it.

One association which might have done much to lead his feet in more relaxing paths is that with the musician, Henry Lawes. Lawes was already a well-known professional figure in London by the time Milton left the University. He had been a member of the Chapel Royal since the accession of Charles I and in 1630 was appointed one of the King's Music, an office which brought him into immediate contact with the court as a performer in the elaborate musical and dramatic entertainments of the time. He was also attached to the family of Sir John Egerton, first Earl of Bridgewater, shortly to be appointed Lord President of Wales. Bridgewater was son and heir to Sir Thomas Egerton, who had died in 1617 as James I's Lord Chancellor. Sir Thomas' widow, the Countess Dowager of Derby, formerly married to Ferdinando Stanley, lived at Harefield, a few miles from the Milton estate. Once a patroness of the poet Spenser, who claimed kindred with her line, this lady was a venerable and distinguished aristocrat whose social influence must have dominated the whole neighbourhood. We have the record of Lawes's visits to this establishment in a surviving account book of 1634.

There were grandchildren living with the Countess, and Lawes was probably employed in their instruction, as he certainly was in that of the son and daughters of Sir John, who had his country seat at Ashridge and paid frequent visits to the Harefield estate on his journeys to and from London. The dates and detail of this relationship we do not know exactly. But it was in all probability Lawes who was called on to produce a dramatic entertainment at Harefield for some occasion in the early 1630s. This was probably before he had taken any leading part in the production of a court masque, though he is believed to have performed regularly in them.

Competition was keen among poets, musicians, and stage designers, and Lawes was probably ambitious to demonstrate his ability to compose and direct a private performance in a family which like the Egertons were themselves involved in the court affairs. For this performance Milton wrote the words, later published under the title *Arcades* and described as "part of an entertainment presented to the Countess Dowager of Derby at Harefield, by some noble persons of her family, who appear on the scene in pastoral habit, moving towards the seat of state." The poem consists of three exquisite lyrics in the Elizabethan tradition of aristocratic compliment and a blank verse address by the Genius of the Wood, a part which we assume to have been taken by Lawes himself and which may have helped establish him in such parts.

This was a literary commission which might have led, had Milton and his times been other than they were, to a court career and to association with fellow artists who, like Lawes, throve briefly in this last manifestation of the culture of the preceding age. As a composer of airs for lyrics of the best poets, as recipient of aristocratic patronage, and as a future dispenser of royal favour, Lawes was already in a position to advance the fortunes of a literary aspirant. We are prepared to find Milton potentially a member of the artistic circles in which Lawes moved. His father's interests, his own contributions to student verse in the Hobson poems, and to national letters in the lines on Shakespeare, point in this direction. Without more knowledge we can only speculate on the part played by the musician in stimulating Milton's activity. The poet was, we believe, highly suggestible to older persons who understood how to deal with him and whose accomplishments he admired, nor was he at all proof against social and artistic glamour. Lawes had good reason to encourage a promising talent and may have made a strong play for Milton's allegiance. The poet's familiarity with court pageantry, already apparent in the poem on a Fair

Infant, suggests that his friend's influence in that direction was of early date. Did he, perhaps, encourage Milton to take the role of Father in the Vacation Exercise, and was it for him that the poet wrote the lyric on May Morning, the poem "At a Solemn Music" and the companion pieces, "L'Allegro" and "Il Penseroso"?

The invitation to write the words for the Harefield entertainment implies some confidence that Milton could adapt himself not only artistically but socially to the requirements of the situation. The necessity of suiting the performance to the tastes of the audience and the interests of the noble actors would naturally have involved consultation with them, and there is no reason to suppose that Milton would not have been present at rehearsals and at the affair itself. The fact that he was accessible in the neighbourhood may have been an added reason for his selection. We know, however, that he was conditioned against any real integration with this society. He already stands poles apart from such a world and the likelihood of its receiving him on his own terms or of his accepting its advances in anything but the most tentative way is slight indeed. No writer of historical fiction, to my knowledge, has undertaken to show us Milton interrupting his studies to present himself at Harefield and exchange courtesies with the awe-inspiring dowager, the socially experienced Lord Brackley, and the soon to be marriageable Lady Alice, but the opportunity to do so obviously exists.

The text which he writes shows perfect familiarity with the tradition in which the Countess herself had been bred and of which she would doubtless have been a connoisseur. If Lawes is responsible for the device, Milton carried it out with a literary finesse beyond the capacities of any living poet. In so doing he finds that his own poetic personality and its familiar symbols have taken on a new radiance. The phrase in *Arcades*,

> Sitting like a goddess bright,
> In the centre of her light,

embodies a Miltonic idea. The imagery of the second song is also very much his own.

> O'er the smooth enamelled green,
> Where no print of foot hath been,
> Follow me as I sing,
> And touch the warbled string,

> Under the shady roof
> Of branching elm star-proof.
> Follow me.

Finally, in the declamation the poet projects himself into a role which has possibilities for him. It is the first time he has spoken in the person of an angel, but not the last. By day the Genius inspires and protects the woodland growth; by night he listens to the music of the spheres,

> which none can hear
> Of human mould, with gross unpurgèd ear.

In the final song, conjuring with a recondite mythology, he bids the nymphs and shepherds dance no more,

> By sandy Ladon's lilied banks,

but come and live where they shall have "greater grace" to serve Arcadia's Queen.

These hints are elaborated in Milton's second and more elaborate masque, which, indeed, centres in the figure corresponding to the Genius, that of the Attendant Spirit, pronouncer of Miltonic doctrine in a more rapt and mystical form than we have hitherto encountered. The occasion of *Comus* was the inauguration of the Earl of Bridgewater as the Lord President of Wales in 1634. It was given at Ludlow Castle in September, Lawes himself taking the part of the Attendant Spirit and three children of the Earl those of the Lady and her brothers. The production would perhaps have striven to rival the royal pageantry of London in its magnificence, for the Lord President was actually a viceroy and his success in ruling the "old and haughty nation" through his council of Welsh nobility depended on prestige. Inaugurations were political acts and in that day no expense was spared to ensure impressiveness. The Bridgewater House records preserved at the Huntington Library, though they contain no data concerning *Comus*, bear sufficient witness to the state maintained both at Ludlow Castle and at Ashridge, and to the elaborateness of the seasonal progresses from London of the Lord President and his train.

The stage version of *Comus* has survived, with directions in Lawes's hand; so too has the score of four of Lawes's songs. There is some evidence of collaboration between poet and producer. Milton has carefully copied back into his own manuscript bits of stage business devised by his friend. And Lawes apparently owed to a suggestion contained in a cancelled passage of Milton's rough draft the idea of transferring the spirit's epilogue to the beginning. He may or may not have had the poet's approval when he shortened some long passages and broke heavy speeches into dialogue. These changes point to a limitation, perhaps an unexpected one, in Milton's adaptability to the masque requirement. The intrusion of his own personality and ideas now becomes conspicuous, resulting in a literary text which would appear to be far too weighty to serve the social purpose for which it was designed.

One fancies that Milton, emboldened by the experience of *Arcades* and having profited by a matter of four years' added growth in wisdom, tended to take matters into his own hands. He may have further studied the masque tradition and perhaps seen Lawes in Carew's *Coelum Brittanicum*, for which he had composed the music and in which two Egerton children had performed amid such animal heads as they were later to confront in *Comus*. He is likely at least to have read Fletcher's *Faithful Shepherdess* after its revival at court in the winter of 1632 and he might have inferred from that play a larger literary possibility for such entertainment. He must have known and had opinions about the recent pastoral enthusiasms of court and the great business of Platonic love which Queen Henrietta was promoting, to the cynical amusement of some of the old hands at it.

In any case, accepting the mythological, allegorical, pastoral tradition of the masque and its prevailing theme of the triumph of some virtue, Milton sets out to improve on it in all respects. The theme of chastity was near his heart and he yearned to preach it. He had not quite done so before, for the gross brutishness which made human ears incapable of hearing the celestial harmony had always been left unspecified. Now was the happy opportunity of defining his purest thought in the Iris woof of poetry, and making the very people who most needed this high doctrine, the courtly youths and maidens of fashionable society, themselves the instruments of promulgating it. The familiar symbol of Circe and her monsters, men transformed by bestial sensuality, afforded the groundwork. Comus the god of revelry, a classic and Jonsonian creation, could be redrawn in the image of dissolute youth which at once fascinated and alarmed him. The Lady is an ideal embodiment of the informed and fastidious innocence which had won him his academic nickname. Her brothers are protective males, already principled in virtue's book. Thyrsis, the Attendant Spirit, is divine guidance, a Platonic angel, descending from the sphere to bring Heavenly counsel and support to mortals.

All the experience and conviction of Milton's youth are here. He has known and weighed the arguments of the enchanter. The Lady's eloquent answer is ready to his lips. It is, I think, no fanciful idea that Milton's *Comus* was written as a more or less official reply to the libertine philosophy of his fellow student, Thomas Randolph. In *The Muse's Looking Glass*, which Milton may well have seen performed, it is reasoned that Nature's bounty is an invitation to enjoyment and that he who would be continent commits a sullen injury against her. Comus rehearses this very argument, thereby prompting the Lady to open her virgin lips in chastity's defence. If the poet had indeed been offended by Randolph in his Cambridge days, to exhibit him thus as the corrupt son of Circe and Bacchus, confuted in his own palace by the voice of innocence and truth, would have been a very proper and a very Miltonian revenge. But there were many other Randolphs, and Milton is indeed standing against the whole lewd tradition of libertine and erotic verse.

The dominant philosophy of *Comus* is obviously a Christian-ised Platonism. The pattern of true love is laid up in Heaven, and earthly virtue is a discipline preparatory to its enjoyment. Reason and knowledge are the sources of right action; the senses enslave; faith is grounded in philosophy; the mind is its own place. More specifically, virtuous and vicious thoughts transform the material or the spiritual substance each to its own essence.

> For of the soul the body form doth take
> For soul is form and doth the body make.

Milton came to this way of thinking partly, as he himself suggests, through Spenser. Amoret in the house of Busyrane in Book III of the *Faerie Queen* is a kindred image of chastity triumphant over lust; the close of Book II is a Platonic myth, based, like *Comus*, on the legent of Circe and her beasts. Spenser, supplying Milton with poetic phrase and imagery, taught him how the poet embodies truth in dreams and directed him with new conviction to the poet among philoso-phers as supplying the mode of thought most congenial to his own idealistic temper.

What satisfaction Lawes and the Egertons took in the presentation of Milton's aspiring poem we do not know. It is probable that any expectation of further collaboration was at an end. Lawes was now involved in composing for and acting in the major masques at court, working successively with Carew, Townsend, Shirley, and Davenant, but Milton had no hand in any of them. There could well have been frustration in this, however much the situation was one of his own making. But Milton had ample defences against any intimation of incomplete success. He cherished the idea that what he had to give was far superior to the tinsel trappings of the stage and that Lawes himself had received and profited by his doctrine. Their relationship, as he conceived it, is the theme of a little allegory in *Comus*, wherein the Attendant Spirit (Lawes himself) tells how he came by knowledge of the magic herb which will make the Lady safe in the halls of the enchanter.

>   Care and utmost shifts
> How to secure the lady from surprisal,
> Brought to my mind a certain shepherd lad,
> Of small regard to see to, yet well skilled
> In every virtuous plant and healing herb,
> That spreads her verdant leaf to th' morning ray:
> He loved me well, and oft would beg me sing,
> Which when I did, he on the tender grass
> Would sit, and hearken e'en to ecstasy,
> And in requital ope his leathern scrip,
> And show me simples of a thousand names,
> Telling their strange and vigorous faculties:
> Amongst the rest a small unsightly root,
> But of divine effect, he culled me out;
> The leaf was darkish, and had prickles on it,
> But in another country, as he said,
> Bore a bright golden flow'r, but not in this soil:
> Unknown, and like esteemed, and the dull swain
> Treads on it daily with his clouted shoon,
> And yet more medicinal is it than that moly
> That Hermes once to wise Ulysses gave;
> He called it Haemony, and gave it me,
> And bade me keep it as of sovereign use
> 'Gainst all enchantments, mildew, blast, or damp,
> Or ghastly furies' apparition.

The shepherd lad is Milton himself; the herb, bearing in more favoured soils the flower of poetry, is the Christian and Platonic ideal of virtue which the mature and gifted Lawes accepted from his lips.

The effects of Milton's moment of participation in the current dramatic movement were more lasting than appears on the surface. His friendship with Lawes continued and we shall have reason to believe that he never quite gave up the idea of marrying the arts of poetry, music, and the stage on the highest level, with the poet in command. Lawes, for his part, joined others in acclaiming Milton's genius. He published *Comus* in 1637, with a dedicatory letter to Bridgewater's son and heir, who had performed in it, describing the poem, though unacknowledged by the author, as a "legitimate offspring, so lovely and so much desired that the often copying of it hath tired my pen to give my several friends satisfaction." A motto, which Milton must himself have chosen, repeats the old deprecation of criticism. The circle of readers was not wide, but it included one who might well have stood in the poet's mind as the best qualified judge then living, that ripe Elizabethan diplomat and man of letters, Sir Henry Wotton, now Provost of Eton College. Milton called on him some time in the early spring of 1638 and, encouraged by his affability, sent him a copy of Lawes's edition after his return to Horton. Wotton's acknowledgment is as just in its appreciation as it is urbane.

I should much commend the tragical part, if the lyrical did not ravish me with a certain Doric delicacy in your songs and odes, whereunto I must plainly confess I have seen nothing yet parallel in our language: *Ipsa molities.* But I must not omit to tell you that I now only owe you thanks for intimating unto me (how modestly soever) the true artificer. For the work itself I viewed some while before, having received it from our common friend Mr. R. in the very close of the late R's poems, printed at Oxford, whereunto it was added, as I suppose, that the accessory might help out the principal, according to the art of stationers, and leave the reader *con la bocca dolce.*

"The late R" is presumably Randolph, who had died in 1635 and whose *Poems* appeared in the year in which Wotton wrote. We have no other knowledge of a single volume containing these two strange Cambridge bedfellows.

Between the writing of *Comus* in 1634 and that of *Lycidas* in November, 1637, there are no poems from Milton's pen, unless the verse epistle to his father was prompted, as it may well have been, by the activities in which he had been engaged. We know from a letter to Alexander Gill, dated December 4th, 1634, that he had written a Greek ode the week before, "the first and only thing" to be composed in that language "since I left your school." He employs himself more willingly, he tells his friend, in Latin and English, since whoever spends study on Greek "runs risk of singing mostly to the deaf." The letter was written "from our suburban residence" but makes an appointment with Gill the following Monday "among the booksellers." There is an unexplained request that Gill use his good offices with the "annual President of the College" in "the promotion of our business," and thanks for a set of hendecasyllabic verses he has sent. This is the last communication to Gill and the last evidence of Milton's continued acquaintance with him. Such usefulness as he had had as a stimulus to creative effort was presumably over. Collaboration with Lawes and the effects of public success as an English poet would naturally have diverted the poet's interest from the relatively sterile fellowship of neo-Latin verse.

The studies of the Commonplace Book may have preoccupied Milton in the next few years. His return to poetry in the autumn of 1637 is heralded by two prose letters to Diodati which reveal a new stage in his emotional relationship with this absent friend. Both are dated from London. In the first, written on September 2nd, Milton speaks of being about to set forth for his country residence; in the second (September 23rd) of looking for a more convenient town dwelling in one of the Inns of Court, where he can find a pleasant walking ground and less cramped quarters. He hopes Diodati will soon return from the north parts, so that they may exchange visits and be neighbours both in town and country. It is evident that the two have not met or corresponded for some time. The fault has not been Milton's, who has never been guilty of not answering a letter in due turn. Diodati, unlike himself, is an easy letter-writer. How does it happen that he has sent letters to the bookseller and to his brother, John, without including one to Milton? The poet complains also that his friend failed of his promise to pay him a visit when he left the city. He himself has gone out of his way to make inquiries and when

Diodati was falsely reported to be in London has dashed to his empty lodgings as if by storm.

When at length Diodati does write, Milton answers, first with a long comment on the six hundred healths which his friend has wished him:

> While other friends generally in their letters think it enough to express a single wish for one's health, I see now how it is that you convey the same salutation so many ways; for to all that you yourself could in former times offer, and which are all that others have to offer yet, you would now have me understand, I suppose, that there is the gigantic addition of your art and all the forces of your medical practitionership.

Professor Dorian, in a recent study of the Diodati family, gives reason to believe that Charles had just begun the independent practice of medicine and that Milton is congratulating him on the event.

> Verily [the poet continues], you must have been made the very steward of the larder, the clerk of the kitchen of Health. . . . Health ought now to be your parasite, you so act the king over her and command her to be obedient. I therefore congratulate you, and find it consequently necessary to return you thanks on double account—your friendship for one thing, and your excellence in your profession for another.

This may well be a bantering felicitation. To me it sounds also like mildly irritated cavilling. One recalls the opening of the sixth elegy eight years before in which Milton wishes Diodati the good health which because of his heavy eating he perhaps lacks. Was there not bound to be a slight admixture of jealousy in Milton's relationship with this exuberant youth who apparently arrived at his goals with so little effort? He reiterates the complaint of the former letter with the additional reminder that Diodati had promised to correspond: "I did, indeed, since it had been so agreed, long expect letters from you." Then he proceeds to idealise his own feeling by the same Platonic formula of love in absence which he had used more lightly years before in addressing Young.

> For I would not have true friendship turn on balances of letters and salutations, all which may be false, but that it should rest on both sides in the deep roots of the mind and

sustain itself there, and that once begun on sincere and
sacred grounds, it should, though mutual good offices cease,
be free from suspicion and blame all life long.

This, surely, is an effort to maintain the imaginary values of a
friendship which has perhaps ceased on one side to have
meaning save as a pleasant memory. Diodati, as was natural,
has been carried along by the realities around him and has
little need of the gentle youth whom he had befriended and
loved at St. Paul's. Milton's sense of injury, if there is one, is
quickly lost in the Platonic explanation of his love in absence.
Forgetting his earlier image of Diodati as a light and sensual
creature, who can admire but by no means attain the Miltonic
way of life and thought, he now makes him an embodiment of
the ideal object of his own quest for goodness, truth, and
beauty. The abstracted love of *Comus* has found a local habitation.

> What besides God has resolved concerning me I know not,
> but this at least. He has instilled into me, if into anyone, a
> vehement love of the beautiful. Not with so much labour—
> as the fables have it, is Ceres said to have sought her daughter
> Proserpina as it is my habit day and night to seek for this
> idea of the beautiful, as for a certain image of true beauty,
> through all the forms and faces of things. . . . Hence it is that
> when anyone scorns what the vulgar opine in their depraved
> estimation of things, and dares to feel and speak and be that
> which the highest wisdom throughout all ages has taught to
> be best, to that man I attach myself forthwith. . . . If, whether
> by nature or by my fate, I am so circumscribed that by no
> effort and labour of mine can I myself rise to such an honour
> and elevation, yet that I should always worship and look up
> to those who have attained that glory, or happily aspire to
> it, neither gods nor men, I reckon, have bidden nay.

It is natural that Milton should pass from this rapture to a
statement of his own poetic plans:

> You make many anxious inquiries, even as to what I am
> at present thinking. Harken, Theodotus, but let it be in your
> private ear, lest I blush; and allow me for a little to use big
> language with you. You ask what I am thinking of? So may
> the good Deity help me, of immortality. And what am I
> doing? Growing my wings and meditating flight; but as yet

our Pegasus raises himself on very tender pinions. Let us be lowly wise!

When Milton wrote these words he may already have been at work on "Lycidas," for the draft in the Trinity manuscript is dated in November. The poem is the culmination of the effort of the Horton period as the Nativity Ode, of which he boasted to Diodati with similar exultation, had been of his literary work at Cambridge. If I interpret it aright, the poem is itself an embodiment of the fervid idealism with which Milton invests his love for his dearest friend. We need not be surprised to find him transferring to the deceased Edward King the emotions which had hitherto been associated with Diodati and in doing so giving these emotions a new refinement and a higher eloquence.

King had been a slightly younger contemporary of Milton at Christ's College and had remained there as Fellow until 1634. Like Milton, he had been destined for the Church. There is evidence of his promise as a scholar; he was certainly much loved, and Milton may have enjoyed intimacy with him. At any rate he must have responded with genuine warmth to the invitation which came to him to join with other alumni in the celebration of his untimely death. King was drowned in the Irish Sea on August 10th, 1637. Milton's poem stands last in the memorial volume of 1638. The poet appears to have known nothing of the detail of his death, for he omits circumstances mentioned by others and is apparently wrong in saying that the vessel went down in a calm. There is indeed little of King as an individual in "Lycidas." He is simply the poet, apparently destined for God's peculiar service and unaccountably cut off before he has begun to fulfil his destiny. As such he becomes a surrogate for Milton himself. He like King has scorned delights and lived laborious days in anticipation of immortal fame. Were it not better to relax to pleasure if life is subject to such accidents? The answer is an act of faith which Milton has no difficulty in performing. True glory dwells with God and is secure against the hand of fate. Lycidas, "sunk low but mounted high," still lives and sings and is rewarded by "the perfect witness of all-judging Jove."

The real starting point and the central theme of "Lycidas" is thus seen to be the personal resolve, the life-long aspiration, with its attendant fluctuation of hopes and fears, expressed by

Milton in the seventh prolusion, in the sixth elegy, in the sonnet on his twenty-third birthday, and now most recently in the letter to Diodati. The death of King and the summons to write have compelled him again reluctantly to anticipate his programme. His lyric apprenticeship is over: his full epic maturity has not yet come. Modestly, he chooses the pastoral but the Virgilian pastoral, capable of almost epic elevation, and he echoes the master's phrase, bidding the Muse "begin and somewhat loudly sweep the string." With matchless skill, he makes his own impatience an artistic motive. The gentle mood of grief gives way again and yet again to a higher strain, as the poet contemplates the problem of death and fame, or denounces the corrupt clergy, or hails Lycidas as a protecting angel. But each time when the pastoral style and genre threaten to be finally disrupted, the poet stops suddenly as if not daring to go on, and reinvokes the spirit of pastoral poetry.

> Return Alpheus, the dread voice is past,
> That shrunk thy streams; return, Sicilian Muse.

It is on this quiet note and strictly in the *genus humile* of pastoral that the poem concludes, as if Milton were saying to himself, as he had said to Diodati, "Let me be lowly wise." An intimation of new things to come—Italy or epic poetry or both —is given in the final couplet.

> At last he rose, and twitched his mantle blue;
> To-morrow to fresh woods and pastures new.

The biographical use which I have tried to make of "Lycidas" leaves much unsaid about the poem as a work of art, but does not actually distort its values. It is, after all, Milton himself who has invited the world to look at his work and his life together. Diodati is to read the poem, if no one else, and Diodati already has the key to the poet's heart and mind. That the poem belongs to the most conventional of genres and is itself a cento of motives from earlier pastoral literature does not invalidate it as a personal expression, for the Miltonic elements are easily discerned. A notable instance is the allusion to the inspired singer Orpheus, torn to pieces by the followers of Bacchus. This is a recurrent symbol like that of the music of the spheres. Milton identifies himself, here by implication, in *Paradise Lost* explicitly, with the son of the Muse, who could move stocks and stones to rapture, but whose art could not reach the savage hearts of men. He had used the myth already, in both "L'Allegro" and "Il Penseroso," in the poem to his father, and in Elegy VI, where Orpheus is listed among the ascetic bards.

The detail of the manifold artistic influences which meet in *Lycidas* is too technical to concern us here. The suggestion which matches it, not with its obvious pastoral predecessors (the Second Idyll of Theocritus, Virgil's Fifth Eclogue, Spenser's "November" in the *Shepherd's Calendar*), but with contemporary musical composition in the Italian recitative style, is, however, important for our present purposes. Lawes, though professionally hostile to foreign music and musicians, had studied the new theories and was himself the leading exponent of English recitative. Milton was later to commend his *Ariadne*. There is no evidence that he set Milton's elegy to music, but the poet may have fancied him as doing it. In any case the idea of a specifically musical inspiration for "Lycidas" commends itself. The changes in mood and rhythm, the alternation of declamatory, lyric, and choric effect have prompted more than one critic to describe the poem in such terminology. And there may be more than pastoral conventions in Milton's saying of his singing shepherd:

He touched the tender stops of various quills.

The lyric impulse which began with the Nativity Ode and digressed under Lawes's influence into pastoral song and masque has now reached its period in a work which must have given Milton new proof of his destiny as a heroic poet. He could hardly have gone further in the relatively secluded environment of Horton. Whatever had been his intention when he took up his residence there, he must by this time have felt the need of mingling with men on terms of independence. The death of his mother may have had something to do with his willingness to terminate this pastoral interlude. Home would perhaps have been made less attractive also by the domiciling at Horton in the spring of 1638 of his newly married brother, Christopher, who was just finishing his training for the Bar and who represented nearly everything that Milton himself did not. The visit, finally, to Sir Henry Wotton at Eton would naturally have served to whet a resolution already in the process of formation to make a trip to the Continent according to the well-established tradition of those times.

CHAPTER FOUR

ITALIAN JOURNEY
1638–9

No EPISODE IN MILTON's life is better known or more appealing to the biographer than his year and three months of foreign travel. It is, indeed, one of the great *Wanderjahre* of literary history, a moment of contact between cultures comparable with the Italian journeys of Erasmus and of Goethe. He was perhaps the last Englishman to go abroad in the spirit of the earlier Renaissance—with dignity and purposefulness, courting only the higher type of experience, seeking out distinguished men with whom he might converse, communicating his own culture, observing and appraising theirs. The experience did much to confirm in him the sense of belonging to the intellectual *élite* of Europe, that republic of letters which maintained its community of interest against the stress of national and religious prejudice, and might, but for its aloofness, have unified the world. But he went also and primarily as a poet, susceptible to new impressions of the eye and ear, quick to transmute reality to the stuff of the imagination, and now confronting an exotic world, opulent with colour, such as he had seen only in his dreams.

Psychologically as well as culturally, Milton returned to England much enriched. He had something to recall with satisfaction in later years, friends to whom he could turn in thought, a storehouse of images and ideas on which to draw, and above all, I believe, a new sense, at least for the time being, of confidence in himself. Had he not been received on terms of equality by scholars, listened to and praised by poets, entertained by patrons of the arts? Had he not also stood firm for his religion in spite of threats and dangers? In the many frustrating experiences which lay before him this moment of freedom and acceptance must always have remained with him as a sustaining memory.

How mighty was I then [he was to write in the "Epitaph of Damon"] when I lay stretched by cool and murmuring Arno, and could now pluck violets, and now sprigs of myrtle, when I listened to Menalcas contending with Lycidas in song.

He specifically attributes a strengthening of his belief in his own
literary capacity and a new impetus of ambition to the encouragement of his Continental friends, who received his
compositions with "written encomiums which the Italian is
not forward to bestow on men of this side the Alps."

I began thus far to assent both to them and divers of my
friends here at home—that I might perhaps leave something
so written to after times, as they should not willingly let it die.

The poems written on the journey and immediately after
constitute a new body of Latin verse, a return to the humanistic
practice largely abandoned in favour of English during the
years at Horton.

In the decision to spend most of his time in Italy, instead of
dividing it with France or making a more comprehensive tour,
as many others did, Milton shows his predilection for the traditions of an earlier epoch. His classical studies had made "the
places trod by the heroes of old" sacred to him. He had learned
Italian and made a special study of Italian history. His imagination had fed on the glories of Dante, Petrarch, Ariosto, and
Tasso. There was, finally, the fact of Diodati's Italian origin
and the desire, as a prospective statesman of Protestant reform,
to see the land of Catholic reaction, to witness, as Luther had
done before him, the magnificence and the corruption of the
Roman Church. It was this Protestant interest also which led
him to Geneva, where Charles Diodati had already studied
and where his uncle, Giovanni, was a leading figure among the
successors of John Calvin. For France, on the other hand,
Milton had little liking. It was, for him, the source of an
objectionable influence in English society, it had produced
little literature which appealed to his imagination, and the
language itself was not greatly to his taste. When called on
later to defend his life courses against the slanders of Du Molin,
Milton asks himself the question: "Why should I rather travel
into Italy than into France or Holland?" and answers thus:
"It was because I well knew, and have since experienced, that
Italy instead of being, as you suppose, the general receptacle
of vice, was the seat of civilisation and the hospitable domicile
of every species of erudition." This is a humanist's rather than
a Puritan's judgment. It is the judgment, also, of an artist.

The first recorded indication of Milton's plan for foreign
travel is to be found in the letter of Sir Henry Wotton, dated

April 13th, 1638. The poet had evidently asked his advice
regarding an itinerary, as well he might in view of Wotton's
long experience abroad. Sir Henry recommends a journey
"through the whole length of France to Marseilles, and thence
by sea to Genoa, whence the passage into Tuscany is as diurnal
as a Gravesend barge." He promises him letters and pleasantly
advises him to follow in his wanderings the advice which he
himself had received from Alberto Scipione, that he should,
if he wished to carry himself without offence in foreign parts,
go with "*i pensieri stretti e il viso sciolto,*" with his countenance
open and his thoughts closed.

How well Milton followed this advice we shall shortly know.
His friend, Lawes, secured a passport for him from the Warden
of the Cinque Ports, something not always easy to obtain. He
went accompanied by a servant, as was the common custom
among the well-to-do. The journey would have cost him
several hundred pounds. He would have travelled mostly on
horseback, by arrangement with *vetturini*, whose agents frequently accompanied groups of travellers and sometimes
contracted for their meals *en route*. There were tricky problems
of exchange of currency, compliance with customs and police
regulations, the securing of decent and reasonable lodgings.
It was recommended as advisable for any long stay that the
traveller buy and prepare his own food. To have accomplished
what he did, Milton must have travelled with considerable
efficiency. We may well believe that he industriously consulted
the large literature of instruction and information—Sandys,
Howell, Coryat, Moryson—which was then available. Other
introductions than those provided by Wotton were arranged
for him in Paris, and we have good evidence that he was not
at all backward in soliciting acquaintance for himself.

The itinerary can be made out with some completeness, for
he gives a quite disproportionate amount of space to it in his
autobiographical statement. We shall quote this statement
piecemeal for the various stages of the journey, interspersing
such relevant information as may be available from other
sources. After speaking of the Wotton letter, Milton goes on
to describe his short stay in France:

The noble Thomas Scudamore, King Charles's ambassador, to whom I carried letters of recommendation, received
me most courteously at Paris. His lordship gave me a card

of introduction to the learned Hugo Grotius, at that time ambassador from the queen of Sweden to the French court; whose acquaintance I anxiously desired, and to whose house I was accompanied by some of his lordship's friends. A few days after, when I set out for Italy, he gave me letters to the English merchants on my route, that they might show me any civilities in their power.

The desire to meet Grotius is symptomatic of Milton's ambitious purposes. This great humanist, now aged fifty-five, after an industrious and adventuresome career, had been sent as Ambassador to Paris, and was certainly the most distinguished man whose presence that city could then boast. Just before the date of Milton's journey, Grotius had propounded to Archbishop Laud through Scudamore a scheme for uniting several of the Protestant Churches on the Continent with the English. The cherishing of this dream, which had originated during his sojourn in England in 1613, would naturally have given him a special interest in any young Englishman, and Milton's fine Latin scholarship must have added to his acceptability. Phillips reports that the great Dutchman took Milton's visit kindly "and gave him entertainment suitable to his worth and the high commendations he had heard of him." It may well be that this acquaintance first directed Milton's interest toward Grotius' Latin drama, *Adamus Exul*, from which he was afterwards to derive suggestions for his own treatment of the subject of the fall of man.

Milton speaks as if it were Lord Scudamore himself who received and made arrangements for him. Wotton, however, says that he has given Milton a letter to Mr. M. B., "whom you shall easily find attending the young Lord S. as his governor and you may surely receive from him good directions for the shaping of your farther journey into Italy, where he did reside by my choice some time for the King, after mine own recess from Venice." This would be Michael Braithwaite, tutor to Lord Scudamore's fourteen-year-old son then resident with his father. One wonders how much further the joint influence of Scudamore and Wotton may have extended in preparing Milton's way. Sir Henry had promised to entertain him with home novelties "in any part where I shall understand you fixed." He was evidently taking a great interest in Milton's enterprise and is perhaps a chief cause why doors were opened to him. Grotius and Wotton were both interested in Galileo, whom Milton was to visit a few months later in Florence, and among Grotius' acquaintances in Paris was Galileo's best supporter outside of Italy, Elia Diodati, a relative of Charles. The two had been active in trying to secure the sale of one of Galileo's inventions to the United Provinces. We have no evidence that Milton knew this Diodati, but the clan kept well together and it is not unlikely. We shall include him among the possibilities when we come to consider through what intermediaries Milton obtained his interview with the astronomer in Florence.

Of the journey through France to the Mediterranean, Milton says nothing. It need not have taken him more than two weeks. He went for some reason to Nice instead of to Marseilles, as Wotton had advised, and from thence to Genoa by sea, then by way of Leghorn and Pisa to Florence which was his destination.

> In the latter city [he continues] which I have always more particularly esteemed for the elegance of its dialect, its genius, and its taste, I stopped about two months; when I contracted an intimacy with many persons of rank and learning; and was a constant attendant at their literary parties; a practice which prevails there, and tends so much to the diffusion of knowledge, and the preservation of friendship. No time will ever abolish the agreeable recollections which I cherish of Jacopo Gaddi, Carlo Dati, Frescobaldi, Coltellini, Bonmattei, Clementillo, Francini, and many others.

The date of Milton's arrival at Florence is conjectural. He may, starting from England in May, have consumed as much as two months getting there. By September 10th, he is already acquainted with at least one of the intellectuals whose friendships he was to set at so high a rate. A letter of that date to Benedetto Bonmattei reveals clearly enough one reason why he found so warm a welcome. It is an expression of enthusiastic interest in a work on the Italian tongue which Bonmattei has in hand and an exhortation to finish it betimes, both for the glory of his own country and for the benefit of foreigners like himself. Milton's attitude is characteristic. He speaks with conviction of the importance of the occupation which his friend has undertaken, and we recognise in his defence of the claims of a mere grammarian to high honour among men the reflection of a deep conviction. Those who wisely form the manners of men and rule them at home and in war with excellent institutes are perhaps to be esteemed first, but next to them come those who "strive to establish in maxims and rules the method and habit of speaking and writing received from a good age of the nation." He calls on Bonmattei to be mindful in his work of those who, knowing Italian only imperfectly, yet count it among their chief delights. Let him, if possible, add to the grammatical portion of his volume a set of judgments on Italian literature—telling who among so many writers can claim the second place to Dante; who is illustrious in tragedy; who happy and sprightly in comedy; who smart or weighty in epistles or dialogues; who noble in history. Speaking for himself, he professes a love and admiration for the Italian genius second only to his enthusiastic reverence for the classics. He writes this letter in Latin only because of lack of skill in his friend's own language and in the hope of prevailing upon him to speed his grammar to completion.

We can well imagine the effect of this letter upon the man to whom it was addressed. Only the deepest dyed of cynics would have read egotism and condescension into Milton's *ex cathedra* manner. Bonmattei and his friends would have taken Milton's impassioned interest at its face value and responded with an unfeigned admiration for the gifted and attractive stranger who had come among them. At any rate, his progress into the centre of Florentine cultural life was swift. The minutes of the Academy of the *Svogliati* record not only his attendance but his reading of a Latin poem at their meeting of September 16th:

> The gentlemen of the Academy being met in sufficient numbers, various compositions were read, and in particular Mr. John Milton, an Englishman, read a very learned Latin poem in hexameters.

The success of this and later exhibitions of his skill in an art so highly prized in humanistic circles is a further evidence of acceptance by the group. It is clear from his references to these occasions in *The Reason of Church Government* that he felt his experience to be exceptional. Other Englishmen were entertained, but few could have fitted in so well.

In the private academies of Italy, whither I was favoured to resort . . . some trifles which I had in memory, composed at under twenty or thereabout—for the manner is that everyone must give some proof of his wit and reading there—met with such acceptance above what was looked, and other things which I had shifted, in scarcity of books and conveniences, to patch up amongst them, were received with written encomiums, which the Italian is not forward to bestow on men of this side of the Alps.

The societies which Milton found so valuable were a unique and widespread institution. There were some seven hundred of them in Italy in the early seventeenth century, the largest number being at Rome. Florence in Milton's time had no less than twenty. They ranged all the way from mere dining clubs to serious literary or scientific organizations, meeting often in the house of some nobleman, and seeking individual distinction by various forms of oddity, especially their names. There were, for example, the *Lincei*, the lynxes; the *Apatici*, the impartial ones; the *Fantastic*; the *Confusi*; the *Inquieti*; the *Negletti*! Milton's *Svogliati* were the disgusted ones, or rather, "those who have lost their zest." The "*impresa*" of the society was capers, with the motto from Petrarch: "*Per chi m'invoglio*," "with these I whet my appetite!" The adoption of this precious device had been achieved the year before Milton's visit after many quaint and curious suggestions had been debated. The club had its origin in a learned *conversazione* in the house of Jacopo Gaddi in 1620, and continued to meet under his patronage. Milton refers to it later as the Gaddian academy. Its interests were philosophy, military art, poetry, politics. Princes and prelates attended its sessions and it was known as the flower of the Florentine academies. The men named by Milton were mostly members. Coltellini, however, was founder and patron of another society, the *Apatisti* or Indifferents, called by him a "university of literati," having many high nobles on its roll. The specialities of this organisation were Latin and Tuscan poetry. The programme began with a *dubbio* or problem proposed by the regent. Orations and recitations of poetry followed in Latin and Italian.

Of the Florentines by whom Milton was so warmly welcomed, the youth, Carlo Dati, evidently deserved and occupied the first place in his regard. As author of a series of lives of the painters, and leading member of many academies, he was to become one of the most widely known and popular of his contemporaries. Dati was at the time of Milton's visit only nineteen years of age. That the poet's friendship for him was warmly returned is shown by their later correspondence. A further evidence of Dati's continued interest in Milton and of the poet's pride in his approval is to be found in the verses published among the *Testimonia* which Milton prefixed to the Latin poems in the edition of 1645. The language is extravagant, but not for that reason insincere. Dati hails him as a new Ulysses who had, whether in mind or body, surveyed the whole world of civilisation, as a polyglot on whose tongue the ancient languages lived again, as a philosopher who had listened to the music of the spheres. The voice of fame is inadequate to divulge his virtues, the astonishment of men too faint a witness to his excellence. The Italians were skilled in nothing so much as in the art of compliment, and Milton, of all men, was the least likely to take their praises at anything less than their face value.

If Dati was or became in retrospect the focal point of Milton's Florentine visit, the other members of the group whom he names with such enthusiasm contributed hardly less by their intelligent and cultured appreciation of his genius to make it a satisfying experience. Jacopo Gaddi was a fellow poet in the Latin tongue and a noted patron of men of letters. As head of the *Svogliati*, he made a point of playing host to strangers at its meetings. Francini, like Dati and Coltellini, was younger than Milton himself, and already enjoyed some reputation as a vernacular poet. He too wrote a tribute, in the form of an Italian ode, for the volume of 1645. Like Gaddi he speaks of the poet's proficiency in languages—"Spanish, French, Tuscan, Latin and Old Greek"—and he pauses to record Milton's gratifying enthusiasm for the Italian Muse. One man of letters in the Florentine circle, Antonio Malatesti, is unmentioned by Milton in the passage quoted from the *Second Defence*. Their acquaintance is, however, attested by his dedication to the English poet of a series of fifty sonnets, entitled *La Tina* and preserved in a manuscript which Milton may perhaps have carried to England with him on his return. It is not surprising in view of the suggestive character of the sonnets that the chaste-minded youth should have failed to value them sufficiently to record Malatesti among the Florentines of whose acquaintance he was proud.

D

The outstanding event of Milton's Florentine visit was a call on Galileo, which we treat here, though it may belong to a second stay at Florence on his return north. It is mentioned in *Areopagitica*, where Milton is speaking of the freedom of the Press and of the discouragement which restraint of publication brings to learned men, contrasting Italy in this respect with England.

> I could recount what I have seen and heard in other countries, where this kind of inquisition tyrannises; when I have sat among their learned men (for that honour I had), and been counted happy to be born in such a place of philosophic freedom, as they supposed England was, while themselves did nothing but bemoan the servile condition into which learning amongst them was brought; that this was it which had damped the glory of Italian wits; that nothing had been there written now these many years but flattery and fustian. There it was that I found and visited the famous Galileo, grown old, a prisoner to the inquisition, for thinking in astronomy otherwise than the Franciscan and Dominican licensers thought. And though I knew that England was then groaning loudest under the prelatical yoke, nevertheless I took it as a pledge of future happiness, that other nations were so persuaded of her liberty.

The actuality of his visit to Galileo has been questioned on the ground that the astronomer was ill when Milton was in Florence, that he was being closely watched by the Inquisition, and that he himself, for fear of consequences, exhibited the utmost docility in his confinement. It is difficult to believe that Milton would have gone out of his way to invent the incident, and the known facts do not warrant us in thinking that the visit was impossible. The men whom Milton knew were the ones most likely to have been able and willing to promote an interview. Carlo Dati, for example, had been Galileo's pupil. In a letter to Milton written some years later he sent the good wishes of a Galileo who is presumably the philosopher's son. It is a tempting speculation that Milton had become a link in the communication between Galileo and Elia Diodati. This member of the international ring of intellectuals had become one of Galileo's best friends and supporters and was in active correspondence with him and about him in the summer of 1638. If Milton did meet him in Paris and expressed the desire or intention to see Galileo, he would certainly have been informed about the situation and given at least verbal messages to bear to this hero and martyr of the advancement of knowledge.

On the other hand, the poet may have got permission to see him through connections he later made in Rome. The difficulties were somewhat greater at the time of his second visit to Florence, but Cardinal Francesco Barberini, who extended courtesies to Milton and was apparently responsible for Galileo's behaviour, might have found such a request quite harmless and given some kind of assurance regarding it.

The chief poetic fruitage of this high moment in Milton's Florentine experience is to be found in a celebrated passage in Book I of *Paradise Lost*, where the poet likens the huge circumference of Satan's shield to—

> the moon, whose orb
> Through optic glass the Tuscan artist views
> At evening, from the top of Fesole
> Or in Valdarno, to descry new lands,
> Rivers or mountains in her spotty globe.

Milton has no authority for making Galileo star-gaze from Fiesole, but there is a tower near Arcetri still pointed out as having once been his observatory. The poet simply transferred the scene of his activities to the more conspicuous and familiar place. Galileo was almost, if not totally, blind in 1638, a fact which Milton does not mention, but he had used the telescope the year before to observe the moon's monthly librations. We can readily conjecture the impression which talk of this recent discovery might have made on the mind of Milton. If in those earlier expeditions to London from Horton to learn some new thing in "music or mathematics" or in talk with the well-informed Wotton, he had not already realised the importance of the revelations, he would do so now. His later discussions of issues between the two systems of the universe reflect the new astronomical knowledge at every point. It has been shown that the arguments advanced at the beginning of the eighth book of *Paradise Lost* are those of Galileo's *Dialogue*; and the following passage involves acquaintance not only with the general truth that planets have their radiance from the sun, but also with Galileo's discovery that Venus has phases like the moon:

> Hither as to their fountain, other stars
> Repairing, in their golden urns draw light,
> And hence the morning planet gilds his horns.

Well might Milton on leaving Florence have said with Adam, "Greatly instructed I depart. . . . Now clear I understand what oft my steadiest thoughts have searched in vain."

Milton is so concerned to memorialise the personal relationships of his sojourn in Florence that he says nothing of the commoner experiences of English travellers in this magnificent city. We may take it for granted that he saw the sights, as he definitely said he did in Rome and Naples. The outstanding exhibit was the ducal palace. By special arrangement, visitors could see the Duke's treasure: his study; the theatre; the picture gallery, with portraits of the Medicean popes; the usual array of arms and clothing; the zoo, containing lions, wolves, tigers, eagles, a mountain cat, birds of India. There were also the Pratoline gardens, the library "where they show maps of Ptolemy done in gold," and the churches, each with its unique and often extraordinary collection of relics. Expeditions to the surrounding countryside there must have been. The common one to Vallombrosa left an echo in a beautiful simile in *Paradise Lost*:

> Thick as autumnal leaves that strow the brooks
> In Vallombrosa, where th' Etrurian shades
> High overarched embower; . . .

Visitors to this place were entertained overnight in the monastery. Milton's two months' stay at Florence must have ended about October 1st. He thus continues his narrative in the *Second Defence*.

> From Florence I went to Siena, thence to Rome, where, after I had spent about two months viewing the antiquities of that renowned city, where I experienced the most friendly attentions from Lukas Holsten, and other learned and ingenious men, I continued my route to Naples.

There is no documentation for the visit to Siena, which was probably brief, but in Rome we know Milton to have had opportunities hardly less memorable than those in Florence. The character of his activity was, however, so far as the records show, somewhat different. Rome was the chief monument of antiquity and the capital of Catholic Christianity. Its buildings and inscriptions and statuary, the geography of Tiber and the seven hills, would have themselves been enough to occupy his attention even if there had been nobody there to interest him or to be interested in him. The mere adventure of living safely in a city filled with prejudice and plottings against Protestant England put him on his mettle and gave him problems of behaviour in which he had already had instruction. The earlier accounts of travel lay great emphasis on the danger to Englishmen from the Jesuits. Moryson, for example, advises travellers to see Rome and Naples first, as being the places where trouble was most likely to be in store for them. His point is that they will be spied on and reported about as soon as they are known and will be in greater danger if a case has been built up against them by their words and actions in other cities. He tells them also to change their lodgings frequently. Innkeepers were said to be invariably agents of the Inquisition, eager to win credit by presenting dossiers which might be used against their guests. Wotton's advice to Milton to keep his visage open and his mouth shut was no mere pleasantry. Had he been the type, it might even have been suggested to him to pretend to be a Catholic. Moryson warns travellers against asking to see relics in churches unless they are prepared to adore them, and tells a fantastic story about getting an interview with Cardinal Bellarmine under such a false pretence.

Milton, of course, did nothing of the sort, but he was at least discreet enough in the earlier weeks of his Roman visit to obtain and survive entertainment at the English Jesuit College. The Pilgrim's Book of that venerable institution records his presence there at dinner on October 30th, 1638, with his servant, in the company of Mr. Carey, brother of Lord Falkland, a Dr. Holding of Lancaster, and a Mr. Fortesque. There was probably nothing special about this, since the guest book records a long and miscellaneous line of English visitors who were evidently welcomed as a matter of policy, irrespective of their faith. The college was committed to the cause of Catholicism in England, and acceptance of hospitality from them might be calculated to do a little something toward softening the intolerance which was the portion of every son of English Protestantism. It is more surprising that Milton should have gone than that he was received. He had described the diabolic activities of the Society in his poem on the Gunpowder Plot and had embraced the general English heritage of dread. If, however, he had gone to Italy to see for himself, he would have been glad of the opportunity to enter the very seminary of English Catholicism. We may well believe that he confronted the martyr tradition of a hundred years unmoved.

The most memorable experiences at Rome belonged, as we shall see, to a second visit there, made on his return from Naples. Milton is either careless or confused in his chronology in speaking as if he met Holsten on the first visit. At least the statement is inconsistent with what we gather from a letter written to this scholar five months later. The other "learned and ingenious men" must have included some to whom he was commended by the Florentines, and these he is likely to have met on his first visit. Cherubini, a young scholar of some distinction, is mentioned in the letter to Holsten as a prior acquaintance. To an obscure Roman poet, Giovanni Salsilli, Milton later addressed a flattering set of Latin verses. He was, as we infer from Milton's lines, something of an invalid. Milton contrasts the unruly climate of his own England with the kindly skies of Italy and expresses the hope that Salsilli may soon be restored to the loving Muses, and charm with his song the neighbouring meadows. Such a poem may well have been written for a meeting of one of the academies in Rome where Milton would naturally have been received, with a recommendation from the Florentine *Svogliati*. We know him to have had also at least one acquaintance among the English travellers.

The great experience of the earlier visit would certainly have been of the city itself. Imperial Rome in beauty and decay left on his imagination an impression in which ancient studies, the emotions of the hour, and the observed actuality are curiously mingled. The mightiest representation of the mother of nations at her height of pride is a passage written nearly thirty years later as a part of Satan's display of the "kingdoms of the earth and the glory of them" in *Paradise Regained*. The opening lines give the geographical setting as only one who had observed it as a scholar and a philosopher of history could do; the rest is as if Milton had gazed on the present scene until its irrelevances dissolved away and each site and ruin resumed its former grandeur:

> He brought our Saviour to the western side
> Of that high mountain, whence he might behold
> Another plain, long but in breadth not wide;
> Washed by the southern sea, and on the north
> To equal length backed with a ridge of hills,
> That screened the fruits of the earth and seats of men

From cold Septentrion blasts, thence in the midst
Divided by a river, of whose banks
On each side an imperial city stood,
With towers and temples proudly elevate
On seven small hills, with palaces adorned,
Porches and theatres, baths, aqueducts,
Statues and trophies, and triumphal arcs,
Gardens and groves presented to his eyes.

Satan expounds the scene as Milton himself might have done
to a newcomer:

"The city which thou seest no other deem
Than great and glorious Rome, Queen of the Earth
So far renowned, and with the spoils enriched
Of nations; there the Capitol thou seest
Above the rest lifting his stately head
On the Tarpeian rock, her citadel
Impregnable, and there Mount Palatine,
Th' imperial palace, compass huge, and high
The structure, skill of noblest architects,
With gilded battlements, conspicuous far,
Turrets and terraces, and glittering spires.
Many a fair edifice besides, more like
Houses of gods (so well I have disposed
My aerie microscope) thou mayst behold
Outside and inside both, pillars and roofs,
Carved work, the hand of framed artificers
In cedar, marble, ivory, or gold."

Such was the ancient city in an imaginative reconstruction the
like of which no artist with mere brush or pencil could depict.
Of its modern glories the greatest was, of course, St. Peter's,
completed not long before Milton's time, and on this he would
have looked with mingled feelings. It came back to him, no
doubt, when he described the structure Satan and his followers
raised in Hell. It is Pandemonium, the home of all the demons,
a monument of inverted worship and blasphemous pride,

Built like a temple, where pilasters round
Were set, and Doric pillars overlaid
With golden architrave; nor did there want
Cornice or frieze, with bossy sculptures graven;
The roof was fretted gold. Not Babylon,

Nor great Alcairo, such magnificence
Equalled in all their glories, to enshrine
Belial or Serapis their Gods . . .
                    from the archèd roof
Pendent by subtle magic, many a row
Of starry lamps and blazing cressets, fed
With naphtha and asphaltus, yielded light
As from a sky.

Leaving Rome in December, 1638, Milton journeyed to Naples. The single incident which he recounts is an unexpected meeting with a literary personality well calculated to symbolise for him the cultural tradition of a preceding age:

I was introduced by a certain recluse, with whom I had travelled from Rome, to John Baptista Manso, Marquis of Villa, a nobleman of distinguished rank and authority; to whom Torquato Tasso, the illustrious poet, inscribes his book on friendship. During my stay he gave me singular proofs of his regard: he himself conducted me around the city, and to the palace of the viceroy; and more than once paid me a visit at my lodgings. On my departure he gravely apologised for not having shown me more civility, which he said he had been restrained from doing, because I had spoken with so little reserve on matters of religion.

It is a striking fact that neither the visit to Grotius nor that to Galileo gratified Milton as deeply or seemed as well worth boasting about afterwards as this visit to a man of far lesser importance and achievement. The explanation may lie partly in the warmth and courtesy of the reception, but his strong emotional reactions should serve also to remind us that Milton was a poet, romantically attached to the memory of his predecessors, and ready to dramatise himself not only as standing on soil made sacred by their presence but as now enjoying favour from one so intimately associated with them. The age of literary patronage was largely over. To Milton, at least, it stood for no practical reality. Emotionally and imaginatively, however, he was still in the tradition. His attitude was determined by the warm devotion of Spenser to Leicester and Essex, the manly gratitude of Jonson to the Sidneys, the allegiance of Henry Lawes to the Egertons. Personally, he no doubt needed such a relationship himself and was unconsciously seeking it. The Italians, in general, came nearer to affording it than anyone in England, and Manso very naturally took his place as the outstanding instance of their acceptance of his talent. He was an old man, a great and wealthy noble, himself a philosopher and poet. Milton found it easy to enhance the situation and fancy himself for the moment a *"vainqeur du vainqeur du monde."*

The Marquis of Villa's relationship with Tasso was, indeed, already the material of high legend. The poet had come to him in his latter days, broken and harassed but famous, and under his kind patronage had completed the *Gerusalemme Conquistata.* He had memorialised his patron by naming him in the epic among the Campanian princes, and by making him one of the interlocutors in his dialogue on friendship. Manso, in turn, had written an intimate life of Tasso, which still stands as one of the most authoritative contemporary records. He had also caused an inscription to be carved in the stone which marked the poet's grave in Rome. More recently he had be-friended the younger poet, Marini. Milton was doubtless familiar with Manso's reputation and particularly with the facts connecting him with Tasso before he went to Naples. It is reported of Manso that he was in his old age much given to religious observance, and Milton's statement that he excused himself for not going further in hospitality on ground of the poet's Protestant professions has the ring of truth. Manso must have said something of the sort, whether sincerely or as a mere way of getting rid of him and at the same time officially rebuking heresy.

The questions of how Milton actually did behave in this regard and how his freedom of utterance was received are interesting ones. His own description of his sturdy attitude, to be quoted in a moment, is touched with boastfulness and represents something of an *ad hoc* statement. The really notable thing is that he was able to associate so freely with persons officially connected with the Church—the Cardinal, the Jesuits of the English College, the monk with whom he travelled. Certainly there must have been some discretion in him. He discussed religion, he says, only if the point was raised, then declared himself quite openly. There is some evidence of a disarming quality in his manner of maintaining the role which he so carefully adopted. In the letter written many years later to Carlo Dati, he asks indulgence for "speaking of your religion

in our peculiar way." Dati himself mentions the difference
between them. That the religious issue was not a barrier to free
intercourse, even with Manso, is proved by the contribution
made by the latter to the sheaf of Latin testimonials prefixed
to the Poems of 1645.

Johannes Baptista Manso, Marquis of Villa, Neapolitan,
to John Milton, Englishman.

Mind, form, grace, face, and morals are perfect; if but
thy creed were also, then not Anglic alone, but truly
Angelic thou'dst be.

The glow of this friendship prompted Milton to new poetic
utterance. His Latin poem "Mansus," written and sent before
his departure from Naples, after recounting Manso's services
to Tasso and Marini, modestly advances the claims of the
English Muse to attention even in this favoured motherland
of culture. Poets, he says, need such protectors; and he fancies
that when he himself shall have fulfilled his mortal task, some
Manso will follow him to the grave and erect a marble statue
in his memory. There is a wistful sincerity in Milton's utterance.
However independent he may later have become, one part of
him always yearned for sympathy, understanding, and support,
and the thought of the relationship of Tasso and his patron
roused in him a deep, emotional response.

A detail of great interest is added to the record of Milton's
association with Manso in the "Epitaph of Damon," written
shortly after his return to England and containing glowing
recollections of the Italian journey. Manso had, he says, given
him two cups "of marvellous artistry, as Manso himself is a
marvel," the design on them being twofold: a Phœnix rising
from its bed in Araby, and Olympus, with Heavenly Love
limned against the clouds. Milton is speaking in the pastoral
manner and cups were a traditional gift of shepherds. What
Manso probably gave him were copies of his works, a characteristic gesture, since he set great store by his own achievements
and did everything he could to perpetuate his fame as a man
of culture. Two of his published volumes were the *Erocallia*,
dialogues dealing in the Platonic fashion with love and beauty
and their moral and spiritual effects on man, and the *Poesie
Nomiche*, a collection which had appeared three years before
Milton's visit. One of the poems does indeed describe the

Phœnix, and an introduction to the volume repeats the arguments of the *Erocallia*. Milton's own deep involvement with the Platonic theory, we have already noted. His responsiveness to Manso's contribution to the subject would have assured the venerable idealist that he could have no better reader.

What the poet says of sight-seeing in Naples with Manso as a guide opens vistas of conjecture. The city itself, "metropolis of the Campania and queen of all south Italy," was above all a spectacle of Spanish military power. Moryson describes the arsenal, the mole, the shipping in the harbour, the streets "pestered with citizens and foreigners in pursuit of their delights and profits, whose ears are daily inured to the sound of the drum and fife, as their eyes to the bounding of steeds and the glistening of armours." The foreign soldiery, he says, "were obeyed with as much love as galley slaves obey those who have deprived them of their fortunes and liberty." Women were not so strictly guarded here as elsewhere in Italy, perhaps, as the English observer suggested, because they were less tempted "in regard of the number of allowed courtesans." Sandys says there were 30,000 of the latter in a population of 300,000. They led a merry life, "feasted at home by their lovers and honoured by all men with respectful salutations." A liberal education for the author of *Comus*! A curious echo of Milton's reaction to this aspect, probably, of Italian life, is to be found in an impression a later traveller picked up in associating with the Florentine intellectuals who knew and remembered Milton:

> The Englishman was even disliked by the Italians among whom he lived a long time, on account of his too severe morals, though he would freely dispute about religion and hit out strongly against the Pope on any occasion.

Is this or is it not important testimony? I myself take it as such, believing that Milton, having made it his special mission to preach "the sage and serious doctrine of virginity" and conspicuously to exemplify it, sometimes did so out of season. It is not at this period that he was replying to slanderous accusations. We may conclude that the later expositions of his principles and the assurances he gives his readers of the purity of his own life are as much sermons as they are defence. Indeed, they are both. At the close of his narrative of the Italian journey in the *Second Defence* he makes, gratuitously enough from our point of view, this blanket statement:

The mention of this city [Geneva] brings to my recollection the slanders of More and makes me again call the Deity to witness, that in all those places in which vice meets with so little discouragement, and is practised with so little shame, I never once deviated from the paths of integrity and virtue, and perpetually reflected that, though my conduct might escape the notice of men, it could not elude the inspection of God.

What gave point to these reflections was the contrast between the civilisation he had just left and the city which Calvin and his successors had disciplined by their theocracy. If he had needed confirmation of things observed at Naples and elsewhere he would have found it in Venice, where, if travellers' reports are to be trusted, a chastity-loving Englishman might occasionally be delivered by a gondolier, not to his destination, but to the house of some courtesan.

Milton mentions the Viceroy's palace as among the sights that Manso showed him. His singling this out suggests that special privileges might have been obtained. The palace was notable for its "large and sweet gardens and delicate walks paved with divers coloured and engraved marbles," its two banqueting houses, the "secret fountains and delicate cages of birds"; it contained "royal and most rich household stuff" and an astonishing array of implements of war. But Manso's special enthusiasm, as Milton well knew, if he had read the life of Tasso, was for the scenery of the Bay of Naples and the classical associations along its shores, a neighbourhood as deeply steeped in ancient memories as Rome itself. His own villa was at Pozzuoli, six miles to the west of the city. It was here that he had entertained the author of the *Gerusalemme*, and his description of the process of bringing the poet back to health and happiness gives us the spirit, if not the exact detail, of his guidance to the younger feet and sturdier mind of Milton. Tasso had surveyed, says Manso, "the verdure of the celebrated Posilippo," "the shores and rocks made glorious by the sepulture of Virgil and Sannazaro, the grotto of Lucullus, the villa of Cicero, the still and bubbling waters of Cumae, the fires of Pozzuoli, all of which sea-side places are protected by the mountains of Baiae, by the promontory of Miseno, by the isle of Ischia, not less famous for the fable of Typhoeus than for its own fertility." In the city itself he had admired the lofty walls which terrified victorious Hannibal, the strength of the castle, with its wonderful location, the diversity of the fountains, the magnificence of public and private buildings, the concourse of foreigners, the throngs of the populace, the pomp of cavaliers and princes, the richness and abundance of the merchandise, the multitude of wines and fruits and flowers.

The most alluring possibility is a visit of Milton to the Solfatara, a half-extinct volcanic crater which then as now was a seven days' wonder of Nature, having well-elaborated associations with the infernal world. It is this phenomenon known from antiquity as the Phlegraen Fields, to which Manso refers as the "fires of Pozzuoli." The case for Milton's having made in this place a visual confrontation of the Hell he describes in the first book of *Paradise Lost* is so brilliantly argued by Marjorie Nicolson that even the hardest bitten critic of historical evidence is tempted to forget that it is a hypothesis.

This so-called *Forum Vulcani* is situated in the very suburbs of modern Naples, a mile or so from the location of Manso's villa. It is described by contemporary travellers in terms very suggestive of the thoroughly volcanic picture which Milton paints to the imagination of the place reserved for the rebel angels by Eternal Wrath. The hot soil is perhaps the key point in the literary parallel. Milton has stepped it up to the level of the miraculous. The fallen Satan rises from the burning lake and steers his course—

> till on dry land
> He lights, if it were land that ever burned
> With solid, as the lake with liquid, fire;
> And such appeared in hue, as when the force
> Of subterranean wind transports a hill
> Torn from Pelorus, or the shattered side
> Of thund'ring Etna, whose combustible
> And fueled entrails thence conceiving fire,
> Sublimed with mineral fury, aid the winds,
> And leave a singèd bottom, all involved
> With stench and smoke: such resting found the sole
> Of unblessed feet.

The lake itself was in the crater, not red, of course, but "full of boiling waters and ready to fright one with their blackness. You would say it was a kettle or cauldron boiling with pitch or rosin. Which forthwith change places, and the waters growing hard on the brim of the cauldron, it is made narrower or wider, as the force and impetuosity of the exhalation is greater or lesser." A further impression Milton would inevitably have received from a visit to this district was that of mineral wealth. "They that labour in making of sulphur, nitre, vitriol, etc. reap much profit thereby." The demons of *Paradise Lost*, under the captaincy of Mammon, become mining engineers and build Pandemonium, using the infernal fires themselves to found their metals. Even more strikingly they concoct the "sulphurous and nitrous foam" to gunpowder. The sources of Milton's imaginative constructions are, of course, highly literary and he had doubtless read such guide-book accounts as the one in Sandys from which quotation has been made. But in the case of scenes Italian, reading and seeing were part of the same process of assimilation. While some impressions bear fruit in allusions like those to Galileo's optic glass and the shades of Vallombrosa, this one results in a broad imaginative transformation of the materials, one of the cornerstones of a great work of art.

Milton evidently stayed something less than a month in Naples. He had intended to follow the less travelled and more romantic eastward route of Sandys, still drawn, no doubt, by the desire to trace western civilisation to its source, but was turned back by disquieting news from home:

> When I was preparing to pass over into Sicily and Greece, the melancholy intelligence which I received of the civil commotions in England made me alter my purpose; for I thought it base to be travelling for amusement abroad, while my fellow-citizens were fighting for liberty at home.

The news which turned him back was of events connected with the resistance of the Scottish nation to the will of Laud and Charles. Before Milton left England, the effort had been made to force the adoption of a prayer-book based on that of the English Church in place of John Knox's Book of Common Order. This to the Scots was the equivalent of destroying their national worship, and nobles and people united in defiant rejection of the innovation. In the first months of the poet's absence awareness of what was going on north of the border became increasingly prevalent in England. The Puritan opponents of Episcopacy accepted the cause of Scotland as their own, and watched with growing alarm the evidences of

Charles's determination to settle the issue, if necessary by force of arms. The kind of letter which brought Milton home would have been written most plausibly by Thomas Young, informing him of the negotiations which preceded the first military expedition of the spring of 1639 and indicating that a crisis in the affairs of the English Church itself was near at hand. It might have been written in November or December and reached Milton some time the next month.

We have no reason to doubt the sincerity of Milton's patriotic reaction or to wonder, as some have done, why he should, in the face of so high a resolution, have taken nearly eight months to return to England. It was not as if war had actually broken out or Parliament again been summoned, but only that events were shaping themselves to a point where a man of his convictions might be of use. He might feel that he would rather be journeying toward than away from the scene of duty and yet see no urgent reason for cutting his time short. The somewhat dramatic interpretation of his decision is characteristic. The passage in the *Second Defence*, where it occurs, was written as a vindication of his life and character against disparagement and is intended as a testimony to the works of Providence in one of His chosen instruments. Such a purpose simply coincided with John Milton's instinct for self-portraiture and released inhibitions which he might otherwise have felt. It also helped determine the kind of thing which he selected for mention in his autobiographical narrative.

These points are well illustrated in the description which follows of the danger to which he was now exposed as a consequence of his open defence of his religion:

While I was on my way back to Rome, some merchants informed me that the English Jesuits had formed a plot against me if I returned to Rome, because I had spoken too freely about religion; for it was a rule which I laid down to myself in those places, never to be the first to begin any conversation on religion; but if any questions were put to me concerning my faith, to declare it without any reserve or fear. I, nevertheless, returned to Rome. I took no steps to conceal either my person or my character; and for about the space of two months I again openly defended, as I had done before, the reformed religion in the very metropolis of popery. By the favour of God, I got safe back to Florence, where I was received with as much affection as if I had returned to my native country.

This touch of romantic adventure must have done much to sweeten and enhance Milton's Italian experience. He was sharing the perils of earlier heroes of Protestant reform as he had shared the honours of the poets in the academies and under the patronage of Manso. The experience was one calculated to give determination to the patriotic resolve with which he was now setting his face toward the scene of a new struggle.

Milton's second period in Rome belongs to the early winter of 1639. He was there, as we shall see, on February 27th and back in Florence before March 17th. On March 30th, he wrote to Lukas Holsten, the Vatican Librarian, to thank him for his hospitality and report on a commission which he had been asked to carry out. The letter contains the most important evidence we have hitherto encountered of Milton's occupations and opportunities in the capital. It is clear that this was his first meeting with Holsten and that the events recounted belong to the second visit to Rome:

> When I went up to the Vatican for the purpose of meeting you, though a total stranger to you—unless, perchance anything had been previously said about me to you by Alexander Cherubini—you received me with the utmost courtesy. Admitted at once with politeness into the Museum, I was allowed to behold the superb collection of books, and also very many manuscripts. Greek authors, set forth with your explanations—some of whom, not yet seen in our age, seemed, in their array, like Virgil's
>
> *penitus convalle virenti*
> *Inclusae animae superumque ad limen iturae,*
>
> to demand the active hand of the printer, and a delivery into the world, while others, already edited by your care, are eagerly received everywhere by scholars: dismissed, too, richer than I came, with two copies of one of these last presented to me by yourself.

Holsten was an authentic humanistic scholar, bred in the severer traditions of northern Europe. A German by birth, he had become Catholic and a naturalised Roman, the convert and protégé of Cardinal Francesco Barberini. In the list of

Milton's acquaintanceship he belongs more nearly, perhaps, with Grotius than with any of the Italians. It was, however, through his influence that the English poet enjoyed the most remarkable of all his contacts with the higher social and cultural circles of Italian life.

I could not but believe that it was in consequence of the mention you made of me to the most excellent Cardinal Francesco Barberini that, when he, a few days after, gave that public musical entertainment, he himself, waiting at the doors, and seeking me out in so great a crowd, almost seizing me by the hand indeed, admitted me within in a truly most honourable manner. Further, when, on this account, I went to pay my respects to him next day, you again were the person that both made access for me and obtained me an opportunity such as, with so great a man —than whom on the topmost summit of dignity, nothing more kind, nothing more courteous—was truly, place and time considered, too ample rather than too sparing.

The family of the Barberini was at this time one of the most magnificent in Rome and by all odds the greatest in the Church. Maffeo Barberini had become Pope Clement IX. The two youthful nephews whom he had appointed cardinals, Francesco and Antonio, were both great patrons of the arts, and Francesco was the Papal Secretary. The Casa Barberini, his residence, contained a theatre which commanded the highest talent in Italy, notably that of Giulio Rospigliosi, who afterwards became Pope Urban VIII. Francesco Barberini was politically interested in the English and made it a point of extending courtesies to them. The son of the English Secretary of State, Windebank, had received an audience from him not long before. Milton's visit, for an ordinary traveller, must nevertheless have been unique.

It was, however, attendance at the entertainment of the day before which constituted the most significant part of the experience. What Milton saw and heard was a performance of one of the earliest of Italian comic operas, a spectacular and memorable occasion of which full records are preserved. We know it to have taken place in the Barberini theatre on February 27th, 1639, before an audience of some 3,500 people, including Cardinal Mazarin and other outstanding representatives of Roman and ecclesiastical society. The stage design

was by Bernini and is described by his biographer as something
of which "the fame will endure for ever in the world." The
piece itself, *Chi soffre speri*, "Let the sufferer take heart,"
written by Rospigliosi and set by Mazzochi and Marazzuoli,
consists of a prologue and three acts with intermezzi, the story
being of Egisto in love with a resistant widow, but finally
overcoming her disbelief in men by acts of extravagant devotion. A girl in her employ, disguised as a boy, falls in love
with Egisto, but turns out to be his long-lost sister. The score
employs a new kind of recitative (*recitativo secco*) with a minimum of melodic character. Between the acts there was the
representation of the Fair of Farfa with a multitude of actors,
extending beyond the stage and into the gardens. There were
buyers and sellers, carts drawn by oxen, lords in carriages, a
charlatan vending wares, dancing, quarrelling, fighting—a
comedy spectacle suggestive of the spirit of Roman carnival.
The performance is said to have lasted five hours. Milton calls
the entertainment an *acroama musicum*, *acroama* being the Greek
and Latin term used of various kinds of entertainment at meals.
His memory apparently played him false regarding Cardinal
Francesco's greeting. According to an eyewitness, it was his
brother, Antonio, who ushered in the guests. Cardinal Francesco went about among them from bench to bench. One young
man who became noisy was thrown out. Altogether it was an
incredible affair for him to have attended.

Our special interest in his presence is, of course, the evidence
it affords of his contact with the newest developments in
Italian "*dramma per musica*." It was not for nothing that the
poet came to Italy from the experience of collaborating with
Henry Lawes. It meant not only that his pilgrimage was
bound to be in part a musical one, but also that he would be
well informed in advance what to look for and expect. In
order to confirm his interest, it is necessary to go a bit beyond
the date of the Roman visit when it probably would have
received its greatest impulse. He sent home from Venice,
according to Phillips, a chest or two of choice music books,
including the works of Orazio Vecchi, composer of the
Amphiparnasso, a "*commedia harmonica*"; of Luca Marenzio, who
is said to have emphasised and defended the principle of letting
the words dictate the musical expression; of Gesualdo, an
outstanding innovator in harmony; and, finally, of Monteverdi,
the greatest composer of the day and the chief inventor of

modern opera. The selection of just these musicians suggests a direction of interest which came naturally to a man of letters and prepares us for the contribution which he himself was to make to the issue between madrigal and the more dramatic manner in a later sonnet to Lawes. The latter composer had ridiculed indifference to meaning, thus helping formulate the reasons which had led even among musicians of the English tradition to the invention of the air to the lute. The idea was of Italian origin. Caccini, in the sixteenth century, had inveighed against musicians who mangle poetry by sometimes lengthening, sometimes shortening, syllables in order to suit the counterpoint.

The chief theorist of these matters and a protagonist of the operatic movement was Giovanni Battista Doni, a man whom Milton certainly met. Following the tradition of the *Camerata*, a famous group of earlier Florentine scholars which included the father of Galileo, Doni advocated the revival of what he believed to be Greek practice of singing not only the choruses but the dialogue of tragedy, also of the use of the Greek modes for the expression of more varied emotion. He was a friend of Cardinal Francesco Barberini and had himself set the *Troades* of Seneca for performance at the Barberini theatre. Milton refers to him in the letter to Holsten, and the records of the *Svogliati* academy indicate that the two men were on the same programme during his second visit to Florence. Doni on this occasion read part of a tragedy. The association takes Milton into the very heart of the most significant artistic activity of the time and was, I believe, to have a striking influence on his own conceptions and his literary plans. The case of the famous *Adamo* of Andreini, seriously to be considered as a "source" for *Paradise Lost*, will be discussed later. There was also a long tradition of oratorio which may have helped to direct Milton's thoughts to a kind of semi-operatic composition more serious than that represented by the English masque.

A concrete piece of evidence of Milton's musical contacts, other than dramatic, is a set of epigrams which he wrote on the singer, Leonora Baroni, whose talents and charm had aroused the admiration of her countrymen to the point of ecstasy. Leonora was the friend and protégée, perhaps the mistress, of Rospigliosi, and writers of Continental temperament have sometimes suggested a similar relationship with Milton. It is enough that he listened to her from afar, "with rapt soul sitting in his eyes," and recognised the celestial music in her voice.

> For if all things be God, and He pervade them all, in you alone He speaks, in all the rest He is present but silent.

He was reminded, too, of Tasso's Leonora and his mad love for her.

> How much more happily would he have been destroyed in your time, Leonora, and for your sake . . . you could by your soul-stirring singing have restored him to himself.

There was a volume of *Applausi Poetici*, published in 1639, containing scores of poems in her praise. Milton's compositions are not among them, but they suggest the closeness of his relationship to the circle of her admirers. It is interesting to find him once again a lover of the beautiful and young, sharing, as if he were himself a Roman, the enthusiasm with which Italians are accustomed to hail their divæ. The episode carries us back to the only earlier evidences of the incursion of a living woman into Milton's world of dreams. The Emilia of the Italian sonnets was a singer, too. But Milton was not then adept, as he is now, in converting the flesh and blood of a desired object into a poetic symbol of his aspiration for the heavenly ideal.

Returning to Florence in early March, Milton stopped as many months as he did before, "except that I made an excursion of a few days to Lucca." Of this second visit we know only that he was warmly received, that he again attended the academies (he was present at the *Svogliati* meetings of March 17th, 24th, and 31st) and that he tried to be helpful to Lukas Holsten:

> The commission which you seemed to give me, relating to the inspection of a Medicæan codex, I have already carefully reported to my friends, who, however, hold forth for the present very small hope of effecting that matter. In that library, I am told, nothing can be copied, unless by leave first obtained; it is not permitted to bring a pen to the tables. But they tell me that Giovanni Battista Doni is now at Rome; having been called to Florence to undertake the public lectureship in Greek, he is daily expected; and through him, they say, it will be easy for you to accomplish what you want.

The excursion to Lucca may have been a pious pilgrimage, especially since it was not *en route*. The city, as Milton recalls in the "Epitaph of Damon," was the ancestral home of Diodati. More than that it was a chief scene of the Protestant episode in Italy and carried the association of Peter Martyr, one of the great reformers. Milton's own later stripe of thought has resemblances to the rationalism of the Italian heretics. He at least knew their place in Reformation history and he knew also of the late attempts to win Venice to the Protestant cause, for Henry Wotton, with Giovanni Diodati, whom Milton was shortly to visit, was engaged in it.

From Florence, Milton went by way of Bologna and Ferrara to Venice, where he spent a month "surveying the curiosities of the city" and shipped his collection of books to England. Thence he proceeded through Verona and Milan and along Lake Leman to Geneva. There is no detail for any part of this itinerary. Did Milton profit by Wotton's long acquaintance at Venice? Did he concern himself with study of the political system, so much admired as an example of the mixed state, the perfect working out of republican checks and balances, capable of transcending the weaknesses of individuals and lasting perhaps forever? It is hard to believe, given his habits, his experience, and his former contacts, that there were no new acquaintances. Monteverdi was Director of Music for the Republic, organist at St. Mark's, and master of the choir. The three new opera houses, the first in Italy, were probably closed at this season of the year, but they could hardly have failed to excite interest. The well-kept Venetian records have never, to my knowledge, been searched and it may be that we shall yet know something of this lost moment in Milton's journey.

If there are no allusions to Venetian scenes in Milton's poetry or prose, he is equally silent about the works of God in the Alps or Lake Leman. He could describe in "L'Allegro," on the basis of no experience of them outside of books—

> Mountains, on whose barren breast
> The lab'ring clouds do often rest.

The actuality of such grandeurs finds no voice. This, of course, is the habit of the times, which had not yet learned to talk enthusiastically about the beauty of mountain scenery. Yet Milton's later imagination may owe more than is demonstrable to such impressions. He is the poet of cosmic spectacles and of the immensities of space. The visions of his blindness are made up out of materials which had formerly been presented to his sight. The case is perhaps the same with his relation to the glories of Italian pictorial art. He nowhere alludes to the work of the great painters which must have confronted him everywhere. But *Paradise Lost* is best illustrated by comparison with these analogous expressions, and its fusion of Christian and pagan imagery, its visualisations of Biblical legend and of classical mythology, its rich perspectives and its profusion of detail, are probably more indebted than Milton himself realised to what his eyes took in on the ceilings of the Sistine Chapel or the walls of the Doge's palace.

At Geneva, the home of Protestant theology, Milton again found welcome from a personality worth his interest. Giovanni Diodati, uncle of Charles, was professor in the Academy there and distinguished as a translator of the Bible into Italian and author of various theological works. He was also noted as an instructor of young men of rank who came from various parts of Europe to board in his house. There Milton himself may have stayed, for he says that he was daily in Diodati's society. He could now at last discourse of politics and religion to sympathetic instead of hostile ears. The environment was one calculated to confirm his Protestantism and increase his determination to be among its champions in England. Diodati was, of course, a Calvinist and a maintainer of the Presbyterian theocracy which flourished at Geneva above all other places. Milton was shortly to advocate such a system, though not for long. His acquaintance extended to other members of the inbred clan of Italian refugees. On June 10th, 1639, he inscribed his name in the visitors' album of the Cerdogni, a family of Neapolitans resident in Geneva since 1608, adding a quotation from *Comus*.

> if virtue feeble were
> Heaven itself would stoop to her,

and the mildly defiant motto,

> *Coelum non animum muto dum trans mare curro.*

It is the Lady's

> Thou canst not touch the freedom of my mind.

Milton says he returned to England by way of France and arrived, after an absence of a year and three months, "at the time when Charles, having broken the peace, was renewing what is called the episcopal war with the Scots, in which the royalists being routed in the first encounter, and the English being universally and justly disaffected, the necessity of his affairs at last obliged him to convene a parliament." This would be in the summer of 1640, but Milton is speaking loosely. He actually reached England about August 1st, 1639, when the King had disbanded the militia and gone home. Strafford had not yet been called from Ireland and the second Scottish expedition, which led to the summoning of the Long Parliament, was still a year away. The poet was therefore an actual witness of the final efforts to force the royal policy on the nation, first by coercing the Short Parliament, then by a renewal of illegal levies without their consent.

Before he left Geneva and perhaps at some earlier point in his journey, Milton must have learned of the death of Charles Diodati in late August, 1638. The Latin pastoral, "*Epitaphium Damonis*," which he wrote in commemoration of this event, was composed after he arrived in England, but the experience which it records is essentially a part of the epoch in Milton's life which is now closing, and the poem is an immediate fruit of the new inspiration which he had received in Italy. His heart was still there when he composed it; and it was written very definitely with the Florentine audience in mind. The expression of grief and loneliness, despite the artificial medium, is as sincere as it is beautiful. Milton recalls their companionship and gives voice to his sense of desolation in the pastoral terms of "Lycidas" but at greater length and with much more of personal emotion. He reproaches himself for being absent from his beloved's deathbed—"Was it worth so much to see buried Rome?"—he recalls his happiness and strength in Italy, and dwells on the anticipation he indulged in of plans to be made for tours when they should be together.

> Say, my good friend, you are not busy are you? Unless, perhaps, something holds thee back, shall we go and lie for a while in the shade of the rustling trees, either by the waters of Colne, or in the countryside of Cassebelaunus?

Then, suddenly, the mood is broken and Milton turns to the forward-looking reality of his own poetic plans. The death of Damon becomes a symbol exactly like the death of Lycidas, a warning challenge to high effort and an occasion for the declaration of the religious faith without which, in the face of death, such effort cannot be maintained.

I myself also—for my pipe was trying to utter some lofty strain (it is now eleven nights and a day)—had chanced to put my lips to new reeds; but they snapped asunder as their fastenings broke, and could not further endure that mighty volume of sound. I fear, too, that I may be conceited; still I will tell the story. Do you, ye woods, withdraw.

Go home, my lambs, unfed; your master has now no time for you. I shall sing, yes, I myself, of the Dardanian ships moving on Rutupian waters, and the ancient kingdom of Imogene, daughter of Pandrasus, and of the chieftains Brennus and Arviragus and of ancient Belinus, and of the Armorican settlers who came at length under the laws of the Britons. And then I shall sing of Igraine pregnant with Arthur through a fateful trick, and those false lineaments, and the wearing of the arms of Gorlois—all this the guile of Merlin. Oh, if then life shall still be mine, you, my reed-pipe, will hang on an aged pine far away, quite forgotten by me, or else, all changed, you shall stridently emit a British note for my native Muses. For consider. One man may not do all things, one man may not hope all things; for me there will be a sufficiently ample reward, a sufficiently great glory (though I then be unknown to fame for ever and altogether without repute in the outside world), if only fair-haired Ouse shall read me and he who drinks of Allan and eddying Humber and all the woods of Trent; and if above all the rest my own Thames and dark-metalled Tamur, and the Orkneys, whose waves are at the end of the world, shall commit my verse to memory.

There was a similar declaration in the epistle to Manso of the intention to write an English epic on legendary British history culminating in the Christian victories of King Arthur. Now Milton says he had actually begun it. What follows in the "Epitaph of Damon" is the most ecstatic version he was ever to write in verse of the theme of heavenly love as the reward of earthly chastity. The passage has already been alluded to as describing the symbolic design on Manso's cups or the content of his books:

On the other side are a wide expanse of sky and towering Olympus; and (who would believe it?) here is Love also with his quiver limned against the clouds, his flashing weapons, his torches, his darts tinged with burning bronze.

And from this point he does not attack trivial souls and the ignoble hearts of the crowd; but, turning hither and thither his shining eyes, he ever shoots his arrows upward towards the stars, and never tires nor looks aside to make a downward stroke. In this way the minds of the elect are inflamed and the shapes of the gods.

The conclusion transfers the soul of Diodati to this Platonic paradise, the mystic garden of the close of *Comus*, the "blest kingdom meek of joy and love" of "Lycidas":

Because the flush of innocence and stainless youth were dear to thee, because thou didst not know the joy of marriage, lo, for thee, virginal honours are reserved. Thou, with thy bright head haloed in glory, and carrying in thy hand a leafy canopy of joyous palms, shalt to all eternity take part in immortal nuptial songs, where music abounds, and the ecstatic melodies of the lyre blend with the choruses of the blessed and the joyous revelry grows ever wilder under the touch of the thyrsus of Zion.

Milton's identification with the subject of his elegy is complete. the Poem may or may not be judged a greater work of art than "Lycidas," but the symbol itself is, for him, much richer. There are really no further steps possible in this direction. When Milton plans and writes another major poem it will not be a lyric.

CHAPTER FIVE

PARADISE SOUGHT

1639-49

WHEN MILTON RETURNED TO England in the summer of 1639, it was with the idea that his period of mere preparation was at last over. Whatever God might have determined for him with regard to his more ambitious purposes, he could at least take steps toward being useful and in so doing provide for partial self-support. Milton was the son of a self-made man and he never showed himself indifferent or unskilled in practical affairs. There is no reason, moreover, for believing that the idea of making provision for marriage was unimportant to him. He had spoken rather theoretically of this in the Letter to a Friend.

> Or if it [his "tardy moving"] be thought an unnatural proneness, there is against that a much more potent inclination, and inbred, which about this time of man's life solicits most, the desire of house and family of his own, to which nothing is esteemed more helpful than the early entering into credible employment, and nothing more hindering than this affected solitariness.

If his concern with chastity in the Horton period and the quality of his friendship with Diodati suggest an ascetic inclination, as I think they do, wider social contacts, greater detachment from his family, and the natural processes of maturation may have done something to overcome it. Celibacy was clearly not in his programme for himself, and he was nearly arrived at the canonical age of thirty-five, which Aristotle suggests as the proper one for choosing a mate. What might be needed to overcome backwardness is another matter, but the motivations for independent earning were in any case sufficient.

The problem was solved humbly enough but in a way congenial to Milton's tastes and not inconsistent with his impersonal aims. It so happened that the husband of his sister Anne had died some years before leaving two sons, Edward and John Phillips, who were in 1639 ten and eight years old respectively. The mother had remarried and the new family was at least moderately wealthy. There was also extensive property from the estate of Edward Phillips, Sr., which had been left in trust to Milton's father for the use of Anne and her children. It was arranged that Milton should teach these boys, the younger having been, in his brother's words, "wholly entrusted to his charge & care." He took lodgings at first with a tailor named Russell in St. Bride's Churchyard, then set up an establishment, with a servant named Jane Yates, in a "pretty garden house" in Aldersgate Street "at the end of an entry and therefore fitter for his turn by reason of the privacy." There were, Phillips adds, few streets in London more free from noise. Both the boys now boarded with him, and after a while he received other pupils. It is clear that Milton never thought of his teaching as more than an incidental occupation. He does not mention it in his own account of the beginning of his active life:

As soon as I was able I hired a spacious house in the city for myself and my books; where I again with rapture renewed my literary pursuits and where I calmly awaited the issue of the contest, which I trusted to the wise conduct of Providence.

He nevertheless was and remained a teacher for many years.

We learn a good deal of his practices from Phillips; more, by inference, from the tractate, *Of Education*, which he was to write four years later at the request of Samuel Hartlib. To this document we shall return, since it gives the theory on which his system was based and forms a part of what Milton regarded as his total contribution to the cause of liberty. Phillips was impressed by the ambitiousness of the programme, which, "through his excellent judgment and way of teaching," carried the students through "authors scarce ever heard of in the common public schools." He lists the Roman and Greek writers on agriculture, medicine, astronomy, geometry, and military affairs; recondite poets like Apollonius Rhodius, and Caliber; the Pentateuch in Hebrew; the Targum in Chaldee; "several chapters of St. Matthew in the Syriac testament"; and finally Villani's Italian history and Pierre Davity's geography in French. Milton said of his programme that it was not a bow for everyone to shoot with. He shot with it, and the boys survived. There seems to be no bitterness in Phillips' suggestive remark that he was able in his teaching to increase his own knowledge, having the reading of these authors as it were by proxy, a procedure which "might possibly have conduced to the preserving of his eyesight, had he not moreover been perpetually busied in his own laborious undertakings of the book and pen." He is not the first or the last scholar-teacher to work this way. In one department of educational industry, at least, there was from Milton's striplings a definite contribution to his research:

> The Sunday's work was, for the most part, the reading each day of a chapter of the Greek Testament, and hearing his learned exposition of the same. . . . The next work after this was the writing from his own dictation, some part, from time to time, of a tractate he thought fit to collect from the ablest of divines who had written of that subject: Amesius, Wollebius, etc., viz. *A Perfect System of Divinity*, of which more hereafter.

Milton and his pupils were thus compiling Sunday after Sunday, year in and year out, basic materials for the Latin treatise, *Of Christian Doctrine*, which was finished and copied two decades later, but remained unpublished till long after its author's death.

A year and a half elapsed before Milton made his first gesture in the public service. He had, he tells us, "other plans" which were interrupted by this call. It is a safe guess that the literary pursuits which he "renewed with rapture" included both a continuation of the Horton programme of historical study and a new attack on the projected masterpiece. The Commonplace Book shows that he now reached the history of England and went through such authors as Holinshed, Speed, and Hall. Another set of notes, included in the Trinity manuscripts of the poems, besides confirming this, gives the record of his literary planning. He lists from his Biblical and his historical reading about one hundred literary subjects, often with suggestions as to treatment and, in a half-dozen instances, with a detailed outline of the plot. The plans are all dramatic, though he remarks incidentally at one point that "a heroical poem may be founded somewhere in Alfred's reign, especially at his issuing out of Edelingseye, whose actions are well like those of Ulysses."

In these plans there appears prominently and for the first time the subject of the fall of man. The notes contain four drafts of a scenario on this theme, the first two being mere lists of characters, the third an organisation of the material in five acts, the fourth a carefully outlined plot. Evidently what Milton has in mind is an oratorio, a religious masque, or an actual *dramma per musica* of the sort that he had perhaps seen in Italy. Voltaire, on what authority we do not know, says that it was a performance of Andreini's famous *Adamo* which inspired him, and there are general resemblances, particularly in the use of such allegorical figures as Labour, Sickness, Death, which make the suggestion of a relationship plausible. We do not, to be sure, know exactly when and where the *Adamo* was ever given after its original presentation on the occasion of the marriage of the Duke of Milan. It had, however, been published with many illustrations apparently depicting the scenes as actually performed. If Milton bought or read this book we have no difficulty in accounting for the form which his ideas now take. Its influence would combine with that of many other versions of the oft-handled story and with the general patterns of oratorio, *dramma per musica*, and opera.

He need not have and indeed had not abandoned either the British subject or the epic form. Three of the plans for a "Paradise Lost" come first in the notes, then a Biblical and a historical list, then elaborate outlines of plays on Abraham, John the Baptist, Sodom, then the final Adam Unparadised, then some "Scotch stories" including a Macbeth, then more from Scripture. There may, of course, have been a parallel manuscript of epic plots. We find the poet still debating both the form and subject at a later time. Nevertheless, a masque-like poem on the fall, with musical features, represents his most probable present intention and may well be among the "other plans" referred to as occupying his mind when he was called to enter the pamphlet war in the spring of 1641. Phillips tells us that he actually composed the opening speech and that ten lines were incorporated in *Paradise Lost* as a part of Satan's address to the sun:

> O thou that with surpassing glory crowned,
> Look'st from thy sole dominion like the God
> Of this new world. . . .

There is no more dramatic or more powerful passage in the poem. A similar invocation opens the second scene of Andreini and a goat-hoofed Satan is depicted on the stage amid hellish smoke, threatening his creator.

Much light is thrown on Milton's public intentions at this time by a passage in *The Reason of Church Government*, to be discussed more fully in another connection. He is speaking of the moral uses of poetry, particularly as an antidote to the "corruption and bane" which our youth and gentry "daily suck in from the writings and interludes of libidinous poetasters." And he calls on the magistrates to provide for more edifying literary entertainment "in theatres and porches" and "in the affable and frequent meetings of academies." The reference to what he had seen abroad is obvious. Knowing the earnestness as well as the scope of Milton's aspirations, one cannot escape the belief that he thought of himself as ready to supply this literature, single-handed or as the head of a group like-minded with himself for whom he might be able to supply the formula. We recall that he had already had the experience of successful masque writing. May he not now have thought that similar collaboration with Lawes or others on the serious treatment of both Biblical and historical subject matter in the new Italian manner would challenge the worthless but still popular Caroline drama and meet the Puritan objection to the stage?

Opera was already in the air in England, but it was Davenant and not Milton who was to be its pioneer. He had petitioned for the building of an opera house in 1639. The first Day's Entertainment at Rutland House produced with Lawes's music in 1653, about as soon as the public situation made it possible, was published with a defensive preface drawing heavily on the Italian theory of sung drama. A connection between his activity and Milton's plans is, of course, highly speculative, but with Lawes as a link it is not out of the range of possibility. If at any time in his career Milton could have communicated freely and hopefully with men of letters and the stage, it was in this moment of confidence and enthusiasm immediately following the Italian journey.

I have suggested the possibility that Milton may have drawn up his list of dramatic subjects as a guide to others as well as to himself. He can hardly have expected to become a Lope de Vega and write on all these subjects. However, the process of setting them down may have been merely part of a laborious act of choosing or the record of a thorough exploration of all the possibilities in a given area of his reading as a reminder for the future.

Enough has been said, in any case, to show that new vigour and a somewhat new direction had been given to Milton's programme of literary action. The content of his message is also in process of enrichment. The dramatic plans for *Paradise Lost* suggest a continuation and a development of his earlier thoughts of chastity and love. He is still the Puritan and Platonist, but the new theme will involve the earthly rapture of the Garden of Eden as well as the Heavenly one of the union of the chaste soul with God. The mere ascetic can hardly enter successfully into this domain. Heavenly Love, Evening Star and a chorus singing the marriage song of Adam and Eve meet us and have a whole act in the third of the dramatic plans. The prologue, wherein Moses excites the audience to vision and tells them they cannot see Adam and Eve in a state of innocence by reason of their sin, shows Milton accommodating this new symbol to his philosophic doctrine. The "muddy vesture of decay" prevents our understanding of true love as it prevents our hearing the music of the spheres. Later, in the *Apology for Smectymnuus*, Milton still talks of entertaining the reader with "the abstracted sublimities" of chastity and of that love—

> whose charming cup is only virtue which she bears in her hand to those who are worthy; (the rest are cheated with a thick intoxicating potion, which a certain sorceress, the abuser of love's name carries about;) and how the first and chiefest office of love begins and ends in the soul, producing those happy twins of her divine generation, knowledge and virtue.

The language applies better to *Comus* than to the completed *Paradise Lost*. The theme does actually survive in the angelic expositions and in the total meaning of the epic, but by the time it was written the centre of Milton's interest had, as we shall see, shifted to human marriage in both its ideal and its perverted forms.

How long the processes of decision would have gone on with Milton without external stimulus or occasion, we well may wonder. He needed an audience, if but a single individual; he needed confidence; he needed a riper personal experience. The activities on which he now engaged, besides giving a wider attachment to his emotions, served more than appears on the surface to provide an outlet for the pent-up thoughts which he had hoped to clothe with nobler language.

The public issues were developing rapidly before his eyes. The Earl of Strafford had come from Ireland, a month after Milton's own return, to undertake the establishment of the absolute supremacy of the Crown. The Short Parliament met and was dismissed. In the summer of 1640, a second ill-advised expedition against the Scots met signal defeat. In October, Charles, confronted with the necessity of raising large sums to buy their army out of England, was forced to summon the Long Parliament. Their revolutionary acts became at once the topic of the hour. The opening debate, after the freeing of such victims of Laud's tyranny as John Lilburne and the dramatic arrest of Strafford, concerned the question of Episcopacy. On December 11th "a world of honest citizens" presented a petition for its abolition "with all its roots and branches." The accompanying pamphlet war between the defenders of the establishment and the now vocal Puritans brought Milton at last out of his personal world into the arena of the times. Here is his own account, written many years later, of the situation as he read it:

> The vigour of the Parliament had begun to humble the pride of the bishops. As long as the liberty of speech was no longer subject to control all mouths began to be opened against the bishops; some complained of the vices of individuals, others of those of the order. They said that it was unjust that they alone should differ from the model of other reformed churches, and particularly the word of God. This awakened my attention and my zeal. I saw that a way was opening for the establishment of real liberty; that the foundation was laying for the deliverance of man from the yoke of slavery and superstition; that the principles of religion, which were the first objects of our care, would exert a salutary influence on the manners and constitution of the republic; and as I had from my youth studied the distinctions between religious and civil rights, I perceived that if I ever wished to be of use, I ought not to be wanting to my country, to the church and to so many of my fellow Christians, in a crisis of so much danger.

We must try to reconstruct the workings of Milton's mind at this crucial moment in his career and to speculate on what it really was which had touched the springs of action in him. Patriotism is the large emotion which is taking possession of him, the divinity which is about to shape his ends. But the individual choices of patriotism, as we well understand today, are complexly determined. Milton's decision to engage in public controversy at just this point may have been precipitated partly by a personal loyalty.

His friend and mentor, Thomas Young, with a group of fellow ministers, had already written a reply to the defence of Episcopacy by Joseph Hall, one of the most literary of the bishops, and this reply had been replied to by both Hall and the learned James Ussher, Archbishop of Armagh. Milton's first pamphlet, *Of Reformation in England and the Causes That Have Hitherto Hindered It*, published in May or June, 1641, stands, to be sure, apart from this immediate exchange. It seems like a voluntary offering, the young scholar's best unaided effort, containing the gist of his study of English history and illustrating his idea of the way in which the case for reformation should be put. The succeeding pamphlets, however, are specifically directed against Ussher and Hall. I believe that Milton, who had long since championed Young in private, is now moved to join him in open battle. Pride and perhaps some sensitiveness about his lay position make him do so independently at first; then with greater confidence he assumes the role of a collaborator. This personal involvement draws him more and more powerfully and is a determining factor in his career. His account of the sequel of his first enlistment in the cause is as follows:

Afterwards, when two bishops of superior distinction vindicated their privileges against some principal ministers, I thought that on these topics, to the consideration of which I was led solely by my love of truth, and my reverence for Christianity, I should probably not write worse than those who were contending only for their own emoluments and usurpations. I therefore answered the one in two books, of which the first is inscribed *Concerning Prelatical Episcopacy* and the other *Concerning the Mode of Ecclesiastical Government*; and I replied to the other in some *Animadversions* and soon after in an *Apology*. On this occasion it was supposed that I brought a timely succour to the ministers, who were hardly a match for the eloquence of their opponents.

The last sentence is very much the point. Milton, the highly cultivated, the man of literature and learning, is to render the true account of his privileges and talent by aiding men of simple goodness against skilled antagonists for whom they are no match. There is a group of guileless Israelites, two Goliaths and one David. It was a controversial role in which Milton was long to fancy himself. The Puritans were, to be sure, men of intellect and erudition, quite capable of holding their own in the debate. But the young scholar liked to think that his long years of preparation had given him something which their more active lives had not enabled them to acquire. He could supplement their learning, refine their arguments, give philosophic breadth and literary colouring to their ideas. He could answer the wittiest sallies of Hall with a quality of vituperation unheard, save in his pamphlets, on either side. He counters, for example, thus when Hall ridicules them for speaking of the "Areopagi," instead of the "Areopagites," a manifest and lamentable slip.

E

A soar-eagle would not stoop at a fly; but sure some pedagogue stood at your elbow, and made it itch with this parlous criticism; they urged you with a decree of the sage and severe judges of Athens, and you cite them to appear for certain paragogical contempts, before a capricious pedantry of hot-livered grammarians.

It is necessary to describe these early pamphlets which came so rapidly from Milton's pen in the years 1641 and 1642 only so far as to indicate how much they contain of his essential thought. Obviously, they divert it from the right line of its development. Milton writes for the most part as one committed to the Presbyterian point of view of Young and his fellow ministers. He argues with them that this system of Church organization is "the one right discipline," divinely ordered and prescribed by Scripture. Actually, Milton is too much a humanist and too deeply imbued with the idea of the spiritual liberty of the individual not to be restive under this doctrine. It has been pointed out, moreover, that there is a difference in emphasis and divergent implications in his statements of the nature of Church government and theirs. They write as ministers, he as a layman. The democratic and individualistic element in Puritanism is therefore more natural to his thought than to theirs. The distance between them in this respect was bound to widen. Both Milton and the ministers speak at this time as monarchists. They argue that a hierarchy of power in the Church may actually be dangerous to the Throne, and see in the Presbyterian system a true conformity to the State of England "where under a free and untutored monarch, the noblest, worthiest, and most prudent men, with full approbation and suffrage of the people, have in their power the supreme and final determination of highest affairs." Milton is later to part company with his old friends on this point as well.

If, however, Milton's alliance with the dominant Puritan groups was a passive and unstable, not to say an unnatural, one, he does manage to say things in these pamphlets which spring from deep conviction and which connect closely with his primary thought about his calling and inspiration. The opening paragraphs of the first tractate, written before he had become enmeshed in the specific defence of Presbyterianism, carry us in a sense back to the Sixth Elegy and to *Comus*. The doctrine of the gospel that the body was purified by the affections of the regenerate soul and that faith needed not "the weak and fallible offices" of the senses to be the interpreters of heavenly mysteries, "save where our Lord in His sacraments ordained," this doctrine had been dragged down to the "new paganism of sensual idolatry," and the inward acts of the spirit brought to the eye-service of the body, "as if they could make God fleshly, because they could not make themselves heavenly and spiritual." The priests thus began "to draw down all the divine intercourse between God and the soul, yea, the very shape of God Himself, into an exterior and bodily form . . . till the soul by this means of overbodying herself, given up justly to fleshly delights, bated her wing downward." This is not precisely the sage and serious doctrine of the Elder Brother but it is a version of it. Milton's further thought that the spiritual liberty offered by the Gospel, "the cheerful and adoptive boldness which our new alliance with God requires," was replaced by servile and thrall-like fear is a Christian amplification of the Attendant Spirit's

> Mortals that would follow me,
> Love Virtue, she alone is free.

Milton's case against the hierarchy is thus grounded in his own need of feeling himself to be an heir of Christ, a free partaker of "that feast of love and heavenly-admitted fellowship" at which he sealed his covenant to the Apostles. And this consciousness is closely associated with his conviction of his own divine calling. He is, in the ecclesiastical pamphlets, not only proclaiming the spiritual equality of all believers, but supporting his own right as a layman to speak of holy things. They are therefore in a roundabout way a part of his great defence. It is not surprising that we should find him digressing more than once from the argument to speak of his own poetic plans or that the passages in which he does so should be the most deeply serious portions of the entire discussion.

The first and perhaps the most remarkable of these outbursts is in the famous prayer at the close of the first pamphlet. He gives thanks to God who "after the impetuous rage of five bloody inundations and the succeeding sword of intestine war" did "build up this Brittanic Empire to a glorious and enviable height, with all her sister isles around her," and implores Him to further deliver it from its present foes.

Then [he continues in an apocalyptic and millennial conclusion, which translates the nation to the starry sphere as
he had previously translated the souls of Lycidas and Damon]
amidst the hymns and hallelujahs of the saints some one may
perhaps be heard offering at high strains in new and lofty
measures to sing and celebrate thy divine mercies and
marvellous judgements in the land throughout all ages.

In thus identifying himself and his function with the nation's
imagined triumph Milton gives a new attachment to his
aspiration, a higher sanction to his art. It is clear that he still
clings in thought to the British subject and will give it up only
in favour of something which gives scope for the expression of
even deeper loyalties.

The next personal digression, a long meditation in *The Reason
of Church Government*, takes up the question of gifts and their
uses at the point where Milton had left it in the Letter to a
Friend. There is now, however, no complaint of unreadiness or
immaturity. The problem is how one who has obtained to
know something of God and His true worship and "what is
infallibly good and happy in the state of man's life" can best
put that knowledge into use, "remembering that God, even to
a strictness, requires the improvement of these His entrusted
gifts." The burden of this decision, Milton continues, is in-
creased when the entrusted knowledge is of a truth unacceptable
to men and when those who have received it, though "selected
heralds of peace," are required like the prophets of old to "take
the trumpet and blow a dolorous or a jarring blast."

It is clear that Milton regards the question of the employment
of his talents as having been settled for him. He is still "by
disposition or what other cause too inquisitive or suspicious"
of himself and his own doings, but these self-questionings now
come after rather than before the fact. He answers them for
himself and others, by a review of his career and a new and
greatly expanded exposition of his purposes. Portions of this
passage have already been quoted. The key thought is that in
rejecting the ministry he has chosen, for himself, a better way.
His vocation is as much of God as that of the inspired prophets.
Poetry, as he conceives it, is itself a divine art, "of power,
beside the office of a pulpit, to inbreed and cherish in a great
people the seeds of virtue and public civility, to allay the
perturbations of the mind, and set the affections in right tune,

to celebrate in glorious and lofty hymns the throne and equipage of God's almightiness and what He suffers to be wrought with high providence in His church." When the land is free from tyranny Milton will return to perform the function which "abilities rarely bestowed," the inspired gift of God, have made his own.

This is the highest point to which Milton's enthusiasm ever carried him in his persuasion of himself. Before he wrote *An Apology*, the last pamphlet in the ecclesiastical series, he had been personally attacked. In view of his early sensitiveness to the remonstrations of his father and his nameless friend and of his long anticipation of public hostility in other forms, it becomes a matter of much interest how he will react. There is actually no new element in his defence, but it is easy to discern a lowering of the tone. The likelihood of his being able to escape easily or soon from the world of bitterness and hate into that of Heavenly Love seems more remote.

His approach to the subject is, as usual, intricate. In speaking against the rancour of an evil tongue he is forced to "proceed from the unfeigned and diligent inquiry" of his own conscience. His hesitations are not serious, but he must argue them out. The best apology against false accusers is perhaps silence and he himself could easily rest in the "inward contentment" of having his friends congratulate themselves on his innocence. He is aware, besides, that most men, in these present times, have little chance to think of their own concernments and have "removed the seat of their thoughts outward to the expectation of events." There is, finally, the example of noble or religious men who have suffered wrong with meekness, in whose honourable society he could easily appease his sense of injury without defence. Against these pleadings of what we to-day are prone to think his better judgement, Milton has a decisive answer. Hall's intent has been not so much to smite him as to render odious the truth which he has written. Milton stands not in his own person, but as the representative of a cause, "a member incorporate of that truth to which I was persuaded." It is his duty, therefore, to leave on his garment "not the least thought or blemish in good name."

There is a great deal more of this, but the reader has surely seen enough now of Milton's processes to be able to appraise them. The most notable and revealing thing which the poet says, as the self-analysis drags on, is that the ministers, through their unnecessary patience, have laid themselves at the mercy of their opponent's style.

> To me it seemed an indignity, that whom his whole wisdom could not move from their place, them his impetuous folly should ride over.

We have a clear consequence in this of the old identification with Thomas Young. It is through this relationship that Milton has now learned how to make himself a cause. He will not soon unlearn the lesson.

It is in this pamphlet that Milton reverts to the circumstances of his college life. Hall has asserted that he was "vomited out" from the University after a riotous and dissolute life. Milton thanks him for giving occasion by this lie to recall "the more than ordinary favour and respect" which he found above his equals from the Fellows, and how after he had taken two decrees they had signified many ways how much better it would content them if he should stay. The words of warmth and friendliness which follow are almost immediately unsaid in terms of the university in general. The contradiction is not merely a matter of rhetoric or a contrast between then and now. It represents a real ambivalence in Milton's feeling.

The specific charge of unchastity which Hall has launched against him opens a floodgate. Milton is prompted to an elaborate review of his personal ideals which easily becomes a review also of his changing literary taste. He speaks of his acceptances and rejections in the sequence we have already partly noted—first the smooth and sensuous elegaic Romans, then Dante and Petrarch, the famous renowners of Beatrice and Laura, then the "lofty fables and romances," finally, in riper years, "the divine volumes of Plato and his equal Xenophon." The passage is puzzling in many ways. One can hardly credit its naïveté. He turned against Ovid and the elegists when he found them "speaking unworthy things of themselves or unchaste of those names which before they had extolled." He read in the literature of chivalry that it was in the oath of every knight to defend the chastity of women, and if these heroes broke that oath in word or deed he judged the author to have "written indecently of the gods." It will not do to assign these reactions exclusively to his boyhood. He is obviously thinking of the literary development of his university and later years, for he marks the exact moment of the sixth elegy in recording the conviction, not long after his occupation with Ovid and the sonnet-writers, "that he who would not be frustrate of his hope to write well hereafter in laudable things ought himself to be a true poem." Spenserian and Platonic ideas of virtue dominate the period of *Comus*, and the proposal now made to entertain the reader with a new version of such sublimities brings us to the present. Milton is obviously not so much defending himself against Hall as he is again explaining the evidence of his calling.

> These reasonings, together with a certain niceness of nature, an honest haughtiness, and self-esteem either of what I was or what I might be . . . kept me still above those low descents of mind. . . . So that even those books, which to many others have been the fuel of wantonness and loose living, I cannot think how, except by divine indulgence, proved to me so many incitements, as you have heard, to the love and steadfast observation of that virtue which abhors the society of the bordellos.

The capstone of the whole edifice is a final paragraph describing his training, "last not in time but as perfection is last," in the chaste and high mysteries of the Christian religion which taught him that the body is for the Lord and the Lord for the body.

> Nor did I slumber over that place, expressing such high rewards of ever following the Lamb with those celestial songs to others inapprehensible, but not to those who were not defiled with women, which doubtless means fornication; for marriage must not be called a defilement.

We are back with the formula of the music of the spheres, the mystic marriage, and the central motive of Milton's youthful art. The final clause is at the moment and in this context an irrelevancy. A little earlier he would not have written it, a little later he would have incorporated it into his thought. It is two years since he has written the ecstatic conclusion to the "Epitaph of Damon." That poem is itself, if I read it rightly, something of a regression. The plans for *Paradise Lost* and the poetic programme of the *Reason of Church Government* are already in advance of it. Hall's attacks have thrown Milton back on himself. His line of healthy emotional and imaginative progress does not lie in this direction.

We come now to the episode of Milton's marriage, the *pons*

asinorum of his biographers. It is with reluctance that one undertakes to add another chapter to the superabaundance of discussion. The case, however, is fairly clear if we attend to all the evidence and do not ask to know the actual secrets of the marriage bed. The date is apparently the spring of 1642, a month or so after the publication of the last pamphlet. The first part of the story, as given by Milton's nephew, Edward Phillips, an inmate of his house and at the time a boy of eleven, is this.

About Whitsuntide it was, or a little after, that he took a journey into the country; no body about him certainly knowing the reason, or that it was any more than a journey of recreation; after a month's stay, home he returns a married man, that went out a bachelor; his wife being Mary, the eldest daughter of Mr. Richard Powell, then a justice of peace, of Foresthill, near Shotover in Oxfordshire; some few of her nearest relations accompanying the bride to her new habitation; which by reason the father nor any body else were yet come, was able to receive them; where the feasting held for some days in celebration of the nuptials, and for entertainment of the bride's friends. At length they took their leave, and returning to Foresthill, left the sister behind; probably not much to her satisfaction, as appeared by the sequel. By that time she had for a month or thereabout led a philosophical life (after having been used to a great house, and much company and joviality), her friends, possibly incited by her own desire, made earnest suit by letter, to have her company the remaining part of the summer, which was granted, on condition of her return at the time appointed, Michaelmas, or thereabout.

No parish record of the marriage has been found and Phillips does not give the year. It cannot have been 1643, as Masson, often careless in his inferences, assumed, for the public situation hardly permitted of the events which the early biographer describes. Before the summer of 1642, actual war between the forces of King and Parliament was not yet certain. After that it was. Charles raised his standard at Nottingham on August 22nd, and those who were to cast their lots with him left London. The Battle of Edgehill took place on October 23rd. Oxford immediately became royal headquarters, an armed camp. Intercourse between the town and London was from then on under strong restriction. The likelihood of Milton's

being able to go there was small, and the social and
psychological barrier to marriage with the daughter of an
Oxford royalist would, one must think, have proved even•
more decisive after blood had once been shed. Phillips' language
leaves little doubt in any case that the outbreak of hostilities
took place between the time of the marriage and Mary's failure
to return. She stayed "a month or thereabout" in Milton's
house, say till July or August. Before the date set for her return,
September 29th, the King "was in some prospect of success,"
and members of her own family were in arms. All this fits
1642. On the face of it, Milton's domestic happiness was a
sacrifice to the passionate loyalties of war.

The difficulties which the bride had in adjusting herself to
Milton's household are understandable enough. He was
thirty-three, she sixteen. They knew nothing of each other and
she, at least, nothing of his way of life. Only love and great
understanding on Milton's part could have bridged the gap.
We know enough of him to feel that this was something he
could not give. Marriage was "no defilement," but he was not
ready to manage it without help. The normal process of
adjustment was interrupted, and serious frustration was the
the result. It is not necessary to accept Mrs. Powells' later
accusation that Milton, "a harsh and choleric man," himself
sent Mary away. (See below, p. 184.)

The writing of the first divorce tract, in the summer of 1643,
was, in the opinion of Milton's friends, a step toward retrieving
this defeat. "He fortified his resolution with arguments," says
Phillips. The early anonymous biographer, who also knew
Milton personally, gives the same judgement, with some interesting modifications:

He, in the interval, who had entered into that state for the
end designed by God and nature and was then in the full
vigour of his manhood, could ill bear the disappointment he
met by her obstinate absenting; and therefore thought upon
a divorce, that he might be free to marry another; concerning
which he also was in treaty. The lawfulness and expedience
of this . . . had upon full consideration and reading good
authors been formerly his opinion; and the necessity of
qualifying himself now concurring with the opportunity,
acceptable to him, of instructing others in a point of so great
concern to the peace and preservation of families, and so

likely to prevent temptations as well as mischiefs, he first writ *The Doctrine and Discipline of Divorce*.

Milton's own version of his new enterprise leaves the personal motivation out of account and makes it what he no doubt sincerely believed it to be, a second calculated step in the liberation of mankind. The statement continues the long defence and rationalism of his career from which I have been quoting:

> When, therefore, I perceived that there were three species of liberty which are essential to the happiness of social life—religious, domestic, and civil; and as I had already written concerning the first, and the magistrates were strenuously active in the third, I determined to turn my attention to the second, or domestic species . . . for he in vain makes vaunt of liberty in the senate or the forum, who languishes under the vilest servitude, to an inferior at home.

All this is very much in accord with the later patterns of Milton's thought. In the sentence which follows he comes as near as one would expect to giving the facts of his own case:

> On this subject, therefore, I published some books which were more particularly necessary at that time, when the man often stayed to take care of his children at home, while the mother of the family was seen in the camp of the enemy, threatening death and destruction to her husband.

Later events—Mary's return and childbearing, John's second and third marriages, dowry litigation with the Powells, the reported bitterness of daughters—provide further ground for speculation as to Milton's domestic competence, and will be dealt with in due course.

In the divorce tracts themselves, his personal reactions are largely swallowed up in the total argument. The whole point is that incompatibility, because it defeats the higher end of marriage, is higher ground for its dissolution than adultery, which is the only reason for divorce by canon law. The elaboration of this case involves all of Milton's earlier philosophising and results in a new and original development of his point of view. There are, however, remarks which may be taken as a reflection of individual experience. Thus, to those who argue that the disposition of the parties ought to be seriously considered before marriage in order that the catastrophe of mismating may be avoided, he replies:

But let them know again, that for all the wariness can be used, it may yet befall a discreet man to be mistaken in his choice: and we have plenty of examples. The soberest and best governed men are least practised in these affairs; and who knows not that the bashful muteness of a virgin may often hide all the unliveliness and natural sloth which is really unfit for conversation? Nor is there that freedom of access granted or presumed, as may suffice to a perfect discerning till too late; and where any indisposition is suspected, what more usual than the persuasion of friends, that acquaintance, as it increases, will amend all? And lastly, it is not strange though many, who have spent their life chastely, are in some things not so quick-sighted, while they haste too eagerly to light the nuptial torch.

These must surely be the terms in which Milton interpreted his own case. His eloquence is expended in the description of the spiritual disaster which results from such an error. Marriage was given to man as an aid to his fulfilment of "the supreme dictate of charity," the desire and longing which God put into Adam in Paradise, "before he knew the sin of incontinence." That other carnal burning, "the venom of a lusty and over-abounding concoction," labour and the abatement of a full diet "may keep low and obedient enough."

But this pure and inbred desire of joining in conjugal fellowship a fit and conversing soul (which desire is properly called love) is "stronger than death," as the spouse of Christ thought: "many waters cannot quench it neither can the floods drown it."

Milton is thus pleading the case, as he had promised to do, of "love which is truly so, whose divine offices begin and end in the soul," but he is pleading it with the new intensity of one who has tried to prove the doctrine valid in his own experience and signally failed. It is remarkable that in the second edition of the *Doctrine & Discipline*, he amplifies this statement by returning to the Platonic imagery of *Comus* and the "Epitaph of Damon," finding an identity between the teachings of the "festival discourse" of Socrates wherein Love is said to be "the son of Penury, begot of Plenty in the garden of Jupiter" and the divinely inspired word of Moses who tells us that it is "the son of Loneliness begot in Paradise by that social and helpful attitude which God implanted in man and woman toward each other." The failure of Platonic love on earth, a problem now first encountered, leads him to a further elaboration of the doctrine out of materials supplied by Plato's *Phaedrus*. "Love, if he be not twin born, hath a brother wondrous like himself, called Anteros," his *alter ego* and true soul mate. Seeking this ideal object he is apt to meet with many "false and feigning desires" who walk about in its likeness. The God is not wholly blind but partly so, "having but one eye and that not the quickest in this dark region here below, which is not Love's proper sphere." He is, moreover, easily misled by the simplicity and credulity which is natural to him. For this reason he sometimes shoots amiss and "embraces and consorts with these obvious and suborned striplings, as if they were his mother's sons, for so he thinks them, while they subtly keep themselves mostly on his blind side." At length, soaring again to his true element and darting out the direct rays of his most piercing eyesight, he recognizes the "impostures and trim disguises that were used against him." His arrows lose their golden heads, his silken braids untwine and slip their knots, and the orginal and fiery virtue given him by Fate all in a sudden gives out, leaving him undeified and despoiled of all his force.

> Thus mine authors sung it to me [Milton concludes], and by the leave of those who would be counted the only grave ones, this is no mere amatorious novel.

The insight which this poetic flight gives us into Milton's experience in marriage is much greater than we could gain from further knowledge of its material circumstances. Milton entered the relationship completely enveloped in a cloud of idealistic thought. The experience must serve the predetermined purposes of his prophetic mission or be abandoned almost without a trial. It was a perfect prophylactic against success. And since the practical realization of his earthly Paradise was a necessary demonstration and fulfilment of his thought, there must be a new attempt. The God of Love must shoot a second time. Discovering the real Anteros at last he is to "kindle and repair the almost faded ammunition of his deity by the reflection of a coequal and homogenial fire."

Descending to the cooler element of prose, Milton reasons broadly, ingeniously, and learnedly through many chapters and in the succeeding tracts. He evidently felt that he had hit on something so important and so essentially his own that it must be carried to a conclusion at all costs. For the second edition of the *Doctrine & Discipline* he did much research in the authorities, greatly elaborated the arguments, and organised the whole into what may well be called a treatise on the subject. It is nearly twice as long as the longest of the ecclesiastical pamphlets. *Tetrachordon*, in which he grapples again with the problem of reconciling the words of Christ and Moses, adds an equal amount of bulk to the discussion. The second and fourth pamphlets are incidental salvos. In *The Judgment of Martin Bucer Concerning Divorce* Milton translates from the weightiest of the Protestant divines who have taken his position, in *Colasterion* he meets the arguments of an anonymous opponent. The entire contribution occupied him from 1643 to 1645, and it is hard to see how his mind could in this period have concerned itself deeply with any other matter.

It is a striking fact that we hear nothing of the poetic plans to which he alluded so frequently in the ecclesiastical tracts. The truth is that Milton is now actually embarked on the enterprise for which he had prepared himself, albeit in a way quite different from his earlier expectation. He feels no necessity for personal digression. That at least is how I interpret the change. Equally significant is the shift in his attitude toward the public reception of his work. Confident that he has made a real discovery he not only expects but invites opposition. His role is that of a pioneer of truth and he rejoices in his isolation. The difference in his present and former situation is clearly indicated in the introductory address to Parliament, which he added in the second edition of the *Doctrine & Discipline*. Custom, he declares, is of all teachers the one which has drawn the most disciples after it, and it is custom in alliance with error which "cries down free reasoning under the terms of humour and innovation." Previously, he says, "under the incitement of men reputed grave," he has defended with others the free industry of the soul against this abuse, now he is himself called on, through the chance of evil or of good report, to be "the sole advocate of a discountenanced truth."

> . . . A high enterprise, Lords and Commons, a high enterprise and hard, and such as every seventh son of a seventh son does not venture on.

With this attitude Milton is not to be injured by calumny, but only by neglect. It is a small matter that a chorus of abuse (which Milton greatly magnified) breaks out against him, a small matter even that the cry has gone up from the very Presbyterians with whom he has been allied. He wishes only that he might see his detractors at any fair meeting; his complaint in *Tetrachordon* is that he has to answer only one who, he is persuaded, has scarce read his book and does not know the man who wrote it. In the introduction to *Colasterion* he describes himself as annoyed by Prynne's merely incidental references to his book "at the tail of anabaptistical, antinomian, atheistical epithets," and as hoping long and impatiently for a serious answer—

> but as I still was waiting, when these light-armed refuters would have done pelting at their three lines uttered with a sage delivery of no reason, . . . at length a book was brought to my hands, entitled "An Answer to the Doctrine and Discipline of Divorce." Gladly I received it, and very attentively composed myself to read.

The nameless answer is itself a disappointment and Milton refutes it lightly. The subject is dismissed unless a serious and public-spirited discussion is forthcoming, though Milton promises, "since Fate exacts from me a talent for sport, which I had thought to hide in a napkin," if this opponent will but give his name, to "endorse him on the backside of posterity" and "rhyme him into such condition as instead of judging good books to be burnt by the executioner, he shall be readier to be his own hangman."

The sincerity of these sentiments is witnessed by their overflow in two sonnets, expressive of the mere disgust of a man who has uttered wisdom to a public too trivial and prejudiced to do anything but rail or wonder at it.

> I did but prompt the age to quit their clogs
> By the known rules of ancient liberty,
> When strait a barbarous noise environs me
> Of owls and cuckoos, asses, apes, and dogs.

If Milton cannot rhyme the individual to death he will at least belabour the group to which he belongs. The other sonnet suggests also wistful fondness for a brain child whose merits its author and a few like him have recognised but which is doomed to follow so many other costly efforts of the human mind into oblivion.

A book was writ of late called *Tetrachordon*;
And woven close, both matter, form, and style;
The subject new: it walked the town a while,
Numb'ring good intellects; now seldom por'd on.

No expressions at all like this result from the ecclesiastical
controversy. It is evident that Milton's creativeness has been
much more deeply engaged. He leaves the subject not with
boredom or weariness but with a sense of futility at having
failed to get a serious hearing for his case, perhaps at having
failed also to leave something "so written to aftertimes that they
would not willingly let it die."

We have outrun chronology by a few years in carrying the
divorce episode to its conclusion. Mary Powell left Milton in
the summer of 1642. *The Doctrine and Discipline* appeared a year
later, the second edition and the *Judgment of Martin Bucer*
followed at six month intervals, and *Tetrachordon* and *Colasterion*,
together, six months after that in March, 1645. Meanwhile he
had published the tractate *Of Education* in June of 1644 and the
great oration on the freedom of the Press, *Areopagitica*, in
November of the same year. Phillips' narrative gives the impression that Milton's domestic life in the period of his second
bachelorhood was anything but an empty one. His father came
to live with him from Reading, where he had been domiciled
with Christopher, and there were additional pupils in the
school. "The studies went on with so much the more vigour as
there were more hands and heads employed." The poet found
diversion in the family of Lady Margaret Ley, a married
woman "of great wit and ingenuity," daughter of the Earl of
Marlborough. The affection and esteem with which he regarded
her is recorded in one of the most gracious of his sonnets. He is
said also to have paid court to a Miss Davis, who rejected his
addresses, a shadowy episode connected by the anonymous
biographer with the writing of the divorce tracts and by Phillips
with the decision of Mary to return. It used to be thought that
another sonnet of this period, "Lady that in the prime of earliest
youth," was addressed to her, but there is some suggestion in the
poem that its subject was a child. In any case, these fragmentary
details forbid us to think that Milton became a recluse. He seems
rather to have been exceptionally active in every way, filling his
time like a wise and resourceful man. Presumably his marriage
experience, however unfortunate, had done him good.

The last bit of self-dramatization as a poet for many a long year comes at the very beginning of the period, in a sonnet written when the royal army under Prince Rupert was nearing London and an assault was momentarily expected. Milton pleads with the imaginary captain or colonel or knight-at-arms who stands before his defenceless house ready to plunder or give it to the flames, bidding him spare it and its inmate for the sake of poetry.

> He can requite thee, for he knows the charms
> That call fame on such gentle acts as these,
> And he can spread thy name o'er lands & seas, . . .
> Lift not thy spear against the Muses' bower:

Masson worries a little over these lines and wonders whether Milton actually pinned them on his door. There is no fear in them, of course; the poet has simply found new occasion for a familiar pose and can, unrealistically enough, entertain for a moment the thought of winning a man of blood to pause and listen to his Pindaric lyre.

The great fruitage of this epoch is *Areopagitica*, a work in which Milton comes as near to the fulfilment of his purposes as it was possible for him to do in prose. He has at last a noble theme and one which transcends the immediate political occasion. His eloquence is untrammelled by any kind of introversion; he has worked out a doctrine perfectly in accord with his conviction. He can be at once the scholar and the enthusiast, the English patriot and the ancient orator, defending liberty and guiding a great republic toward its destiny. The oration grows directly out of the divorce tracts but reflects equally the drama of public events and enrols Milton decisively with the more liberal movement of his times.

The English Parliament, having broken the ecclesiastical hierarchy, had summoned in 1643 a representative assembly of the Church to sit at Westminster and advise them concerning the reformation of religion. The great majority of this body, which included Young and all his fellow Smectymnuans in high triumph, was Presbyterian and disposed to follow the pattern of the Scots in setting up a uniform and inclusive national church under the one right discipline laid down in Scripture. They had no more thought of toleration than Laud himself. There were included in the Westminster Assembly, however, some representatives of the Congregational or

Independent left, who promptly began to plead for recognition of the separatist tradition. Outside there were scattered members of more extreme democratic and sectarian groups, ready to make their voices heard and now rallying their forces in support of the Assembly minority. Roger Williams had already suffered for conscience's sake in Massachusetts and was preparing to champion religious freedom and the complete separation of Church and State. Henry Vane, who had defended the antinomian Anne Hutchinson against the Boston Clergy, was in the Assembly as a lay member. Milton responded to these influences because he had by publishing the divorce tracts already enrolled himself as an individualist in doctrine, parting company once and for all with Thomas Young. In advocating a specific freedom he had become of necessity involved in the larger cause.

Concerned for their own security, Parliament undertook to silence opposition, whether from the right or left, by passing in June, 1643, an act requiring the licensing of all books by an official censor. Milton's first divorce tract was published in defiance of this order. Mentioned along with objectionable sectarian publications in a sermon before Parliament on August 13, 1644, it had become the object of a petition by the Stationers Company on August 24th. *Areopagitica* may or may not have been begun before this event. It was published in November.

The work is addressed to Parliament in the hope of influencing it to repeal a decree so inconsistent with its own history and purposes as the restorer of English liberties. After adroitly complimenting this body on its past achievements and excusing himself for venturing in a private capacity on this criticism of their recent act, Milton reviews the history of licensing from ancient times, showing that it has always gone with tyranny and associating its modern form with the reactionary Catholic Council of Trent. The aim is to prove the practice suspect in its origins and a product of the very forces which Parliament has overthrown. Secondly, Milton enters on a noble defence of the benefit of books freely used, showing how necessary is reading of every sort to the attainment of experience in a world where good and evil grow up indiscriminately together. Next, he deals with the impossibility of the attempt to make men virtuous by external restraint. Corrupting influences are present everywhere and can be met only by building inner discipline and the power of rational choosing. This from now on is to be a fundamental tenet of Milton's ethical philosophy. The shift from emphasis on virtue as the only real freedom, to freedom as the necessary condition of real virtue has come about through his half-accidental discovery of the theory of divorce; and this in turn goes back to his earlier insight into the true nature of love and marriage.

In the new argument he is carried far beyond the limited and more or less personal conclusions he had reached hitherto. He speaks now for revolutionary England as he had tried to do in the ecclesiastical pamphlets, but with the more immediate conviction of the divorce tracts. He is for the time being a political Utopian. After arguing more specifically that the new law will be ineffective, even as applied to publication, Milton finally attacks the order as a discouragement to intellectual activity and to the cause of truth. Here again the connection with the divorce idea is close. Milton was himself such a discoverer. He had not himself been suppressed and was perhaps not likely to be. But it is easy for him to see himself as silenced and his truth lost to the world, easy also for him to identify his case with others. It is in this context that he pleads for a resolute faith in the competence of human nature and particularly of English nature to work out its own intellectual salvation; in the divine property, also, of Truth itself, which is sure to prevail over error if the two are allowed to grapple. He expresses with extraordinary forcefulness the resentment of the mature mind at being kept under watch and ward, and vividly displays the results of such a policy in spiritual stagnation and a "starched conformity of opinion." Most remarkably of all, Milton suggests at one point that truth herself may have more faces than one. He thus recants or partially recants the doctrine of the "one right discipline" and opens for himself paths of speculation which only a mind freer than his ever became could follow.

The spirit which speaks through Milton is the spirit of English Protestantism in its main advance. It is not quite the spirit of democracy or science. He is carried by his opposition to the Presbyterians into alignment with the left-wing sectaries, as he had previously been led to make common cause with the Presbyterians against the bishops. His real defence of freedom is nevertheless in behalf of learned men like himself, however charitably he may be disposed to the vagaries of mere individualists. We need not expect to find him going with any mass

movement when that movement shows signs of falling into the
hands of men like Lilburne. He had in the *Doctrine and Discipline
of Divorce* made a damaging analysis of such sectaries as the
familists, whose strange opinions he sees as resulting from sexual
frustration. He would not, of course, unsay this now. It is for
"those who have prepared their minds above the vulgar pitch"
that he primarily pleads the liberty of thought and publication.
The rest are those whom he brackets as "children and childish
men" and of whom he says, speaking of freedom of access to
literature of every kind, "they may well be exhorted to abstain,
but forcibly hindered they cannot be." His full vision would
seem nevertheless to comprehend a nation of adult minds. The
waxing and waning of his hopefulness regarding the trust-
worthiness of the average man to use and not abuse freedom is
easily paralleled in other individuals and in other times.

Our real question as to Milton's democratic validity, even
here where his thought is clearest and best, rises not from any
limitation which he puts on the moral and political autonomy
of the individual or any failure to glorify the divine average
in human nature. It is due rather to his assumptions regarding
the content of those "unwritten or at least unconstraining laws
of virtuous education, religious and civil nurture" on which he
relies to raise the minds of men above the vulgar pitch. Milton
believed in education as intensely as any theorist of pure
democracy. He trusted too much, however, to the efficacy of
an *élite* leadership, and a leadership trained in too exclusively
a moral and intellectual ideal. He did not understand the
actual workings of human personality and therefore did
not understand how the individual could be remade. This
is a large question and cannot engage us here. We have,
however, in the Tractate *Of Education* his programme for the
disciplining of the mind of the English gentry, the men who are
to rule. It is a carefully worked out system with many liberal
features which commend themselves. He defines education
functionally as that which fits a man to perform justly, skilfully,
and magnanimously all the offices, public and private, of peace
or war. He allows music and recreation, joins books and
observation, requires understanding of agriculture and the
mechanic arts, deprecates the merely verbal skills and omits the
whole programme of scholastic disputation, though not the
humane discipline of rhetoric, in which he had himself been
trained. What is lacking is a recognition of the wisdom to be

acquired from life itself and the need of taking experience as a starting point, rather than as something to be conformed to the traditions of excellence handed down by nations which have been industrious after wisdom. The end of education is to "regain to know God aright" and out of that knowledge to love and be like Him. This knowledge is to be won by "orderly conning over the lower and visible creature."

Well enough. But in Milton's assumption the patterns all exist, whether in Scripture or in the Greek and Roman classics. Even divorce, like heroic verse unrhymed, is the rediscovery of ancient liberty. It is not sufficient, and the absence in Milton of a really exploratory instinct keeps him from saying the modern word about education that we wish to hear. His boys are to be made Christian scholars; they could easily fail of becoming human beings. Aside from this limitation, Milton gives almost the perfect cultural and humanistic programme. It is remarkable first of all for its integration. Milton regards ancient civilisation as a unit and requires that it should be studied in all its aspects. Knowledge of tongues is for the sake of acquiring the "solid things in them." Literature is not belles-lettres only; style is not a thing apart. The whole fabric of science, politics, morality, and art is humanly related. Virgil is both a poet and an agriculturalist. The words of Christ are at once beautiful and a rule of life. Milton's merits and defects in this are those of the Christian Renaissance, of which he is in many ways the perfect representative. His doctrine is the noble, classic one of the free individual, crowned and mitred sovereign of himself; his programme for producing him is the main-tenance and promulgation of all excellence according to the image in the mind of God. "Truth came indeed once into the world with her divine master and was a perfect shape most glorious to look on." The programme for its recovery is essen-tially disciplinary and selective. Neither Milton nor any others of his tradition had or have the idea of nurturing something which grows from roots of grass.

Areopagitica and *Of Education* are Milton's first but by no means his last great songs of hope. The Utopian moment was promptly lost in disappointment, but it returns to animate the *Second Defence of the English People* and the conclusion of *Paradise Lost*. The humanistic Christ of *Paradise Regained* finally embodies Milton's faith in the efficacy of reason, weaponed with the experience of "those who have been most industrious after wisdom," to produce happiness for all mankind. Both works apparently fell on deaf ears. At least they went unnoticed in the diurnal flow of pamphlet journalism. Thanks to Herbert Palmer's notice, the divorce scandal attached itself permanently to Milton's name—a lesson in the ways of publicity which stayed with him to his dying day, giving content to his earlier abstract philosophising about fame.

Baillie and Edwards, watchdogs of orthodoxy, gave a curious turn to the pamphlets in connection with the rise of feminine fanaticism. They remembered Anne Hutchinson of Massachusetts and the argument of Samuel Gorting that "it is lawful for every woman to desert her husband if he is not willing to follow her in the church way." Edwards dug up the horrible example of a woman preacher named Attaway, who had justified herself in adultery by quoting Milton's pamphlet. Two gentlemen of the Inns of Court, who had interviewed her out of curiosity at one of her conventicles, reported her as saying that Master Milton's ideas on divorce were a point to be considered, "and that she, for her part, would look more into it, for she had an unsanctified husband, that did not walk in the way of Sion, nor speak the language of Canaan." Following up on this interesting lady with the thoroughness of a modern reporter, Edwards learned that she did actually leave her husband and cohabit with a Baptist preacher named William Jenney. He even documented the story with Jenney's letter to his deserted wife and Mrs. Attaway's to the distressed and hesitating Jenney, inviting him to go with her to Jerusalem and repair that city in anticipation of bringing to it all the saints. Milton, who knew that "fanatic dreams, . . . having full swing, do end in the satisfaction of the flesh," could hardly have enjoyed being associated with this episode. As a philosopher he understood how to put it in its place; as a human being he can hardly have escaped a sharp reaction of cynicism against the irresponsible reception of his ideas.

We have now to record the renewal of Milton's domestic life, through the extraordinary and unexpected return of Mary Powell to his bed and board. Phillips' story of the event is plausible enough. The King's cause, after Naseby, was obviously bankrupt. Wise cavaliers were looking for ways to save themselves, their families, and their possessions. Milton's own friends were uneasy about his separation—uncertain, perhaps, what kind of indiscretion he might commit, if not with the sensible Miss Davis then with some more compliant subject. A conspiracy is set on foot. The return of Mary is arranged. Before the actual surrender of Oxford, say in August of 1645, she is dispatched to London and presented in a tearful mood to her husband at the home of one of his evening hosts.

He making his usual visit, the wife was ready in another room, and on a sudden he was surprised to see one whom he thought to have never seen more, making submission and begging pardon on her knees before him. He might probably at first make some show of aversion and rejection; but partly his own generous nature, more inclinable to reconciliation than to perseverance in anger and revenge, and partly the strong intercession of friends on both sides, soon brought him to an act of oblivion, and a firm league of peace for the future.

Milton was on the point of moving to a larger house in a neighbouring street, the Barbican, and Mary was domiciled with the mother-in-law of Christopher Milton till it was ready. There is no hint of any further interruption of their life together. A first child, Anne, was born about a year later on July 29th, 1646; a second, Mary, October 25th, 1648; a third, John, who died in infancy, March 16th, 1651; a fourth, Deborah, on May 2nd, 1652. Mary herself died three days after this last event. After the fall of Oxford, June 24th, 1646, the Powell estate was sequestered, and the family, including several brothers and sisters, moved to London and took up residence with the Miltons, while Powell engaged in the necessary legal activities incident to making composition for his delinquency and thereby recovering a part of his possessions. The Miltons had an interest in this matter, since Powell owed him £500 on an original debt of £300 which long antedated the marriage and £1,000 as the marriage portion agreed on for Mary in 1642. Christopher Milton was also engaged in suing for his property at the same time, he having been officially in the royalist service. In 1647, both Powell and Milton's father died. After the latter event the poet, giving up any larger plans for teaching, moved to a smaller house in High Holborn, "among those that open backward on Lincoln's Inn Fields." The two Phillips boys perhaps remained members of the household.

One might speculate at length on the human implications of these events and relationships. The material for assessing their effect on Milton's personality, though scanty, is reasonably clear. He published his collected poems in January, 1646. (The title page date, 1645, is, of course, old style.) The publisher, Humphrey Moseley, maintained an almost unique interest in belles-lettres amid the flood of pamphlets and sermons which had been issuing from the presses and which had, as Milton said in *Areopagitica*, rendered almost every other kind of literature unvendible. The close of the civil war gave him opportunity, and Milton's volume was only one among many which were now issued under his imprint. Waller's poems had preceded it in 1644 and Suckling's *Fragmenta Aurea* were to follow in 1646. In his commendatory Preface, Moseley writes, "The author's more peculiar excellency in these studies was too well known to conceal his papers or to keep me from attempting to solicit them from him." They are, he continues, "as true a birth as the Muses have brought forth since our famous Spenser wrote, whose poems in these English ones are as rarely imitated as sweetly excelled." The Virgilian motto, "Crown his brow with ivy, lest some evil tongue injure the future bard," is in the vein of earlier deprecations and must be Milton's own selection.

We have every reason to believe that Milton cherished this publication. The materials are carefully arranged and edited. He sent copies of it to his friends, and he was to have it reprinted with additions the year before his death. The kind of welcome it was likely to receive from individuals may well have been anticipated as a grateful solace from the jangling comments on the tracts. The copy which went to Francis Rous, librarian at Oxford, was lost and Milton sent a second with an inscription in the form of a graceful Latin ode. He addresses the volume itself, "book in twin parts rejoicing in a single cover," the work of a youthful hand, careful, but not yet a master poet, and bids it take its place in the groves of the Muses to be read among the lofty works of Greece and Rome. A stanza in the poem prays that some god may take away hideous civil strife and call back the Muses now banished from almost every part of England.

> And the unclean birds whose claws are almost upon us
> may he pierce with arrows from Apollo's quiver.

The date is given as January 27th, 1647, which would be a few days after the death of Richard Powell.

From the time of the appearance of this volume Milton published nothing for three years, but he wrote considerably more verse than in the preceding six. The last lines of the second divorce sonnet, written presumably in 1646, give his inevitable comment on the civil war which has just come to an end.

> Licence they mean when they cry Liberty;
> For who loves that must first be wise and good;
> But from that mark how far they rove we see,
> For all this waste of wealth, and loss of blood.

A savage denunciation of the "new forcers of conscience under the Long Parliament" belongs to the same period of acute Parliamentary conflict over the establishment of Presbyterianism. The full tide of Milton's bitterness is directed against the enemies of toleration who have renounced their prelate lords only to set up a new ecclesiastical tyranny of their own. Individually he assails Edwards and Baillie who have insulted him on the divorce issue. The personal reference in the following lines is too clear and too Miltonic to be misunderstood.

> Men whose life, learning, faith and pure intent
> Would have been held in high esteem with Paul
> Must now be named and printed heretics
> By shallow Edwards and Scotch what d'ye call.

A new note is struck two years later in a heroic sonnet celebrating the victories of Fairfax in the second civil war. In this "soul animating strain" Milton salutes a great commander and calls on him, as he was later to call on Cromwell, to turn after victory to the nobler tasks of peace.

> For what can war, but endless war still breed,
> Till truth and right from violence be freed,
> And public faith cleared from the shameful brand
> Of public fraud. In vain doth valour bleed,
> While avarice and rapine share the land.

The poet is vindicating his Pindaric power to call fame on the deeds of men of action. He is also assuming the role of counsellor and inspirer of civic leadership, not now in prose orations addressed to a democratic body, but in his own high medium and to an individual.

Except for these utterances Milton passed over in silence the victories of the Parliamentary armies, the capture of the King, the radical petitions of the new model sectaries, the flight of Charles to Carisbrooke, the new royalist rising, the final

collapse of the royal cause, the illegal exclusion of the Presbyterian members from Parliament by Colonel Pride and his
musketeers. "He lived," says Phillips, "a private and quiet life,
still prosecuting his studies and curious search into knowledge,
the grand affair perpetually with him." We learn from Milton
himself in his later summary of his career in *The Second Defence*
that he had begun a history of Britain and had finished four
books by the time of his summons to employment by the
Council of State at the end of the period we are discussing. This,
and no epic or drama on either a historical or a religious subject,
was the main occupation of the years of his developing and
changing family life.

In one sense the work is a kind of commutation, though
certainly no fulfilment, of his earlier enthusiastic promises.
It represents a return to the spirit of his studies in the first year
after his return from Italy and to his intention of being doctrinal
to the nation, but with a new conviction about England borne
in on him by the events which had been enacting themselves
before his eyes and were now threatening to end in disappointment and frustration. In the first book he subjects to sharp
analysis the mythical story of pre-Roman Britain which had
once appealed to him as material for imaginative recreation.
He evidently enjoys recalling the legends but feels, as a sober
historian, a little uneasy about doing so. Such fables, he argues,
have sometimes been found to contain relics of truth. He will
tell them over with a plain and lightsome brevity, if only for the
benefit of our English poets and rhetoricians, "who by their art
will know how to use them judiciously." At the beginning of the
second book he gives by implication the reason why the *History
of Britain* is not what he had once hoped to write, the something to be heard among the hallelujahs of the saints in celebration of a glorious fulfilment of his country's destiny. Great
utterance goes with a great age.

> When the esteem of science and liberal study waxes low
> in the commonwealth, we may presume that also there all
> civil virtue and worthy action is grown as low to a decline:
> and then eloquence as it were consorted in the same destiny,
> with the decrease and fall of virtue, corrupts also and fades.

Milton desired and worked for the great age of England because
he wanted to report it. Such an age had seemed to beckon him.
The hope is fading and his eloquence is mute.

With the third book Milton enters on a subject having contemporary relevance as containing "accidents as various and exemplary as the intermission or change of government hath anywhere brought forth." The late civil broils have cast England "into a condition not much unlike the Britons themselves then were in when the imperial jurisdiction departing left them to the sway of their own counsels." He ominously concludes ("to speak a truth not often spoken") that Britain is a land "fruitful enough of men stout and courageous in war but not over fertile of men able to govern justly and prudently in peace," trusting only in their own mother wit and failing to consider that the qualities which make men fit to rule grow only in minds "well implanted with solid and elaborate breeding." Such qualities are in this soil "in a manner outlandish" and must, like wine and oil, be imported from abroad. Liberty itself, sought out of season in a corrupt and degenerate age, can bring a people only to a farther slavery.

> For liberty hath a sharp and double edge, fit only to be handled by just and virtuous men.

This and the lessons to be derived from examples of ecclesiastical and royal corruption are the heart of Milton's *History*, and make it a further contribution to the cause, but the contribution of a man balked of soaring purposes and obliged to play the part of a day labourer in the vineyard of the Lord.

That the gentler strains of the poetic art are still in Milton and capable of being aroused by personal affection is evidenced by two new sonnets, one addressed to Henry Lawes on the publication of his airs, dated February 9th, 1646, the other a memorial to Mrs. Catherine Thomason, wife of his bookseller friend who left the collection of contemporary tracts now in the British Museum and had received those written by Milton from the author's hand. The first praises the musician, as others praised him, for joining words and notes lovingly together and thereby doing justice to the poet's art. As usual in the sonnets, Milton enshrines a jewel of remembered literary beauty, an allusion so exquisitely appropriate as to cast a glow on the entire poem and the relationship which it commemorates.

> Dante shall give Fame leave to set thee higher
> Than his Casella, whom he wooed to sing,
> Met in the milder shades of Purgatory.

Milton lived by things like this, and, as Marvell with his garden imagery, Donne with his metaphysics, and George Herbert with the symbolism of the Church, wove what he loved into the texture of his verse. The sonnet to Mrs. Thomason is a normal expression of religious faith. Milton's poetic raptures on the subject of death and immortality belonged to the past. The only other verses are English translations, in common metre, of eight psalms, done in April, 1648.

The almost total absence between 1646 and 1649 of utterances expressive of Milton's characteristic eloquence and fervour finds its most obvious explanation in his disappointment with the course of public events. It may well be due also to the pressure of novel and exacting household cares. Milton had performed a great act of rationality, had deserved more truly than anywhere in his life before Wordsworth's description of his character—

> And yet thy heart
> The humblest burdens on itself did lay.

Such an accommodation in a man like Milton is in itself an absorbing effort, having its ultimate rewards and no doubt its present relaxing satisfactions, but also painfully distracting from other purposes, and requiring both stamina and ingenuity to pass through with gain rather than a permanent diminishing of personality. Something of the inner situation is revealed to us in a single letter of this period to Carlo Dati, the most intimate of Milton's Italian friends. The date is April 21st, 1647, after the death of Mr. Powell and the elder Milton, but before the removal from the larger house in the Barbican to the smaller one in Holborn. Milton had sent Dati a copy of "Epitaph of Damon," printed perhaps as early as 1640. The Italian had written three letters which had failed to reach him. Milton's letter is in reply to a fourth, which he has just received. There is no mistaking the genuineness of his delight or the poignancy of the memories which this reminder arouses in him.

> Very sad to me . . . was that departure, and it planted stings in my heart which now rankle there deeper, as often as I think with myself of my reluctant parting, my separation as by a wrench, from so many companions at once, such good friends as they were, and living so pleasantly with each other in one city, far off, indeed, but to me most dear. I call to

witness that tomb of Damon ever to be sacred and solemn to me. . . . I call that sacred grave to witness that I have had no greater delight all this while than in recalling to my mind the most pleasant memory of all of you, and of yourself especially.

These stirrings produce a bitter reflection on the present.

When I came upon that passage where you write that you had sent me three letters before, which I now know to have been lost, then, in the first place that sincere gladness of mine at the receipt of this one began to be infected and troubled with sad regret, and presently a something heavier creeps in upon me to which I am accustomed in very frequent grievings over my own lot: the sense, namely, that those whom the mere necessity of neighbourhood, or something else of useless kind, has closely conjoined with me, whether by accident or by the tie of law, they are the persons, though in no other respect commendable, who sit daily in my company, weary me, nay, by Heaven all but plague me to death whenever they are jointly in the humour for it, whereas those whom habit, disposition, studies, had so handsomely made my friends, are now almost denied me, either by death or by unjust separation of place, and are so for the most part snatched from my sight that I have to live well-nigh in a perpetual solitude.

We have here, I believe, the true inwardness of Milton's life with Mary Powell and her family, the image of his loneliness and longing. The passage, granted that it represents a passing mood, does much to explain the end of his exuberance, the giving up of teaching, the resort to scholarship, the return to miscellaneous versifying, the translation of the psalms, the occasional poetic outbursts.

Other things in the letter recall the sensitive side of Milton's nature, which is the counterpart of his violence. He sent copies of the epitaph to his Florentine friends, hoping that he might lure some of them to write to him—

for if I wrote first, either I had to write to all, or I feared that, if I gave the preference to anyone, I should incur the reproach of such others as came to know it.

He congratulates himself on the thought that his and Dati's concern for each other's welfare is mutual, "the existence of

which on my side only I was perhaps claiming to my credit."
He has hesitated to send his printed poems on account of the
harsh sayings in some of the pages against the Pope of Rome and
hopes Dati will obtain indulgence from his other friends "whenever I may be speaking of your religion in our peculiar way."
We get from the letter, finally, a new comment on the effects on
his mind of the turbulent state of affairs in England.

> What safe retirement for literary leisure could you suppose
> given one among so many battles of a civil war, slaughters,
> fights, seizure of goods.

One thing among his afflictions which Milton does not mention
to Dati is the symptoms which he had already noticed of
approaching blindness. These began about 1644 with the left eye
and were accompanied by some kind of digestive disturbance,
as he tells us in an elaborate medical description, quoted in full
below. The right eye began to fail him some five years later.

To insist on the complications of living which Milton had
now encountered and to find him labouring heavily under them
is not to attempt, beyond the evidence, to reconstruct the facts
or emotions of his private life. His father's presence in his home
may or may not have been an important factor in helping him
go on with the marriage. His death may have made the
situation easier or more difficult.

The role of the Powell widow is equally conjectural. The
early anonymous biographer adds to Phillips' story of the
marriage the detail of Mary's pleading on her return that her
mother had been the chief cause of her frowardness. It may well
be so, and a maternal change of front may be the chief cause of
her becoming a reasonably successful wife. We do not know
just when Mrs. Powell and her other children left the household.
The tone of the passage quoted from the letter suggests that they
were still at hand. Milton carried on lawsuits against her in
later years and there are other stigmata of a divided family.
The eldest daughter was a cripple. "A brave girl," says Phillips,
"though, whether by ill constitution or want of care, she grew
more and more decrepit." A similar formula appears again in
his account of the death of the third child in 1651, "through the
ill usage, or bad constitution, of an ill chosen nurse." Are
the Powells being made to shoulder blame for these calamities
and is Phillips reflecting the opinions of Milton and his friends?
Such attitudes, with the attested hostility of the girls themselves

to Milton, may have developed after the later marriages. Nevertheless, the case for a serene and happy household in the Barbican or High Holborn is not good. The facts which have been set forth would seem to justify us in feeling that Milton has undergone a severe discipline of reality, successfully, though at a heavy cost.

When Milton returned to the world of action and of public utterance it was to take the momentous step of writing himself regicide. The final scene of the stately tragedy of Charles I was about to be enacted. The King had been abducted from his refuge on the Isle of Wight, and brought, a close prisoner, first to Hurst Castle, then to Windsor. The army had marched to London firmly resolved to put an end to negotiation and bring Charles to trial. The recalcitrant Presbyterians were excluded from their seats in Parliament, and the House converted into a body willing to give legal colouring to what was in essence an act of martial law. The trial began at Westminster Hall on January 20th, 1649, and lasted a week. On January 30th, Charles was beheaded. How long before this event Milton began *The Tenure of Kings and Magistrates*, we do not know. The pamphlet was actually on sale by February 13th. It contains allusions to the Parliamentary purge of December 7th, to the protests and appeals of the Presbyterian clergy, and apparently to the trial itself. Milton's own account of its composition, in *The Second Defence*, is as follows:

> When at length some Presbyterian ministers, who had formerly been the most bitter enemies to Charles, became jealous of the growth of the Independents, and of their ascendancy in the Parliament, most tumultuously clamoured against the sentence, and did all in their power to prevent the execution, though they were not angry so much on account of the act itself, as because it was not the act of their party; and when they dared affirm, that the doctrine of the Protestants and of all the reformed churches, was abhorrent to such an atrocious proceedings against kings, I thought that it became me to oppose such a glaring falsehood; and, accordingly, without any immediate application to Charles, I showed, in an abstract consideration of the question, what might lawfully be done against tyrants.

The argument is one familiar in the liberal political theory of the Middle Ages and the Renaissance and is destined to play an important role in the revolutionary movements of the next age. Men are by nature free, born to command and not to obey. Falling among themselves to wrong and violence and foreseeing that such courses must lead to the destruction of them all, they "agreed by a common league to bind each other from mutual injury" and chose magistrates, "not to be their lords and masters . . . but to be their deputies and commissioners," and they invented a system of laws, "either framed or consented to by all, that should confine and limit the authority of whom they chose to govern them." The power of kings and magistrates is derivative and transferred; it remains fundamentally with the people and cannot be taken from them, without a violation of their birthright. It follows, therefore, that the people may "as oft as they shall judge it for the best, either choose him or reject him or depose him, though no tyrant, merely by the liberty and right of free-born men to be governed as seems to them best."

Such is the abstract doctrine, supported by divine and human authority and by the example of ancient and modern societies. But Milton comes closer home than this. When the sovereign has become a tyrant, one regarding neither the law nor the common good, and reigns only for himself and his faction, then it is lawful and has been held so through all ages, "for any who have the power" to call him to account and "after due conviction, to depose and put him to death, if the ordinary magistrate have neglected or denied to do it." The high-handed proceedings of the army and the Rump Parliament would be steps in such an extra-legal process. Milton rests the case at this point. That he does not name Charles by no means prevents his having become the chief theorist and defender of the immediate event, gratuitously incurring a responsibility which had terrified some of the stoutest and most aggressive of the earlier leaders of the rebellion.

The motive force of his action, beside conscience and conviction, is personal animus against the Presbyterians, the old allies who had turned against him and whose defeat had become for the time being a ruling passion of his life. The *Tenure* is thus linked with the divorce tracts, with the plea for toleration in *Areopagitica*, and the concentrated denunciation of Old Priest become New Presbyter in the sonnet on the Forcers of Conscience. Milton deals with their position analytically and at length in the new tract. The old motives recur.

Being slaves within doors, no wonder that they strive so much to have the public state conformably governed to the inward vicious rule by which they govern themselves. For, indeed, none can love freedom heartily but good men; the rest love not freedom but licence, which never hath more scope than under tyrants.

While the hope of becoming "classic and provincial lords" led them on, "while pluralities greased them thick and deep," then to fight against the King was good and lawful. But when they saw that truth and conscience were to be freed, tithes and pluralities to be no more, then "in a new garb of allegiance, which their doings have long since cancelled, they plead for him, pity him, protest against those that talk of bringing him to the trial of justice." Meanwhile, "sincere and real men," have been engaged beyond the possibility of a retreat. It is with these that Milton identifies himself and is to be identified henceforth. He will not be as those who "shiver at the majesty and grandeur of some noble deed, as if they were newly entered into a great sin," or who "let mild and tender dispositions be foolishly softened from their duty and perseverance." His place is rather with those worthies who, when God and a good cause have given them a victory which draws after it alteration of laws, change of government, downfall of princes with their families, are as "the soul of that great enterprise, to be sweat and laboured out amid the throng and noises of vulgar and irrational men." He could hardly be anywhere else than here. If he has come alone and by a devious and even questionable path, it is none the less God's leading.

Except in a few places the *Tenure* lacks the eloquence and hopefulness of *Areopagitica*. The winning of freedom has become grim business. It is the hour of victory, but no new horizons have been lifted. The vision of a "noble and puissant nation rousing herself like a strong man after sleep, and shaking her invincible locks" is not so clear. Milton cannot be merely scornful of the Presbyterians. He is sure there are many good and faithful Christians among them, though misled by some of turbulent spirit.

I wish them, earnestly and calmly, not to fall off from their first principles. . . . Let them not oppose their best friends and associates, who molest them not at all. . . . Let them fear therefore, if they be wise, rather what they have done already than what remains to do, and be warned in time they put no confidence in princes whom they have provoked, lest they be added to the examples of those that miserably have tasted the event.

He seems aware, in this pleading, of the treacherous foundations of popular sentiment on which the consummated republic must try to stand. There is realism in this, beyond any earlier assessment of a public need for services which his pen can render. His effort, accordingly, is practical and sober. It brings him closer to a real alignment with the cause which he has adopted and prepares him for an authentic association with its leadership. The heavenly song which was the dream of his youth and early manhood may well, if he still thought of it, have seemed as remote as the intimate felicity of earthly companionship which he had sought in marriage.

CHAPTER SIX

DEEDS ABOVE HEROIC
1649–60

THE EXECUTION OF CHARLES on January 30th, 1649, high moment in the spacious drama of revolution, was a turning point also in Milton's personal career. He was now to be the appointed servant of the cause for whose triumph he had worked. He had once before stood side by side with friends who shared or seemed to share his purposes. When he ventured forth on divorce he became, as we have seen, a lonely fighter, frustrated at first by an "undervaluing silence," then goaded to further effort by accents of abuse coming incredibly from the very ranks he had defended. At length, for the time being, effort ceased. It must have been an immense relief to write again and to find his new offering accepted. The effect of his appointment to public office was bound to be one of invigoration. To be shown what was to be done, then allowed to do it in his own way, to have new tasks crowd upon him before the old were finished, to feel the warmth of approval from men whose leadership he admired, to be of their innermost counsels, to know how real was their need of his loyalty and skill—this was

F

indeed to have scope and stimulus for the exercise of the talent which was life to use and death to hide. If ultimately he came to chafe at the limitations of his position, to find the cause as great as ever, but the men themselves not able rightly to maintain it, it is only because his nature made conformity impossible for very long. The world must in the last analysis bend to him, not he to it; he must exhort it as long as there was hope, and when hope failed retire within himself and implore the coming of a kingdom not made with hands. We feel in the Preface to *Eikonoklastes*, Milton's first great commission from the Council of State, an accent of assured competence altogether lacking in the opening addresses to Parliament of the earlier tracts. The laboured technique of the classical exordium is put aside, the personal note is sounded only briefly. Milton drives hard for his objective from the first.

His own account, in the *Second Defence*, of the spirit in which he had laboured in the cause of liberty and of his surprise at being appointed Secretary of State for Foreign Tongues, is an unconscious revelation of his real yearning for just the situation in which he now found himself.

All this service of mine, now to the Church, now to the State, I gave gratuitously within my own private walls; from neither Church nor State had I anything in return beyond personal safety; a good conscience, a good reputation with good men, and this honest liberty of speech, were independent possessions: some people about me were drawing wealth to themselves, others honours, without trouble; but no one ever saw me going about, no one ever saw me asking anything among my friends, or stationed at the doors of the Court with a petitioner's face, or haunting the entries of lesser assemblies: I kept myself almost entirely at home, managing on my own resources, though in this civil tumult these were often in great part kept from me, and contriving, though burdened with taxes in the main rather oppressive, to lead my frugal life. All this past and done, imagining I should now have abundance of leisure, I turned myself to the task of drawing out, if I could, in a continuous thread of narrative, the history of my country from its first beginnings to the present times. I had finished four books, when lo!, Charles's kingdom having been formed into a Republic, the Council of State, as it is called, then first set up by the authority of

Parliament, invites me, dreaming of nothing of the sort, to a post in connection with it, with a view to the use of my services chiefly in foreign affairs.

The period of the secretaryship naturally divides itself into two parts: the years before his blindness had become complete, and those which followed. This catastrophe, together with the illness which attended it, marks, as we shall see, a crisis in his public position and in his inner life. We shall review first the story of his official career and then the series of private events which constituted the basic, though less explicitly recorded, element in his maturing experience at this time.

The office to which Milton was appointed on March 15th, 1649 is variously called that of Latin Secretary to the Council of State or Secretary of State for Foreign Tongues. On the surface, it implies only the duty of actually drafting the foreign correspondence of the Commonwealth. In reality, the Council expected to employ Milton's energies in a variety of ways and above all to make him the public defender of its acts. His salary was fixed at £288 13s. 6½d. a year. The position was evidently considered of much less importance than that of the General Secretary, who received £730 a year, or even of the Assistant Secretary, who received £365. Masson infers that Milton was sworn the oath of secrecy regarding the Council's deliberations; he was present at some, but by no means all, of their sessions. It was enough that he should know in general what was going on, receive instructions regarding his particular duties, and occasionally report on the investigations assigned him. We find in the records such routine commissions as the following:

That the letters brought in by Mr. Watkins to be viewed by Mr. Frost [the General Secretary] or by Mr. Milton, to see if any of them contain anything concerning the exportation of any prohibited goods.

That the French letters given to the House by the Dutch Ambassador be translated by Mr. Milton.

That Mr. Milton do examine the papers of *Pragmaticus* and report what he finds in them to the Council.

Increasingly, as time went on, Milton was asked to phrase in Latin the letters and dispatches of the Council to foreign powers. To what extent he merely translated and to what extent he made use of his own eloquence and ideas, it is not easy to determine. On January 2nd, 1652, he was ordered to prepare a letter in Latin "*of the substance* of what was now here read in English, to be sent to the Duke of Tuscany." On January 26th, the instructions read "that Mr. Milton do *translate in Latin* the Answer of the Council to the First Paper of the Lords Ambassadors of the United Provinces." The Latin State Correspondence was ultimately to be published under his own name, and we may certainly regard at least the great letters written during the Protectorate as representing, in Carlyle's phrase, "what Oliver Cromwell meant and John Milton said."

Congenial as this activity may have been, Milton first really finds himself in his new employment when he is given a free hand to combat the menace of the controversial war which was being waged from every quarter against the usurping government. Whatever the Council may have thought about it, Milton regarded this as his great opportunity and obligation. Here he could turn loose his powers with assurance that his efforts were really needed, and feel, as well as know, the truth that speech is a weapon not inferior to the sword.

The great immediate danger to the new government lay, of course, in the deep and irrational public sentiment which had, in spite of his misdeeds, clung to the person of the King, and which was outraged by his execution. The latent flame of this emotion had been fanned to the danger point by the publication in February, 1649, of the *Eikon Basilike*, "The True Portraiture of his Sacred Majesty in his Solitudes and Sufferings." This work, purporting to be a private record of the self-communings of Charles in his last years, but really the fabrication of Bishop Gauden, achieved at once an enormous circulation. The image of the King as a model of conscientiousness and piety—loyally Protestant, given to earnest prayer, tender of his family, solicitous for the good of his subjects—found ready acceptance in the hearts of the people. To undo the havoc it was working was an almost impossible task, but Milton cannot have hesitated in his resolution to undertake it. He was doubtless instructed to do so, though the order does not appear in the minutes of the Council.

Eikonoklastes, "the Image-Breaker," was published in October, 1649, seven months after Milton's appointment as Latin Secretary. The poet hints a suspicion that the work he is attacking is not authentically the King's, but he nevertheless treats it as though it were. His indictment, therefore, becomes one of Charles himself as a falsifier of the facts, as a sentimentalist and hypocrite. Milton recognises the role which he is playing as an ungracious one and characteristically disclaims all satisfaction in assuming it. "To descant on the misfortunes of a person fallen from so high a dignity, who hath paid his debts both to nature and his faults, is neither of itself a thing commendable, nor the intention of this discourse." It is not "the vanity to get a name by writing against a king" which impels him, but patriotic duty and the need of undeceiving those who worship "the gaudy name of majesty." Once embarked in the career of image-breaking, however, he does not stay his hand. He intimates that the King's piety is but an example of the deepest policy of a tyrant and instances the religious dissembling of Shakespeare's Richard III as a precedent. In reply to the King's question, "Whose innocent blood have I shed, what widow's or orphan's tears can witness against me?" he recalls the many cruelties of the time: "Not to speak of those many whippings, pillories, and other corporal inflictions wherewith his reign also before the war was not unbloody; some have died in prison under cruel restraint, others in banishment, whose lives were shortened through the rigour of that persecution wherewith so many years he afflicted the true Church." The blameless life of Charles in his peaceful years he calls "voluptuous," "idle," "without care or thought, as if to be a King had been nothing else in his apprehension but to eat, and drink, and have his will, and take his pleasure."

We hear in all this the harshness of the Puritan, and Milton nowhere does greater violence to the gentler traditions in which he had been brought up than when he is thus zealously saying his worst of Charles. He shows himself equally callous to the demands of chivalry in the famous passage in which he shows that one of the prayers which the King "popped into the hand" of Bishop Juxton on the scaffold and which was included as his own in the *Eikon* was in reality stolen from "that vain and amatorious poem, Sir Philip Sidney's *Arcadia*." "It hardly can be thought upon without some laughter," he writes, "that he who had acted over us so stately and so tragically should leave the world at last with such a ridiculous exit as to bequeath among his deifying friends that stood about him such a piece of mockery." We are reminded, by way of contrast, of Milton's friend Marvell's lines on Charles's death, graciously incorporated

in a poem in praise of Cromwell written at the very time of
which we are speaking.

> He nothing common did, or mean,
> Upon that memorable scene,
>   But with his keener eye
>   The axe's edge did try;
>
> Nor called the Gods with vulgar spite
> To vindicate his helpless right;
>   But bowed his comely head
>   Down, as upon a bed.

The prayer did indeed come from the *Arcadia*, and Milton's
discovery is rightly held to have been one of the most damaging
small points in his case against the royal "martyr." But the
price of controversial victory must be thought a heavy one, for
Milton was himself quite capable of sharing the noble sentiment
of Marvell's lines, of admiring the prayer itself, as he had
certainly in times past admired the work from which it was
taken, and of finding some more generous way of explaining
its presence in the King's devotions.

The King's Book, written in the mother tongue and appealing
to the emotions of personal loyalty and love, was menacing only
in England, and Milton's answer was intended for English ears
alone. But the Commonwealth was on the defensive not only
at home but also in the forum of European opinion. Foreign
princes, sensing danger to their own power, were ready enough
to mobilize against the usurpers. Charles II was on the
Continent, plotting a return and doing his best to secure support
for his cause. It was important for his purposes that the case
against the English parricides should be drawn up in such
compelling form as to set the best minds abroad firmly against
the Commonwealth. With this object, he secured the services
of a noted French scholar, Claude Saumaise, or, to use his
Latin name, Salmasius, and within ten months after the
execution of Charles I (i.e. in November, 1649) there appeared
in Holland an elaborately constructed work in Latin entitled
Defensio Regia pro Carolo I, containing the whole case against the
Commonwealth. The book was dedicated to Charles II and
printed at his expense. Every attempt was made to secure for
it an international audience among the learned, who in turn
would influence the popular and official mind, particularly of

Holland and of France. It was not expected that the work would be influential in England itself, but by November 29th, 1650, we find the Council taking steps to prevent the importation of copies. Something over a month later (January 8th, 1650) the memorable order is entered in the minute books "that Mr. Milton do prepare something in answer to the Book of Salmasius and when he hath done it bring it to the Council."

The poet had at last received his great commission. The reply would naturally be in Latin. It would be addressed, not to provincial ears, but to that wider European republic of letters whose attention was the object of humanistic ambition and whose approval Milton had coveted from boyhood. The knowledge that his antagonist was the most famous scholar of his day was not a discouragement, but rather an incentive. The greater the opponent, the greater the stimulus to high endeavour. Milton went to work at once, and in spite of sickness, the increasing weakness of his eyesight, and the pressure of other duties, including the preparation of a second edition of *Eikonoklastes*, completed his task by the end of December. The reply was proudly and defiantly entitled *John Milton's Defence of the English People against Claude Saumaise's Defence of the King*. It was later to be regarded by Milton as his greatest public act, a noble and famous achievement, hardly second in importance to the winning of a decisive military victory. He was to look back, in blindness and defeat, upon its accomplishment as something which justified the efforts of a lifetime and secured for him a place among the heroes and benefactors of mankind.

Reading the *First Defence* to-day, we find it hard to accept the estimate which Milton put upon it. In some ways it is the least interesting and worthy of his works. Salmasius had exhausted the resources of his learning and his eloquence in the attack. In twelve chapters he had descanted upon the hideousness of the crime, marshalled all the authorities in favour of the inviolable rights of kings, analysed the nature of the English Constitution, defining the traditional prerogatives of the King, the Parliament, the Church, inveighed against the Independents and their principles, and, finally, defended the character and conduct of King Charles. Milton answers all the arguments with an equal display of knowledge and in-genuity. But his best and worst efforts are expended in defaming the personality of Salmasius himself. He pours scorn on his learning and his Latinity; he bespatters him with abusive

epithets—fool, beetle, ass, blockhead, liar, apostate, idiot—
employing a picturesque Latin vocabulary unknown to the age
of Cicero and Virgil; he introduces all the scandal he could
collect from public rumour of Salmasius' subservience to his
wife. For any real defence of the principles of popular sovereignty, except for paragraphs here and there, we search in vain.
Milton was possessed of the devil of controversy, his sole object
being to slaughter the "Great Kill-Cow of Christendom," to
render him and his efforts forever ridiculous in the eyes of those
who might be gulled by him. In dealing with the person of the
King, Milton goes even beyond what he had said in *Eikonoklastes*. He now openly accuses him of the poisoning of his
father, likening him to Nero, and asserting that he was steeped,
with the Duke of Buckingham, in all sorts of viciousness and
incontinence.

It is difficult to judge the actual effect of Milton's work on the
European mind. If he sought continental notoriety he certainly
obtained it, for the book enjoyed a huge *succès de scandale* and
Milton was hereafter to be chiefly known as the antagonist of
Salmasius. But one is not impressed by the satisfaction which
such zealous fellow scholars as Heinsius and Vosius took in the
humiliation of their fellow countryman as representative of
sober foreign opinion, and the fact that Salmasius himself, after
a fit of empty rage, retired in sullenness and despondency from
public life is an evidence of his weakness rather than of Milton's
strength. It was, however, inevitable that all those who were
already predisposed to side with the Commonwealth against the
King should believe in the importance and success of Milton's
effort, and the congratulations which came in to him from
foreigners resident in London were enough to give him the
illusions of a universal acclaim. The final confirmation of his
success came to him three months after the publication of the
First Defence in the form of official recognition from the Council.
An entry in the Order Book for June 18th, 1651, reads as
follows: "That thanks be given to Mr. Milton on behalf of the
Commonwealth, for his good service in writing an answer to
the Book of Salmasius, written against the proceedings of the
Commonwealth of England. And it is ordered that the sum
of . . . hundred pounds be given to him as a reward from the
Council."

The publication of the *First Defence* marks the culmination of what must have been, in spite of his truculence in

controversy, a relatively happy period of extraverted activity in Milton's life. There are in the writing of these two years no evidences of any attempt to influence those above him in their management of public affairs, no references to personal plans and ambitions, no expressions of annoyance at his family, and, significantly, no poetry. The complaint of ill-health in the *First Defence* points forward, however, to trouble, and the record of the year 1651 is one of continuous decline in Milton's efficiency in office. Within the next few years, he was to skirt perilously near the border of personal catastrophe. The conspiracy of circumstances which threatened him and the inner resources by virtue of which he successfully passed through the crisis, it is now our business to detail.

Throughout the year 1651, Milton had included among his official duties the task of censoring and supervising the publication of *Mercurius Politicus*, the chief official journal of the Commonwealth, edited by Marchamont Needham. Masson and others have traced his hand in the actual composition of some of the leading articles. The usual assignments continue to be made him in the Order Book, but he is not called on, nor does he volunteer, to answer the pamphlets which were launched in that year against the *Eikonoklastes* and the *First Defence*. In a letter written to Hermann Mylius in December, he speaks of "what is now an almost perpetual enemy of mine, ill-health," and of removal, on account of ill-health, from his official residence to another house. Since we know that a threat had previously been made against Milton's tenure of his official quarters in Whitehall, it is possible that the removal to Petty France, Westminster, was a forced one, and it may well be taken as the first indication of a change in his standing with the Council. During the whole of December, he was absent from the meetings of that body, after a very irregular attendance during the preceding five months. In January, 1652, he resumed his duties but in March he was apparently again ill and the papers with which he was to deal had to be sent to him by a messenger. On March 11th the Council designated one Wekherlin as his assistant. In November, Wekherlin having declined in health or been found inefficient, the new General Secretary, Thurloe, was instructed to help Milton with his duties.

Behind this situation undoubtedly lies the central fact of Milton's blindness, which had been coming on for years, and which we know to have been complete by 1652. Its full psychological consequences were yet to appear, but the composition in that year of the sonnets to Cromwell and Vane is symptomatic. In these poems Milton is again speaking for himself. They are no mere expressions of enthusiastic admiration, but attempts to encourage and even guide the leaders under whom he has been working. It is as if Milton, no longer satisfied that he is fully useful to the Council of State, must needs, though with restraint and subtle tact, begin now to advise it. This role he was, as we shall see, to play again more openly in the *Second Defence*.

There is, however, more important evidence of a change in Milton than his non-attendance at Council meetings or his resort to poetry. In the summer of 1652, there had appeared in Holland an anonymous reply to his *First Defence*, the *Regii Sanguinis Clamour adversus Parricidas Anglicanos*, "The Cry of the King's Blood against the English Parricides," an abler work than that of Salmasius, and one which contained a terrific attack upon Milton personally. He was ordered to answer it and his every instinct must have demanded of him that he begin at once. That he did not do so demonstrates clearly enough the degree of his temporary defeat. When, finally, he had recovered his self-possession a year later and undertaken the delayed obligation, he looked back upon this moment, and analysed the situation in which he then found himself. "At that time," he says in the *Second Defence*, referring to a date late in 1652, "I was at the very worst, under the pressure of severe anxiety occasioned by diverse causes at once—infirm health, the domestic grief of two funerals, and the now total loss of my eyesight; and moreover, outside there was impending that prior adversary of mine [Salmasius, himself, who was known to be preparing a new onslaught] whom preference was to be decidedly given over this one—which prior adversary was threatening more and more every day an attack upon me with his whole strength."

We have Milton, then, all but ready to retire before his time from the field of battle. Reading the *Clamor* he would have found all the questionable passages in his early life ripped up by someone as competent and well informed as he was hostile. Expelled from the University of Cambridge for profligacy, an advocate of the dissolution of marriage at pleasure, writer of a blackguardly book assailing the person of the King, afflicted by God with a punishment suited to his crimes, and rendered thereby "a monster hideous, ugly, huge, bereft of sight"—the outrageous charges must have broken through his weakened defences and made him even doubt the validity of that conception of himself which it had taken a lifetime to build up.

The story of the next year is one of readjustment and recovery, culminating in a new fury of egotism and eloquence. That Milton could not again be as he had been during the first period of his secretaryship is obvious. He will rather fluctuate between brooding resignation and excited energy. We can expect of him greater things than he has hitherto accomplished, but only as the isolated and supernormal individual, forever separated from the possibility of participation on terms of equality in the enterprises of his fellow men.

We may note, as a first outward step in his adjustment, an inclination to depend on the services of those who were willing to assume a position of subordination. John Phillips, brought up by Milton from childhood, was commissioned to write an answer to a minor attack on him from abroad. This is the first time the poet has called on any pen except his own to participate in his defence. In February, 1653, we find him turning to Andrew Marvell, and petitioning Bradshaw that this youth, rather than anyone appointed by the Council itself, be allowed to serve as his assistant in the secretaryship, "though for my part," Milton adds, "I find no encumbrance of what belongs to me, except it be in point of attendance at conference with Ambassadors, which I must confess in my condition I am not fit for." Marvell was not appointed and, after the interval above alluded to, Milton's work as Secretary went on. On October 17th, however, Philip Meadows, already "employed by the Council in Latin translations," was commissioned "to assist Mr. Thurloe [not Milton] in the despatch of Foreign Affairs." In the following eight months there are but four letters included in the collection of Milton's published correspondence for the Council of State. The period undoubtedly represents in Milton's life history one of rest and recuperation. He speaks gratefully in the *Second Defence* of the indulgence of the Council in letting him go on without reducing his emoluments.

What finally brought him back to a dynamic state was, so far as external events are concerned, the *coup d'état* of Cromwell. Though in the new secretariat, Philip Meadows is definitely designated Latin Secretary and Milton continued on the pay-roll without title, he must have felt in the coming rule of the single strong personality, not only a new hope for the welfare of the State, but a new opportunity for him to exert his personal powers and influence. He was always stimulated by change of leadership, and, though he by no means abandoned his predilection for aristocracy, he must have seen the present necessity of a dictatorship. Subsequent events actually proved that Cromwell, as an individual, could better use and value the kind of service which Milton was now fit to render, than the Council had shown itself inclined to do since his collapse. It would, moreover, be relatively easy for Milton's imagination to portray him as standing by the Protector's side, in his old capacity of inspirer and celebrator of great deeds. He was evidently now ready to accept a subordinate position officially, and to gird his loins for special services which no other could perform.

In the Council Order Book, from now on, his name hardly appears at all, and for the first six months of the Protectorate there is not a single State letter from his pen. He had at last taken up the long delayed answer to the *Clamor* and into it he now threw all his powers. This *Second Defence of the English People*, published May 30th, 1654, is a document of entirely different character and inspiration from the other. In the *First Defence* Milton's ardour is in part factitious; he is more the controversialist, using the accepted weapons of the day. In the *Second Defence*, he is John Milton himself, rising in wrath and dignity against the enemies of truth. There is, to be sure, an abundance of personal vituperation against Alexander More, an associate of Salmasius, whom Milton persisted in assuming to be the author, even after he had been authoritatively informed that he was not. There is also a certain amount of casuistical debating of the old issues regarding the sovereignty and the person of King Charles. But the core of the work is something different. Milton's purpose is, on the one hand, personal defence and self-aggrandisement, on the other, the satisfaction of his early ambition to become the celebrator and interpreter of heroic deeds, the philosopher of true liberty, the wise and eloquent guide of men of action. The *Second Defence* is rather a monumental oration than a controversial pamphlet. In the opening paragraphs, Milton dwells at length on the magnitude of his task, congratulating himself that he has been born in this day of his country's grandeur, and now is called upon again to defend and celebrate the cause of liberty. Enthusiasm for his subject rouses him "to a loftier and more daring strain than an exordium" and he conjures before his imagination the immense audience, "an aggregrate of all the meetings and conventions of the gravest men, cities, and nations—crowded countenances innumerable," who have listened to his former plea and now with eager expectation are prepared for this. He feels himself to be, like Triptolemus of old, "importing among the nations the produce of my own land, only a produce far nobler than any gift of creeds— disseminating, to wit, through cities, kingdoms and peoples, the restored enjoyment of free civil life."

There is surely something more than rhetoric in this. It represents, indeed, the beginning of a new cycle of self-exalta- tion, which has followed as a natural reaction from the de- pression of the preceding years. The state of mind in which Milton was might easily prove dangerous, and it is fortunate for him that the occasion and his eloquence made possible a free externalising of his emotion. In the personal passages which occur later in the discourse the poet passes in review his entire career, elaborating more fully than he had ever done the portrait of himself as he wished the world to know him. Most remarkable of all, and representing a new development in his self-dramatisation, is what he says of his blindness. I have already suggested that his first reaction on reading the *Clamor* was one of surrender. By now, however, his old assurance of a divinely guided destiny, of a special appointment as prophet of God, had returned to aid him. He rouses himself, throws off the intimations of despair, and turns the great affliction which has come upon him into a final seal of consecration.

To exhibit his grapplings with this emotion, his almost desperate but fully successful attempt to regain his spiritual footing, we must quote at length. After repeating his adversary's sordid epithets—"puny, hideous, pale, shrivelled and bereft of sight"—and almost childishly boasting of his youthful and vigorous appearance, he proceeds as follows:

I wish that I could with equal facility refute what this barbarous opponent has said of my blindness; but I cannot do it; and I must submit to the affliction. It is not so wretched to be blind, as it is not to be capable of enduring blindness.

But why should I not endure a misfortune, which it behooves every one to be prepared to endure if it should happen; which may, in the common course of things, happen to any man; and which has been known to happen to the most distinguished and virtuous persons in history. . . . And with respect to myself, though I have accurately examined my conduct, and scrutinised my soul, I call Thee, O God, the searcher of hearts, to witness that I am not conscious, either in the more early or in the later periods of my life, of having committed any enormity, which might deservedly have marked me out as a fit object for such a calamitous visitation. . . . When I had to contend with the pressure of sickness, and with the appreciation of soon losing the sight of my remaining eye, and when my medical attendants clearly announced, that if I did engage in the work, it would be irreparably lost, their premonitions caused no hesitation and inspired no dismay. I would not have listened to the voice even of Esculapius himself from the shrine of Epidauris, in preference to the suggestions of the heavenly monitor within my breast; my resolution was unshaken, though the alternative was either the loss of my sight, or the desertion of my duty. . . . But, if the choice were necessary, I would, sir, prefer my blindness to yours; yours is a cloud spread over the mind, which darkens both the light of reason and of conscience; mine keeps from my view only the coloured surfaces of things, while it leaves me at liberty to contemplate the beauty and stability of virtue and of truth. How many things are there besides which I would not willingly see; how many which I must see against my will; and how few which I feel any anxiety to see! There is, as the apostle has remarked, a way to strength through weakness. Let me then be the most feeble creature alive, as long as that feebleness serves to invigorate the energies of my rational and immortal spirit; as long as in that obscurity, in which I am enveloped, the light of the divine presence more clearly shines, then, in proportion as I am weak, I shall be invincibly strong; and in proportion as I am blind, I shall more clearly see. O! that I may thus be perfected by feebleness and irradiated by obscurity! And, indeed, in my blindness, I enjoy in no inconsiderable degree the favour of the Deity, who regards me with more tenderness and compassion in proportion as I am able to behold nothing but Himself. . . .

Such thoughts as these were to continue long with Milton; it only remained for them to be transmuted into poetry. The two sonnets on his blindness, written in the succeeding year, begin the process; the great personal utterances in *Paradise Lost* complete it. To these we shall return. The importance of the *Second Defence* is that it exhibits the actual struggle which led Milton to his final victory. We may note the extension of that old habit of identifying himself with the great figures of classical or Biblical legend, whose lot of suffering and whose triumphant greatness he seems to share. In the passage which immediately follows the one quoted, he alludes to the tenderness with which he is now treated by his friends, and to the favour of the "highest men in the Commonwealth" who, reflecting on the chances of human life, indulge him as one who has served out his time. "If I have any honourable distinction, they do not take it away; if any emolument therefrom they do not reduce it, kindly judging that, though I am not so useful now as I have been, the provision for me ought not be less: in short, treating me with as much honour as if, according to the custom of the Athenians of old, they had decreed me public support for my life in the Prytaneum."

Sustained by these thoughts, Milton recovers his courage and his eloquence. He launches forth into the praise of the great leaders of the Commonwealth, commending without reservation the deeds and personalities of Bradshaw, Fairfax, and others with whom he had been associated in the Council of State. When he comes to the Protector, he shows, as he had done in the sonnet of 1652, that not mere panegyric but the exertion of influence is his real objective. Accepting *in toto* Cromwell's assumption of the dictatorship and finding wisdom and public spirit in his most undemocratic acts, Milton recalls to his mind the difficulty and the ideal purposes of the task of government which the Protector has undertaken and subtly warns him of the dangers of false policy. Specifically, he bids him, first, not to try to rule alone but to associate with himself men of the highest stamp; such men, indeed, as Milton has already named. It is as if he himself were appointing the Protector's chief advisers. In all this the poet is clearly promoting his fixed ideas—derived from contemplation of the ancient constitutions of Rome and Athens, and the modern one of Venice—of the superiority of aristocracy over all other forms of government. He advises him, secondly, against the dangers of attempting to set up an established Church, another principle which had been and was to continue to be his own unalterable conviction. He cautions him further against over-legislation and against any attempt to restrict the freedom of thought and speech, thereby proving that the fundamental principles of *Areopagitica* are still strong in him. He outlines, finally, a programme for education, including the setting up of free schools in every community and the restriction of university opportunity to those who are really worthy of profiting by it.

In a majestic peroration, Milton turns to the English nation at large, bidding them persevere in the state of liberty which they have achieved, and warning them that this, without high effort, they cannot do. Unless they exterminate ignorance and superstition, unless they subjugate the propensity to avarice, ambition, dissension, jealousy and lust, they will be judged unfit both by God and mankind, to be entrusted with so precious a possession as liberty and the administration of government, "but will rather, like a nation in a state of pupillage, want some active courageous guardian to undertake the management of your affairs." "For myself," Milton concludes, "I have delivered my testimony, I would almost say erected a monument that will not easily be destroyed, to the reality of those singular and mighty achievements, which were above all praise. . . . I have heroically celebrated at least one exploit of my countrymen; I pass by the rest, for who could recite the achievements of a whole people? If after such a display of courage and vigour, you basely relinquish the path of virtue, if you do anything unworthy of yourselves, posterity will sit in judgment on your conduct. . . . They will see that there was a rich harvest of glory, and an opportunity afforded for the greatest achievements, but that men only were wanting for the execution; while they were not wanting who could rightly counsel, exhort, inspire, and bind an unfading wreath of praise round the brows of the actors in so glorious a scene."

Others may fail; Milton himself has fulfilled his function gloriously, and stands firm with God. He must have laid down his pen with a deep satisfaction, prepared henceforth to "stand and wait." We know, however, that he will be ready to perform such humble duties as occasion may require, to lend his hand as best he can in new crises, and above all to interpret for the world the deeper vision of spiritual truth which has begun to come upon him in his solitary communion with the Most High.

The remainder of Milton's public activity under the Commonwealth covers a period of six years, but only at the end does he again attempt to make himself powerfully felt in liberty's defence. There was a reply by Morus (*The Fides Publica*, 1654–5) to the *Second Defence*, denying the authorship of the *Clamor*, endeavouring to clear his character of the scandals which had been heaped upon it, and defaming Milton. The poet answered it within six months in the *Pro Se Defensio*, but without zeal or inspiration. It is clear enough that for him the business of mere personal vituperation had lost its interest, and after the *Second Defence* there was nothing of real importance left to say.

With the return of health, he resumed his activities as Latin Secretary, though no longer in the multifarious form of the earlier years, his talents henceforth being employed only for the drafting of foreign correspondence. In this function he now reached his height of power. The hundred-odd letters written during the years of the Protectorate (1653–9) are over double in number those written during the period of Milton's official occupation before that time. They include utterance on State matters of the highest interest and importance, and in some instances are infused with a dignity, eloquence and passion that can be none other than Milton's own. The most memorable are ten written between May 25th and July 29th, 1655, voicing the English protest to the states of Europe against the massacre of the Protestant Waldensians by the Piedmontese subjects of the Duke of Savoy.

The Latin oration, addressed to the Duke himself, which may also be from Milton's pen, shows him completely possessed by the subject and reveals the deep sources of inspiration of the grandest of his sonnets. The expression in the prose and in the poem are remarkably parallel. "Houses smoking everywhere, torn limbs, the ground bloody! Ay, and virgins ravished and hideously abused, breathed their last miserably; and old men and persons labouring under illness were committed to the flames: and some infants were dashed against the rocks, and the brains of others were cooked and eaten. . . . Verily, verily, Angels are horror-struck, men are amazed; heaven itself seems to be astounded by these cries, and the earth itself to blush with the shed blood of so many innocent men."

Avenge, O Lord, thy slaughtered Saints, whose bones
Lie scattered on the Alpine mountains cold;
Even them who kept thy truth so pure of old,
When all our fathers worshipped stocks and stones,
Forget not: in thy book record their groans
Who were thy sheep, and in their ancient fold
Slain by the bloody Piemontese, that rolled
Mother with infant down the rocks. Their moans
The vales redoubled to the hills, and they
To heav'n. Their martyred blood and ashes sow
O'er all th' Italian fields, where still doth sway
The triple Tyrant; that from these may grow
A hundredfold, who, having learnt thy way,
Early may fly the Babylonian woe.

The whole episode proves the renewal of Milton's capacity for noble emotion, unconnected with the narrower thought of self, and the sonnet marks in a notable way his return to poetry.

It is a striking fact that even before Milton had thus proved himself as serviceable as ever in the clearest requirement of his office, he had received new indications that he was not to continue to enjoy its full dignity and emolument. An order of the Council on April 17th, 1655, proposed to reduce his salary to £150 and to put the management of foreign affairs henceforth entirely in the hands of Thurloe, with Meadows, as Secretary for the Latin Tongue, officially under him at a salary of £200. The sum voted Milton is designated as being "for life." The intention was evidently to pension and retire him. It is noteworthy, however, that this order was not wholly carried out, for Milton is found in receipt of £200 at the end of the Protectorate and he goes on writing letters for Oliver Cromwell and the succeeding governments up to the very moment of the Restoration. Masson's conjecture that the Protector himself may have insisted on continuing Milton in active service and taken care that he be not reduced in salary below the amount allotted to Meadows, would seem to be well founded. Two years later, Milton was at last granted his wish of having Andrew Marvell associated with him in the secretaryship, not, to be sure, officially as his subordinate, but as a fellow employee with himself and Meadows under Thurloe.

The fact that Milton received even this partial assurance of security and support in office and was consequently enabled to retain his sense of utility and importance in the political life of his country, prepares us for the final flare-up of his public energies in the anarchy which followed Cromwell's death. In 1658 he published a new edition of the *Second Defence*, appending a postscript in something of the old strain of self-gratulation and affirming that, while he can now "gratefully enjoy" contemplating the merits and success of this "highest fruit of my labours proposed for myself in this life," he is looking to the accomplishment of "yet greater things, if I have the power—and I *shall* have the power if God be gracious." In speaking of this great achievement yet to come, Milton is more likely to be thinking of *Paradise Lost*, which we know to have been by this time already under way, than of any further piece of political writing.

With the accession to power, however, of a new Protector and the summoning of a new Parliament, the impulse to exert his influence at the moment of opportunity comes again, and he launches in February, 1659, the brief tract, *A Treatise of Civil Power in Ecclesiastical Causes*, in support of his old conviction that it is unlawful for the magistrate to use force in matters of religion. The argument, which is largely Scriptural, is addressed, like the treatises written before his official employment, to Parliament itself. By its plain intimation that the very existence of an established church is objectionable, it implies a renewed condemnation of that part of Cromwell's policy against which, as we have seen, he had always, in his inner thought, protested. Milton is evidently looking again to the old Republican party, which, in the persons of men like Vane, Bradshaw, Harrison, Fleetwood, was well represented in the new body. Such a return was natural, when the one-man power passed from the hands of the mighty Oliver to his feeble son. Milton's inability to win his point of policy with the Protector had made his acquiescence in his rule an uneasy one and must have confirmed him in the idea that an aristocracy was after all more manageable. He knew the principles of such men as Vane to be identical with his own in the matter of Church and State and if they refused to move, it was only because they lacked the conviction or the courage. With this he might supply them.

The restoration of the Rump Parliament in May of 1659 brought Milton still further toward his old position. Though he had praised Cromwell for his dissolution of this body, it was

entirely logical for him to rejoice, now that Cromwell himself
was gone and Richard's power swept away, in what must have
seemed to him a revival of the old Republic for which he had
contended in his days of free and independent service. The
motion toward disestablishment which followed immediately
on the assembly of the Rump, brought from him another
advisory pamphlet: *Considerations touching the likeliest means to
remove Hirelings from the Church*. The opening address to Parliament indicates Milton's ability to accept the new order with
inveterate hopefulness. The body of the work puts him finally
on record as holding the extreme sectarian position that the
preaching of the Gospel should be a wholly voluntary and
unbound task. He is being driven by the logic of his hatred of
any form of Church establishment to a distrust of all organised
religion. His real conviction, based on the sufficiency of his own
experience, is that the spiritual life is an affair between the
individual soul and God.

We can follow the movement of Milton's mind from this
point pretty clearly through the chaotic changes which were
bringing England speedily to the Restoration. It is evident that
he watched the fluctuation of events with intense concern.
When Lambert seized the reins of government and suspended
the Rump, Milton wrote a letter to a friend expressing his
amazement and distress that the army, which had proved its
loyalty to the Good Old Cause by "restoring the old famous
Parliament," should now dissolve it. He calls upon their leaders
to declare and publish the cause of their action, and then
proceeds to construct a programme for the restoration of order
in the present anarchy, his advice amounting simply to the
recalling of Parliament or the establishment of a new Council
of State and the swearing of an oath between Army and Council
not to desert each other till death. Milton is willing to accept
"for the extremities wherein we are" an "annual democracy"
if need be, though he clearly leans to the idea of a perpetual
aristocracy. The thing which alarms him is that the nation in
its present weakness may become the servant "of one or other
Single Person, the secret author and fomentor of these dis-
turbances."

With the arrival of General Monk in London and the second
restoration of the Rump, Milton set himself to draft more fully
a plan of Republican government to avert the crisis. In this
last desperate effort of his statesmanship, *The Ready and Easy*

Way to Establish a New Commonwealth, he again recommends an oligarchic General Council—"one and the same Parliament in perpetuity of membership for life"—with a smaller Council of State as its executive, and provision for local self-government throughout the realm. The pamphlet was written while the situation was outwardly such as to make it conceivable that a Republican programme might still be tried. Before it was published, the secluded Presbyterian Members of Parliament had been readmitted and all rational expectation of the further pursuit of Miltonic policy was at an end. The poet, nevertheless, bravely protests that he rejoices to hear declared the resolution of all those that are now in power not to return to the old bondage. That he still entertains, against the patent facts, some hope of practical success, is proved by a private letter addressed to Monk himself, containing a brief abstract of his plan; by his resolute answer to a sermon of Dr. Griffith against the proposals; and finally by the publication of a second edition of *The Ready and Easy Way*, with the arguments enlarged and the objections answered, on the very eve of the Restoration. He must, however, in his deeper consciousness have realised, even as he penned the original pamphlet, that the Good Old Cause was lost. The concluding passage, particularly in the revised version, is as much a tragic farewell to the great enterprise of liberty as it is an excited last attempt to rally the routed forces of the Republic.

Thus much I should perhaps have said, though I was sure I should have spoken only to trees and stones; and had none to cry to, but with the prophet, "O earth, earth, earth!" to tell the very soil itself what her perverse inhabitants are deaf to. Nay, though what I have spoke should happen (which thou suffer not, who didst create mankind free! nor thou next, who didst redeem us from being servants of men!) to be the last words of our expiring liberty. . . . But I trust I shall have spoken persuasion to abundance of sensible and ingenious men; to some, perhaps, whom God may raise up of these stones to become the children of reviving liberty; and may reclaim, though they seem now choosing them a captain back from Egypt, to bethink themselves a little, and consider whither they are rushing; to exhort this torrent also of the people, not to be so impetuous, but to keep their due channel; and at length recovering and uniting their better resolutions, now that they see how insolent and unbounded the insolence and rage is of our common enemies, to stay these ruinous proceedings, justly and timely fearing to what a precipice of destruction the deluge of this epidemic madness would hurry us, through the general defection of a misguided and abused multitude.

A tempest of abuse attended Milton's last pamphlet. If he were fool enough to write himself irreconcilable, now that vengeance upon the English parricides was at the door, there were plenty who were ready to make use of the opportunity to win favour with the new régime by exposing and defaming him. If he heard the cries of such "asses, apes, and dogs," he no longer attended to them. The fight was over and its standard bearers at last ready to seek personal safety.

On May 5th, 1660, three days before Charles II was proclaimed in London, Milton executed the transfer of a bond for £400 to Cyriack Skinner, perhaps in the anticipation of a need for ready cash. Where he was or how he felt a month later when cheering throngs greeted their returning monarch we have no means of knowing. The Mayor of Dover put the English Bible into Charles's hand and accepted at face value the answer that it was the thing he loved above all things in the world. "He failed," says Trevelyan, "to perceive that the comic spirit had landed on the coast of Britain." But the English people, whom Milton had tried so desperately to sway, were as ready to applaud the new company for a season as they were to pursue with execration the great tragedians who had played their piece and were departing. They went "undismayed by the howling and the fury, wrapped in the dignity of self-dependent virtue, Republicans without fear, without repentance, without hope." Milton alone among them had the resources necessary for a new achievement. He had, as we shall see, already begun work on *Paradise Lost*. Its completion required physical security, which he had little reason to expect, and the reconstruction of at least a minimum of domestic peace.

Phillips informs us that Milton escaped immediate reprisal by going into "retirement and abscondence" in Bartholemew's Close and remaining there till the passage of the Act of Oblivion in August. Of his real danger there can be no doubt. The House, zealous to prove its loyalty, was busy expanding the list of those who were to suffer proscription. Milton's hand was

dyed in guilt, not only and primarily because he had served
the Commonwealth and continued to fight the Stuart return
up to the end, but because he had publicly justified the deposition and execution of Charles I. It is pointed out by Masson
that men who had less to answer for were named among those
to be excepted from the royal clemency.

Why then did Milton escape? Phillips says that it was
"through the intercession of some that stood his friends both
in Council and in Parliament: particularly in the House of
Commons, Mr. Andrew Marvell, a member for Hull, acted
vigorously in his behalf and made a considerable party for
him." A later tradition, reported by Richardson, imparts the
secret that "'twas Sir William Davenant who obtained his
release, in return for his own life, procured by Milton's interest
when himself was under condemnation, *anno* 1650." Masson,
conjecturing that there must have been some more powerful
influence at work, suggests that the Chancellor, Edward Hyde,
admiring Milton's scholarship and, moved to pity by his
blindness, supported the movement to spare him. It may not,
however, have been so much a matter of pity as of good policy.
The execution or life imprisonment of Milton could have done
only harm to the popularity of the Stuart régime, and cooler
heads would inevitably have recognised this fact. The method
actually taken for satisfying the cry for justice and yet procuring
Milton's safety implies deliberate manœuvring. While the
debate regarding the Indemnity Bill was going on in the
Commons, an order was issued that the Attorney-General
draw an indictment against him for the *First Defence* and the
Eikonoklastes, and the sergeant-at-arms was instructed to take
him, together with John Goodwin, into custody. The subsequent royal proclamation reports that no endeavours used for
his apprehension have been effective, and orders his treasonable
books to be burnt by the common hangman. At some later
time, he was actually imprisoned. We have the order on
December 15th that "Mr. Milton, now in the custody of the
sergeant-at-arms attending this house, be forthwith released,
paying his fees." This, apparently, was the end of the whole
matter. No one could say that Milton's case had been over-
looked, though there might be those who wondered why he
had not been made to pay the full penalty.

It was something of a satisfaction to have a notorious figure
left alive, to be referred to on all occasions as a criminal of the

old régime, who had undeservedly escaped hanging. Those who had consented to spare him might enjoy the consciousness of their own gratuitous clemency toward one who, however guilty, was now impotent, and might yet become an honour to his country.

This ends the story of Milton's stormy career through the Commonwealth and the Protectorate. It remains to review the purely domestic and personal conditions which surrounded him in this period and which co-operated with his involvement in the public situation to determine his activity. In 1649 Milton's wife was still living; his first two daughters were in infancy; he had given up teaching and was residing in a comparatively simple establishment in High Holborn. The Phillips boys were perhaps still domiciled with him, though Edward had begun to keep terms at Oxford.

Financially, Milton was now entering on a new period of prosperity. His relationship with the Powell family had long since hardened into one of cold self-protection. He had claims on Sir Richard's widow to the amount of £1,300—the unpaid dowry of £1,000, and a balance of £300 still due on the original debt owing to the Miltons since 1627. For the latter sum he held as security a mortgage on the Powell estate at Wheatley. From the income of this estate with which he was paying himself, he had been paying to the widow a sum of £26 as her third. The legal complications which grew out of the sequestration of the Powell estate and Mrs. Powell's attempts to recover it gave him an opportunity to refuse continuation of this payment, in spite of her claim that it was all she had to keep her children from starvation. She petitioned on July 16th, 1651, to the Commissioners that she be allowed to receive her portion. The following notation on the document, written by some agent or official in her behalf, reveals her bitterness and suggests the implacability of Milton's attitude. "By the law she might recover her third without doubt; but she is so extreme poor she hath not wherewithal to prosecute; and besides Mr. Milton is a harsh and choleric man, and married Mrs. Powell's daughter, who would be undone if any such course were taken against him by Mrs. Powell, he having turned away his wife heretofore for a long space upon some other occasion." We cannot, in view of his own deep sense of injury, be surprised at Milton's position. Mary's dowry of £1,000 he never expected to collect. He had probably persuaded himself that Mrs.

Powell was not so poor as she made out. In any case, he was ready to stand on his legal rights, indifferent to any effect his attitude might have on the feelings and behaviour of his wife. His will was evidently set against any emotional reconciliation with her except on the basis of her complete submission. In general, then, Milton's domestic situation in the first period of his secretarial employment must have continued strained and unhappy.

The birth in 1651 of his third child and only son, John, may temporarily have done something to improve it. The record is duly entered in Milton's hand in the family Bible: "My son John was born on Sunday, March the 16th, at about half-past nine at night: 1650" (i.e. 1651). Phillips says, doubtless echoing the family gossip, that he died "through the ill usage or bad constitution of an ill-chosen nurse." The reference to the "domestic grief of two funerals" includes the death of this child about June 16th, 1652, as recorded in the Bible, and that of Mary Powell shortly after the birth of Deborah on May 2nd of the same year. The general period of these events is that of the publication of the *Clamor*, of the crisis in Milton's secretary-ship, and of the coming on him of total blindness.

The importance of Milton's loss of sight and of the whole physical and mental cycle involved in it is so great that the biographer must use all the resources available to him to take account of it. Modern opinion is uncertain regarding the exact nature of Milton's disease. In his own time, the trouble was confidently diagnosed as amaurosis or "gutta serena," an affection of the optic nerve. The humoral pathology which then dominated scientific thought explained this disease roughly as follows. A redundant humour in the brain flowed down into the optic nerve and congregated there, preventing the "spirits of sight" from finding access to the eyeball. This humour was itself the "gutta serena" or clear drop—clear because it could not be seen outwardly. There is an implied contrast with "gutta obscura," cataract, a correlative disease in which the drop remains in its liquid state until it has passed through the nerve or otherwise found its way into the empty space which was still mistakenly supposed to exist between the cornea and the crystalline lens. This dark drop was, of course, the cataract, visible as a clouding of the eye. Milton himself was certainly aware of the relation between the two types of blindness and perhaps he had some doubt as to whether his trouble was really amaurosis and not cataract in some less common form. At any rate, he gives the alternative explanations when referring to his loss of sight in the passage already cited from *Paradise Lost*:

> So thick a drop serene hath quenched their orbs,
> Or dim suffusion veiled.

Suffusio or suffusio nigra was another technical term for cataract, so used since ancient times. But it is characteristic of Milton to put things in this way. His habit of mind made him as tentative in scientific matters as he was dogmatic in politics, morals, and religion. If he had had any serious thought that he had cataract, he might perhaps have submitted to an operation which there were plenty of doctors ready enough to perform.

The most interesting document connected with Milton's blindness and his physical health generally is his own account of his symptoms and the less complete evidence of the character and supposed effects of the remedies employed. By the time his blindness became complete he seems to have given up all hope of recovery. Two years later, however, a Greek friend domiciled in Paris, Leonard Philaras by name, urged him to resort again to medical aid. With some reluctance and little faith he did so, writing out a careful statement of the facts, to be transmitted by Philaras to a French physician whom it has been possible at last to identify. The letter is a model patient's account of his own symptoms and as such may rank among the classic descriptions of disease. Milton was interested impersonally as well as personally in medical matters. He had read deeply on the subject, presumably consulted no end of doctors, and associated with some of the men who were making the new science—if not directly with his great contemporaries, Harvey, Glisson, and Sydenham, at least with men belonging to their circle. He uses no technical terms in the letter to Philaras, but his meaning is conveyed with scientific precision. Here are the pertinent sections of the statement, translated from the Latin:

> As you have, therefore, suggested to me that I should not give up all hope of recovering my sight, and told me that you have a friend and close companion in the Paris physician, Thevenot, especially distinguished as an oculist, and that you will consult him about my eyes if I furnish you with means for his diagnosis of the causes and symptoms, I will

do what you advise, that I may not haply seem to refuse any chance offered me providentially.

It is ten years, I think, more or less, since I felt my sight getting weak and dull, and at the same time my viscera generally out of sorts. In the morning, if I began, as usual, to read anything, I felt my eyes at once thoroughly pained and shrinking from the act of reading, but refreshed after moderate bodily exercise. If I looked at a lit candle, a kind of iris seemed to snatch it from me. Not very long after, a darkness coming over the left part of my left eye (for that eye became clouded some years before the other) removed from my vision all objects situated on that side. Objects in front also, if I chanced to close the right eye, seemed smaller. The other eye also failing perceptibly and gradually through a period of three years, I observed, some months before my sight was wholly gone, that objects I looked at without myself moving seemed all to swim, now to the right, now to the left. Inveterate mists now seem to have settled in my forehead and temples, which weigh me down and depress me with a kind of sleepy heaviness, especially from meal-time to evening; so that not seldom there comes into my mind the description of the Salmydessian seer, Phineus, in the *Argonautics*:

> All round him then there grew
> A purple thickness; and he thought the Earth
> Whirling beneath his feet, and so he sank,
> Speechless at length, into a feeble sleep.

But I should not forget to mention that, while yet a little sight remained, when first I lay down in bed, and turned myself to either side, there used to shine out a copious glittering light from my shut eyes; then that, as my sight grew less from day to day, colours proportionally duller would burst from them, as with a kind of force and audible shot from within; but that now, as if the sense of lucency were extinct, it is a mere blackness, or a blackness dashed, and as it were inwoven, with an ashy grey, that is wont to pour itself forth. Yet the darkness which is perpetually before me, by night as well as by day, seems always nearer to a whitish than to a blackish, and such that, when the eye rolls itself, there is admitted, as through a small chink, a certain little trifle of light.

And so, whatever ray of hope also there may be for me from your famous physician, all the same, as in a case quite incurable, I prepare and compose myself accordingly; and my frequent thought is that, since many days of darkness, as the Wise Man warns us, are destined for everyone, my darkness hitherto, by the singular kindness of God, amid rest and studies, and the voices and greetings of friends, has been much easier to bear than that deathly one.

This should, one would think—when taken in connection with the general facts of Milton's medical history: his headaches and eyestrain from boyhood on, his indigestion, his death from gout—be enough. But there are evidently too many complicating possibilities to allow the modern expert to arrive at certainty regarding the causes of Milton's blindness. The layman who reads the picturesque variety of theories which have been given in the medical journals thanks heaven that the diagnosis of ocular diseases is no longer dependent on what the patient can tell about himself. Glaucoma, myopia, detachment of the retina, or these combined, have been the leading explanations, but congenital syphilis and brain tumour have also been suggested. The weight of recent opinion seems to favour glaucoma.

The doctor to whom Philaras referred him was François Thevenin, a distinguished Parisian surgeon and ophthalmologist, the exact individual to whom a well-informed Continental would have referred an Englishman of that time as a final authority and last medical hope in an apparently desperate case. This Dr. Thevenin was royal oculist at the court of Louis XIV, where Philaras was resident as an envoy from the Duke of Parma. He died in 1656, leaving a manuscript work on surgery which was eagerly seized upon by the profession. Guillaume Parthon, himself court oculist and nephew and heir to the more famous Thevenin, had the official copy, but others had apparently got access to it or taken down its substance from the master's lectures. Parthon says he would gladly have kept it for the private use of himself and his friends, but, learning that it might be published surreptitiously and imperfectly, he decided to give it to the world. He did so in a handsome folio issued in 1658, with a dedicatory letter to the Deans and Doctors Regent of the Medical Faculty at Paris. The work was important enough to be reprinted in quarto in 1669.

There is no evidence that Milton ever came under the actual care of Thevenin. It was just as well, for that worthy could have done nothing but add to the punishment which he had already undergone in vain. The domestic verdict in Milton's later life was that physic had actually done him more harm than good. We have this from two reliable sources. Edward Phillips, Milton's nephew and an intimate of his home, writes in his memoir of the poet: "It is most certainly known that his sight, what with his continual study, his being subject to the headache, and his perpetual tampering with physic to preserve it, had been decaying for above a dozen years before." The anonymous biographer, a man who evidently knew Milton well, gives more specific information: "And the issues and setons, made use of to save or retrieve that [i.e. the sight of his left eye] were thought by drawing away the spirits which should have supplied the optic vessels, to have hastened the loss of the other."

What these tamperings were like, whether indulged in under professional direction or attempted by Milton on the basis of his own considerable research, we read all too clearly in the medical literature of the time. Thevenin gives a description of the operation of setoning, which was standard for inveterate headaches and severe inflammation.

> The patient is seated on a stool. He bends his head back a little so that the skin and fleshy panicle may be loosened. Then an assistant, taking the skin with both hands just below the hair, either vertically or horizontally, lifts and pulls it up, and the surgeon with the seton pincers, formed like a waffle iron, broad at the ends and pierced, pinches the skin hard to deaden a little for the patient the pain of the burning, then passes through the holes in the pincers a hot cautery, having a diamond point; and when he draws out the cautery he passes with the needle through the same holes a four or five ply cotton thread dipped in white of egg and rose oil and puts a compress over it moistened with oxecrat and charged with the same remedy, continuing this till the suppuration is made and the inflammation past.

It is plausible to suppose that this was but one of many pretty experiments which the wretched poet had tried on him. The variety of possibilities was endless. William Vaughan says amaurosis is incurable but the humour being yet unsettled, various remedies should be tried: "purgation with pils of Iods, with Trochisks of Alhandall, Hydropticks, Mascatoria." Violent errhines are "not to be neglected." Also the brain must be dried with a cap, cauteries must be applied at the root of the ear, and "beware you forget not to use cupping glasses." When the eye is exasperated anoint it with fresh butter, woman's milk, and a special kind of mucilage "drawn in the decoction of Mallowes, Holy-hockes, Violets," etc. Richard Bannister, most intriguing of English writers on diseases of the eyes, prescribes blood-letting, cupping, a caustic applied to the back of the head, bags and coifs filled with all manner of fearful and wonderful concoctions. He is opposed to the use of salves. There is obviously some method in all this madness. The humours must be dried or thinned out and drawn off through various outlets. External applications are, in this disease, for temporary relief only. The initial treatment for cataracts was much the same. It is not surprising if Milton ended, as a statement of John Aubrey implies, by largely renouncing physic. In any case, it is apparent that the fact of blindness, once it had been accepted, was less perturbing than vain hope and the continued attempts to find a cure.

Milton saved himself in part by a great religious rationalisation, the progress of which we have already witnessed, in part by spiritual discipline and the wise cultivation of various forms of relaxing occupation. In 1652 he wrote the sonnets to Vane and Cromwell. The same year he renewed his private correspondence with friends. In 1653 he cultivated the society of Roger Williams, exchanging language lessons and expounding his theories of linguistic education. At this time also he took up again the translation of the Psalms. We recall that the earlier renderings belonged to a similar period of distress and interruption. The activity was at once a means of renewing contact with the universal source of hope and comfort and an exercising of the skilled technique on which he had once relied and still relied for the achievement of immortal fame. His return to poetry is indicative of a realisation that he must revive his old employments if he is to be able again to answer the call of public duty.

The most successful carrying forward of this programme belongs to the year 1655, when Milton had already fulfilled his heavy task of answering the *Clamor*. We learn from Phillips, in a passage which can be taken as referring primarily to this year, that "he was frequently visited by persons of quality, particularly My Lady Ranelagh (whose son for some time he instructed), all learned foreigners of note (who could not part out of this city without giving a visit to a person so eminent), and lastly by particular friends that had a high esteem for him: viz. Mr. Andrew Marvell, young Lawrence (the son of him that was President of Oliver's Council), Mr. Marchamont Needham, the writer of *Politicus*, but above all by Mr. Cyriack Skinner." The fruitage of these associations and of Milton's recovery of health is a renewal of creative energy, evidenced in the composition in 1655-6 of five great sonnets, the one on the Piedmont massacre, the two on his blindness, and the two of genial friendship and good counsel to the younger Lawrence and to Skinner. The last mentioned are beautiful expressions of the philosophy of temperate self-indulgence in the intervals of labour, which Milton always held but had—in his period of discouragement and stress—forgotten. They may be quoted as evidence of the poet's regained wisdom for himself.

Lawrence, of virtuous father virtuous son,
Now that the fields are dank, and ways are mire,
Where shall we sometimes meet, and by the fire
Help waste a sullen day, what may be won
From the hard season gaining? Time will run
On smoother, till Favonius reinspire
The frozen earth, and clothe in fresh attire
The lily and rose, that neither sowed nor spun.
What neat repast shall feast us, light and choice,
To hear the lute well touched, or artful voice
Warble immortal notes and Tuscan air?
He who of these delights can judge, and spare
To interpose them oft, is not unwise.

Cyriack, whose grandsire on the royal bench
Of British Themis, with no mean applause,
Pronounced and in his volumes taught our laws,
Which others at their bar so often wrench;
To-day deep thoughts resolve with me to drench
In mirth, that after no repenting draws;
Let Euclid rest and Archimedes pause,
And what the Swede intend, and what the French.

To measure life learn thou betimes, and know
Toward solid good what leads the nearest way;
For other things mild Heav'n a time ordains,
And disapproves that care, though wise in show,
That with superfluous burden loads the day,
And, when God sends a cheerful hour, refrains.

The poems on his blindness have a deeper meaning for the psychology of Milton's later years. The first expresses true religious acceptance—something quite different from the conviction of God's special favour proclaimed in the *Second Defence*. It is not necessary on this account to assign the sonnet to a period before 1655, which appears to be established by its position in the 1645 *Poems*. Milton's moods are shifting, and the meditations with which he sustains himself vary with the occasion and the imagined audience. Here we have the self-communing of a man of sober faith, meeting the incipient protest of his heart in the same way he had done years before when he wrote the sonnet "On Being Arrived at the Age of Twenty-Three."

When I consider how my light is spent
Ere half my days, in this dark world and wide,
And that one talent which is death to hide,
Lodged with me useless, though my soul more bent
To serve therewith my Maker, and present
My true account, lest He returning chide;
"Doth God exact day-labour, light denied?"
I fondly ask; but Patience, to prevent
That murmur, soon replies: "God doth not need
Either man's work, or his own gifts; who best
Bear His mild yoke, they serve Him best: His state
Is kingly; thousands at his bidding speed
And post o'er land and ocean without rest;
They also serve who only stand and wait."

In the second poem Milton recounts explicitly the outward loss, and gives expression to more human consolations—the small thought that his physical beauty is unimpaired, a soldier's sense of duty done, awareness of the resounding fame of his achievement.

Cyriack, this three years' day these eyes, though clear,
To outward view, of blemish or of spot,
Bereft of light, their seeing have forgot,
Nor to their idle orbs doth sight appear
Of sun, or moon, or star, throughout the year,

Or man, or woman. Yet I argue not
Against Heav'n's hand or will, nor bate a jot
Of heart or hope; but still bear up and steer
Right onward. What supports me, dost thou ask?
The conscience, friend, to have lost them overplied
In Liberty's defence, my noble task,
Of which all Europe talks from side to side.
This thought might lead me through the world's vain mask
Content, though blind, had I no better guide.

These utterances mark Milton's subjugation of his own most intimate experiences to the uses and demands of art. It is but a step to the renewal of steady work on the poetic masterpiece. Such a step he was soon to take. One may suspect, however, that the influence of his second and third marriages was somewhat essential to the happy fulfilment of this task. The union with Katharine Woodcock took place on November 12th, 1656, after the poet had been for over four years a widower. His second wife lived only a year and four months, giving birth to a daughter on October 19th, 1657, and dying, with the child, the February following. There is no reason to doubt that this marriage experience was a happy one, or that Milton gained from it a truer insight into the relationship than he had thus far possessed. We have the final sonnet, "On His Deceased Wife," to witness the poignancy of his memory and regret.

Methought I saw my late espousèd saint
Brought to me like Alcestis from the grave,
Whom Jove's great son to her glad husband gave,
Rescued from Death by force, though pale and faint.
Mine, as whom washed from spot of child-bed taint
Purification in the Old Law did save;
And such, as yet once more I trust to have
Full sight of her in Heaven without restraint,
Came vested all in white, pure as her mind:
Her face was veiled, yet to my fancied sight
Love, sweetness, goodness, in her person shined
So clear, as in no face with more delight.
But oh! as to embrace me she inclined,
I waked, she fled, and day brought back my night.

With the death of his second wife we may close the record of Milton's personal life before the Restoration. Conditions were

G

increasingly favourable, in spite of the revival of pamphleteer-
ing in 1659, for a return to the activities and interests of earlier
years. If Phillips is to be trusted, he took up again, shortly after
the completion of *Pro Se Defensio* in 1655, two projects which he
had long had under way: the *History of Britain* and a new
Thesaurus Linguae Latinae after the manner of Stephanus. This
Latin dictionary, "a work which he had long been collecting
from his own reading," was continued throughout his lifetime
and remained unpublished at his death. The *History of Britain*,
which may be regarded as a partial fulfilment of the early
ambition to celebrate the past glories of his native land, was
carried through the Anglo-Saxon period before 1657 and
finally published in that form in 1670. A long digression in
Book III on the parallel confusion which resulted from the
withdrawal of the Roman legions from Britain and that which
attended the closing of the Civil War in 1648 was excised by
the censor and printed separately in 1681. The *Of Christian
Doctrine*, Milton's great digest of theology, for which he had
been gathering Biblical texts since the days of his school
teaching in the Barbican, was also probably completed at this
time. Tasks of this sort, involving constant consultation of
authorities, must have been immensely difficult to carry out in
blindness, and their prosecution implies a constant use of
amanuensis assistance; they are, however, just the kind of
patient activity which would be best suited to give Milton a
reposeful occupation between the moments of more passionate
or creative thinking.

The outstanding event of the epoch was the poet's resumption
of the great theme of the fall of man, laid aside in 1641 and, so
far as we know, left untouched through the years of public
service. The date at which he actually began the composition
of the poem in epic form is uncertain, but Aubrey's statement,
on the authority of Edward Phillips, that it was "about two
years before the King came in" (i.e. about May, 1658), seems
right. The insolent and lofty vein of Books I and II is a poetic
counterpart of Milton's prose eloquence in the *Second Defence*.
The feeling for varied types of heroic personality suggests the
nearness of the author's days of close association with Cromwell
and his Council. The representation, finally, of indomitable
courage and resolution in a hopeless cause, of wrestling against
defeat, of keen intelligences concocting ingenious but futile
plans, seems like a dramatising of the poet's own emotion as he

battled, at first with others, then alone, in the interest of the already lost Republic. The beginning of Book III, the invocation to light, combines and further sublimates earlier reflections on his blindness. He now implores rather than vaunts the inner light. The sense of deprivation in the second sonnet is voiced with a deeper beauty. Common sights and sounds of nature have the distance of romance. But there is no longer need of stoic resolution. The Heavenly Spirit has found use for him and he rests happy in the enjoyment of its gift of power.

> Thus with the year
> Seasons return, but not to me returns
> Day, or the sweet approach of Even or Morn,
> Or sight of vernal bloom, or Summer's Rose,
> Or flocks, or herds, or human face divine;
> But cloud instead, and ever-during dark
> Surrounds me, from the cheerful ways of men
> Cut off, and for the book of knowledge fair
> Presented with a universal blank
> Of Nature's works to me expunged and rased,
> And wisdom at one entrance quite shut out.
> So much the rather thou, Celestial Light,
> Shine inward, and the mind through all her powers
> Irradiate, there plant eyes, all mist from thence
> Purge and disperse, that I may see and tell
> Of things invisible to mortal sight.

Whether Milton wrote these lines before or after the expiration of his last hope for England, they stand as the record of his own spiritual victory. The mood of exalted serenity which gave rise to such contemplations was always for him the highest mood of poetic inspiration. It was not always present to sustain him. If it declined and became irrecoverable in the succeeding years, it is because life cannot long remain on such a level and because man's spirit, like his body, suffers loss with time.

CHAPTER SEVEN

THE HEAVENLY MUSE
1660–7

THE OUTWARD CHANGES IN Milton's life after the Restoration are the result not only of the closing of all avenues of public activity against him, but of a great decline in his material fortunes. His salary as Secretary, even at £200, added to the income from his father's estate, had made him for a time really affluent. Masson says he possessed about £4,000 in investments, and this calculation is, if anything, too low. His total income could hardly have been less than £600 a year at the end of the Protectorate, the equivalent of many times that amount at the present day. We learn from Phillips that he lost £2,000 which he had invested in government securities and "another great sum by mismanagement and for want of good advice" or, according to the statement of his granddaughter, by the dishonesty of a money-scrivener. Finally, his house in Bread Street was burned in the great fire of 1666. His estate at death, given by Phillips as £1,500, actually amounted to less than £1,000. Obviously, Milton could no longer, with the same freedom as before, buy books, engage skilled literary assistance, provide for his family, entertain his friends.

We can see one effect of this change in circumstances in a remark made in the single personal letter which we have from his pen in the Restoration period. "I will close," he writes to Heimbach on August 15th, 1666, "by begging you to lay the blame for any faults in spelling or lack of punctuation upon the boy who writes this at my dictation, and who knows no Latin at all. I am obliged, much to my annoyance, to spell out the letters one by one as I dictate." There is other proof that Milton was obliged to depend henceforth on casual assistance in his literary activity. From 1657 to about 1661 he evidently had working for him a very competent scribe, one Jeremie Picard. His trained secretarial hand appears in several of the surviving fragments of amanuensis material between those dates and in the extensive Latin manuscript of the *Of Christian Doctrine*. One imagines him to have been a paid employee. After 1661, the hands which write for Milton are various and for the most part inferior. The interlineations of several scribes who follow Picard in the *Christian Doctrine* manuscript are at times almost illegible. So also are the later entries in the *Commonplace Book*. We have bits of writing by Edward and probably by John Phillips—who, however much they may have owed to Milton, had by now their own plans and purposes—also the work of Daniel Skinner, a clever but worthless youth whom Milton attached to himself in his latest years. It was natural for him to make use of the services of friends and pupils, but he must have felt the need of steadier and more reliable help.

The effects of relative poverty on Milton's happiness were certainly not mitigated by anything in his relations with his children. Edward Phillips's account of his attempt to use his two younger daughters as readers reveals only too clearly his inability to cope with the situation which his misfortune or his unwisdom had created.

And those he had by the first [wife] he made serviceable to him in that very particular in which he most wanted their service, and supplied his want of eyesight by their eyes and tongue. For though he had daily about him one or other to read to him; some persons of man's estate, who of their own accord greedily catched at the opportunity of being his readers, that they might as well reap the benefit of what they read to him, as oblige him by the benefit of their reading; others of younger years sent by their parents to the same end; yet, excusing only the eldest daughter by reason of her bodily infirmity and difficult utterance of speech (which to say the truth I doubt was the principal cause of excusing her), the other two were condemned to the performance of reading, and exactly pronouncing of all the languages of whatever book he should at one time or other think fit to peruse; viz. the Hebrew (and I think the Syriac), the Greek, the Latin, the Italian, Spanish, and French. All which sorts of books to be confined to read, without understanding one word, must needs be a trial of patience almost beyond endurance; yet it was endured by both for a long time. Yet the irksomeness of this employment could not be always concealed, but broke out more and more into expressions of uneasiness; so that at length they were all (even the eldest also) sent out to learn some curious and ingenious sorts of manufacture, that are proper for women to learn, particularly embroideries in gold or silver.

The eldest daughter, Anne, was fourteen at the close of their father's public career, the two others, Mary and Deborah, were twelve and eight respectively. Phillips does not say when the disciplining of them into eyes and tongue for languages began or how soon the poet gave up the experiment. Masson thinks they remained in his household till about 1670. In any case the full extent of the domestic damage in Milton's family relationships must have revealed itself only gradually. The poet had been left a blind widower with three children under six, one of them a cripple, another a newborn infant. He had gone through trying changes of circumstance, involving removals from one residence to another and dependence on the aid of others for his very safety. The mother-in-law on whom care of the household would naturally have devolved was already at feud with him. A systematic programme of educating the children might have seemed to go well enough for a time but met increasing difficulties as they reached adolescence.

Meanwhile, on February 24th, 1663, Milton married for a third time, his bride being Elizabeth Minshull, a virgin, aged twenty-four. She had, according to Phillips, been sought out for him by his friend, Nathaniel Paget, the physician, to whom she was related. There is a suggestion here, as in the earlier visits of Lady Ranelagh, of Milton's being an object of solicitude. He must, indeed, have seemed thoroughly pitiable and obviously to have needed nothing so much as the ministrations of a good wife. We have in the testimony of the poet's maidservant, Elizabeth Fisher, given under oath in the legal proceedings relative to Milton's will, a distant echo of this event as it was anticipated by the poet's household.

That this respondent [Elizabeth Fisher] hath heard the deceased [Milton] declare his displeasure against the parties ministrant his children, and particularly the deceased declared to this respondent that a little before he was married to Elizabeth Minshull his now relict, a former maidservant of his told Mary one of the deceased's daughters and one of the ministrants, that she heard the deceased was to be married, to which the said Mary replied to the said maidservant, that that was no news to hear of his marrying, but if she could hear of his death that was something.

With the children, or perhaps only with the two older ones, the case was apparently hopeless, but Elizabeth could at least provide for the creature comforts of the family. For Milton himself she could do much more in supplying him with a sorely needed object of affection. In a later chapter we shall have occasion to present, again out of the court records, very specific evidence of their good relations. The marriage, if not one of romance, gave Milton an excellent wife, who was to do her duty by him most conscientiously all the rest of his life. She lived to cherish Milton's memory and to report to John Aubrey many details of his later years. She preserved his letters "from learned men of his acquaintance, both of England and beyond the sea." His pictures (the portrait done by Janssen at the age of ten and that of Milton as a Cambridge scholar), his Bible, his tobacco box, and "2 books of paradice" are inventoried among her possessions after her death. Aubrey describes her as "a gentle person," of "a peaceful and agreeable humour." Bishop Newton learned from one of her friends that her hair, like Eve's, was gold. Her frugal hospitalities in Nantwich, whither she retired in later life, gave rise to the expression "Mrs. Milton's feast, enough and no more." It is a far cry from the design of spiritual companionship which the poet had given in the divorce tracts and the lack of which, he said, might lead to "a repining, even to atheism." But Milton had long since discovered and accepted the efficacy of another love. He had dwelt with Eve in Eden and he received the nightly visitations of the Muse.

Paradise Lost was published in 1667. The manuscript stood complete, however, at least two years earlier, as we learn from the memoirs of Thomas Ellwood, a Quaker youth who had studied with Milton and come apparently to be loved and trusted by him. The whole episode of the poet's acquaintance with this simple-minded boy is famous in literary history, and deserves to be studied closely as giving the only intimate view we have of the poet at the moment of fulfilment of his most cherished literary hope.

Having turned Quaker under the influence of Isaac Pennington and become ambitious to improve himself in Greek and Latin, Ellwood had in 1662 sought the assistance of Milton and been admitted to come to him "not as a servant to him (which at that time he needed not), nor to be in the house with him, but only to have the liberty of coming to his house at certain hours when I would and to read to him what books he should appoint me."

He received me courteously [says Ellwood of his first visit] as well for the sake of Dr. Paget, who introduced me, as of Isaac Pennington, who recommended me; to both of whom he bore a great respect. And having inquired divers things of me with respect to my former progression in learning, he dismissed me, to provide myself of such accommodations as might be most suitable to my future studies. I went, therefore, and took myself a lodging as near to his house (which was then in Jewin Street) as conveniently I could, and from thenceforward went every day in the afternoon (except on the first day of the week), and sitting by him in his dining-room, read to him in such books in the Latin tongue as he pleased to hear me read. At my first sitting to read to him, observing that I used the English pronounciation, he told me, if I would have the benefit of the Latin tongue, not only to read and understand Latin authors, but also to converse with foreigners, I must learn the foreign pronounciation. To this I consenting, he instructed me how to sound the vowels so different from the common pronounciation used by the English (who speak *Anglice* their Latin) that, with some few other variations in sounding some consonants in particular cases—as *c* before *e* or *i* like *ch*, *sc* before *i* like *sh*—the Latin thus spoken seemed as different from that which was delivered as the English speak it as if it were another language I had before, during my retired life at my father's, by un-wearied diligence and industry so far recovered the rules of grammar, in which I had once been very ready, that I could both read a Latin author and, after a sort, hammer out his meaning. But this change of pronounciation proved a new difficulty to me. It was now harder for me to read than it was before to understand when read. But *Labor omnia vincit improbus*: "Incessant pains the end obtains." And so did I. Which made my reading the more acceptable to my master. He, on the other hand, perceiving with what earnest desire I pursued learning, gave me not only all the encouragement, but all the help, he could. For, having a curious ear, he understood, by my tone, when I understood what I read and when I did not, and accordingly would stop me, examine me, and open the most difficult passages to me.

After six weeks of study, Ellwood fell sick, returning to find his master "heartily glad" and ready to take up the old routine,

"I reading to him, and he explaining as occasion required." Another interruption was occasioned by the Quaker's imprisonment at Newgate, the horrors of which experience, as they are detailed in his *Life*, he must have recounted to his master. The brief period of renewed study was finally brought to an end by Ellwood's employment as tutor to the Pennington children in Chalfont. We can imagine how deeply Milton felt the loss, for Ellwood was as lovable as he was docile. It is interesting to note that the poet's third marriage followed within a month after his separation from this new and engaging pupil. Their association was renewed at Chalfont St. Giles, whither Milton, as we have seen, retired in August, 1665, to escape the plague. Ellwood was again in prison on his arrival. When at length he visited him, it was to receive from his hands the completed text of *Paradise Lost*.

> After some discourses had passed between us [writes Ellwood], he called for a manuscript of his; which being brought, he delivered to me, bidding me take it home with me and read it at my leisure, and, when I had so done, return it to him, with my judgment thereon. When I came home and had set myself to read it, I found it was that excellent poem which he entitled *Paradise Lost*. After I had, with the best intention, read it through, I made him another visit, and returned him his book, with due acknowledgment of the favour he had done me in communicating it to me. He asked me how I liked it and what I thought of it; which I modestly, but freely, told him: and, after some further discourse about it, I pleasantly said to him, "Thou hast said much here of Paradise Lost, but what hast thou to say of Paradise Found?" He made no answer, but sat some time in a muse; then brake off that discourse, and fell on another subject.

Later, after Milton's return to London, Ellwood was given the completed manuscript of *Paradise Regained*: "This is owing to you; for you put it in my head by the question you put to me at Chalfont, which before I had not thought of." Ellwood's interpretation of his role as confidant may seem self-flattering, but he was incapable of wilful misrepresentation, and I have little doubt that Milton said to him something like what he is reported to have said. The significance of the incident, aside from the concrete information it gives us, lies in the suggestion it affords of Milton's use of an accepting personality, almost casually encountered, for encouragement and support, in the absence of a satisfactory environment at home. We recall his dependence on the approval of older persons in his youth. The roles for some reason are now reversed. It is the promising or the docile pupil in whom he seeks his satisfactions.

We may postpone, to a later chapter, consideration of Milton's other personal relationships and of the scanty detail of his outward life in the Restoration. The great problem before us is the interpretation of his poetic masterpiece, and for this our information, so far as it lies in the interplay of personality and circumstance, is as complete as we can expect to have it. The biographer would gladly know how much of *Paradise Lost* was actually written before the Puritan cause collapsed and the poet encountered the immediate material consequences of his political crimes. Scholarly opinion differs widely on this point. The first passage which by common agreement reflects the poet's situation after 1660 occurs in the invocation in Book VII. It is the old confrontation of difficulties and discouragements, but with an apparently direct allusion to his new isolation in a hostile world.

> More safe I sing with mortal voice, unchanged
> To hoarse or mute, though fall'n on evil days,
> On evil days though fall'n, and evil tongues;
> In darkness, and with dangers compassed round,
> And solitude; . . .
> But drive far off the barbarous dissonance
> Of Bacchus and his revellers, the race
> Of that wild rout that tore the Thracian bard
> In Rhodope, where woods and rocks had ears
> To rapture, till the savage clamour drowned
> Both harp and voice.

If we believe, as we well may, that this personal utterance marks a resumption of the poem after the blow had fallen, and at the same time we accept the early biographers' accounts of when it was begun, we are left with the conclusion that not only the portrait of Satan and the council in Hell, but the idyllic description of the life in Eden, the angel's visit, and the war in Heaven all belong to the period between the *Second Defence* and the new outburst of pamphlet writing under the Protectorate of Richard Cromwell—a matter of four years, at most. I personally believe this to be the case. The evidence is against Milton's being able to concentrate on a great work of the imagination while other excitement was driving him to constructive action. The one was a substitute for the other. It is difficult, also, though not impossible, to believe that he could compose when his life and freedom were in immediate danger. He was ordered into custody by Parliament on June 16th, 1660; a royal proclamation was out against him in August. He was arrested perhaps in September and released on December 15th. During the months following, he was domiciled in Holborn, amid turbulent and horrid scenes (the mob around the bodies of Cromwell, Bradshaw, and Ireton exhibited in the neighbouring Red Lion Inn) and "in perpetual danger of being assassinated." This was obviously a make-shift residence after his concealment in Bartholomew Close. Not before he was removed from the scene and domiciled in the quieter neighbourhood of his earlier residences can we easily suppose him to have communed continuously and fruitfully again with the Heavenly Muse.

To carry hypothesis a step further, the recovery of anything like the security and comfort which we would think necessary for great creativeness is most likely to have come when a wife and housekeeper and a final well-chosen residence had been provided for him. It was approximately two and a half years after his marriage, when the Great Plague had begun in London, but was not yet at its height, that the Miltons moved to the pretty box in Chalfont which Ellwood had found for them, and about two months later, in September, 1665, that the poet let him read the completed manuscript. I submit that the second half of *Paradise Lost* was composed in this period. If any part of it is earlier, the occupation of hours of idleness, waiting in concealment in some friend's house, or in prison, or in temporary bachelor's establishments (we learn that Milton also lodged in this interval with the bookseller Millington), it would have been the seventh and perhaps the first part of the eighth book, didactic and relatively pedestrian matter. There is new and lyric inspiration in Adam's narrative of his own and Eve's creation and their nuptials, beginning in Book VIII, line 249. The mood not only of Book IV, but of the sonnet on his deceased wife, which, if our chronology is acceptable, would be somewhere near contemporary with it—this mood and the inspiration which went with it are recaptured.

> She disappeared, and left me dark; I waked
> To find her, or for ever to deplore
> Her loss, and other pleasures all abjure.

A wilderness of such crude literary parallels as have been brought to this episode from Sylvester and elsewhere cannot blind us to its personal fervency. Adam's thanks are poured out to the Creator for a blessing which Milton himself well understands, one which, I believe, he has received or is about to receive with the augury of a new and heavenly hope.

> This turn hath made amends. Thou hast fulfilled
> Thy words, creator bounteous and benign.
> Giver of all things fair, but fairest this
> Of all thy gifts, nor enviest. I now see
> Bone of my bone, flesh of my flesh, myself
> Before me; Woman is her name, of Man
> Extracted; for this cause he shall forgo
> Father and mother, and to his wife adhere;
> And they shall be one flesh, one heart, one soul.

Biographically, then, *Paradise Lost* is two poems, and if we were surer of the facts would be entitled to close examination in this aspect. As the matter stands, we have to take it as a unit, written, to be sure, on both sides of a great personal and public crisis but deriving from an experience in large part completed and matured before this crisis was encountered. We must assume also that Milton composed the parts of the poem substantially in the order in which they stand. There is a theory that he did not. To this, Phillips's statement that the ten lines of Satan's speech in Book IV were written for the early dramas lends some colour. I believe, however, that if Milton worked the other way, we should have learned of it. And I believe that a systematic planning and carrying through of the work would be for him a more natural procedure. The Muse came unimplored, but she did the bidding of his mind. The inconsistencies of plot which have been pointed to as evidence of piecing together materials fragmentarily composed seem for the most part trivial or wholly imaginary. Undoubtedly *Paradise Lost* offers great variety of style and mood, contrasting markedly in these respects with *Paradise Regained* and *Samson Agonistes*. Its inspiration fluctuates and its high creative moments are themselves of diverse character. There are, moreover, as we shall see, unresolved contradictions in Milton's attitude and point of view, contradictions which have persistently suggested that he was divided against himself on the fundamental issues which the poem presents. All this, however, only confirms what we already know, that the work was written in an epoch of disturbance and that it embodies long-accumulated energies of thought and feeling, passionate reactions which defy complete harmonization in either an artistic or a philosophic pattern.

Knowing, then, only that *Paradise Lost* has behind it the greater part of Milton's experience of life, we may undertake to study it as a large projection of this experience. The attempt is intellectually hazardous, but it would be mere stultification not to make it. The best way to approach the subject is to present the story of the fall of man as Milton received it from tradition, reconstructing it as it would naturally have been retold by a Protestant learned writer who happened under God to have been a poet but who did not happen to be Milton. The individual stamp which he put upon it will then be clearer, and its significance as a revelation of his personality may be more confidently assessed.

The main features of the narrative might have been much the same in other hands. Its outlines were determined, first of all, by the Biblical texts, which must be preserved intact in every detail, then by the elaboration and interpretation of that material in preceding literature. This elaboration had been the work of centuries. It is necessary to consider only sources which Milton might plausibly have known. Even this subject would require a volume, and volumes have actually been written on it. My belief is that the Italian and Latin dramatic versions, whether read or seen, were a primary factor in his decision to employ this subject matter. But this does not mean that the patterns of treatment were solely or principally determined by them. The essence of what they gave may be illustrated by a brief oratorio from Milan, which proceeds through the following lyric scenes: 1. Adam contemplating creation; 2. Satan (Lucifer) rousing his followers; 3. the loves of Adam and Eve; 4. Eve's distressful premonitions of evil, with Adam comforting; 5. the Temptation and Fall; 6. Satan glorying in his work; 7. Adam and Eve despairing and repentant. This is the simplest possible visualisation and humanisation of the Fall, with the serpent of Genesis identified with the rebel angel, leader of the hosts who fell in the Apocalypse. The more elaborate dramas on this theme include an amplification of the plot in two directions, bringing them more nearly to the scope of Milton's early dramatic plans and of *Paradise Lost* itself. Thus Andreini begins the *Adamo* with an account of the creation of the world and the placing of Adam and Eve in Paradise, and he exhibits the consequences of the Fall in the continued battle of good and evil for the soul of man, with a prophecy of the redemption. Grotius handles the material even more comprehensively but with the concentration made possible by his use of the structural principles of classical tragedy. The plot of his *Adamus Exul* is as follows:

Act I

Satan tells of the fall of the angels and the creation, expresses his enmity to God, and announces his intention to seduce man from his obedience.

Act II

Adam learns from a friendly angel of the wonders of creation and the state of his own being. He is warned against the serpent. A second scene portrays the life of Adam and Eve in Paradise.

Act III

Satan vainly proposes to Adam an alliance against God.

Act IV

Assuming the form of a serpent, he approaches Eve with subtle arguments and persuades her to eat the forbidden fruit. She offers it to Adam, who at first resists but finally yields to her importunity.

Act V

In Scene 1, Satan exults over his victory. In Scene 2, Eve passionately endeavours to maintain Adam in his sinful state. God declares him guilty and pronounces judgment, revealing at the same time the programme of salvation. The tragedy ends with the departure of Adam and Eve from Paradise.

The emphasis in Grotius is on the temptation and fall of man, a human story, albeit involved in and involving total cosmic history. It is another part of the great saga that forms the theme of the Dutch poet Vondel's famous *Lucifer*. Lucifer, the *Stadtholder* of Heaven, envious of newly created man and outraged by God's declared intention to set him through the incarnation of Christ above the angels, plans rebellion. The organisation of the revolt, the attempts by loyal angels to forestall it, and the battle itself occupy nearly the entire drama, but the fall of man is narrated in the last half of the fifth act, and a final chorus sings of the redemption.

From these works (Grotius and Andreini almost certainly, perhaps not Vondel) Milton received an impression of the literary values in the material and suggestions of structure and motivation which are easily recognised in *Paradise Lost*. His final decision to use the epic form made possible a more balanced development of the related themes of the revolt in heaven, the Temptation and Fall of man, the consequences of original sin, and God's plan of the redemption. The completed poem involves the broader tradition of Scriptural paraphrase and exegesis which constituted the material of religious and literary culture and in which the dramas themselves had their origin. The chances are that having decided to write on this subject, Milton not only read literary versions of the story whenever he came across them, but in his continuous direct study of Scripture paid interested attention to the exegesis of such commentators, Christian or Rabbinical, as were available to him. There was also the interpretative material in the general theological writings of the Church fathers and the Protestant divines, which presented the problems of the fall from every conceivable angle, except, indeed, that of the unbeliever. Even world history, as written, for example, by Sir Walter Raleigh, dealt liberally in the Hebrew story of mankind. The whole programme of salvation was, of course, involved in the fall of man and was therefore explicitly or by implication included in almost every Christian treatment. The scope of Milton's story is represented by the cyclical guild plays of the Middle Ages, which centred in the death and Resurrection of Christ, but began with creation and carried the story through the main events of Biblical history to the Day of Judgment. These no longer survived in Milton's time except fragmentarily in the puppet shows. Milton speaks in *Areopagitica* of the "artificial Adam of the motions," showing that he, like Goethe, had encountered the elements of his majestic poem in this humblest of all their incarnations.

For our purposes the most relevant embodiment of this larger theme is to be found in a long poem which we have reason to believe Milton knew from childhood (see above, p. 31). This is Joshua Sylvester's *Divine Weeks*, a translation of *La Sepmaine* by the Huguenot Du Bartas, an example of the so-called hexaemeric literature which had its origin in antiquity and was vigorously revived in the sixteenth and seventeenth centuries. The detailed resemblances of this work to *Paradise Lost* are too close to be accidental. It is hard to believe Milton could have greatly admired it in his mature years, but it may nevertheless have served him as a starting point for the epic version of the Fall, something which had once impressed his imagination deeply and which he returned to as the outstanding English example of a Biblical paraphrase of cosmic scope, aiming like the dramas at the realisation of literary values in the material, but suggesting the possibility of a larger comprehensiveness. The divine weeks in the poem are two, the first comprising the six days of creation and the seventh of rest, the second a series of moments in cosmic history leading to the Messiah. Adam's fall and its immediate consequences are events in the first and second days of the second week. The narrative does not include the war in Heaven except by allusion. Within this framework the author has included all manner of philosophical, religious and scientific discussion, after the cyclopædic manner of the times. The narrative, indeed, is quite overwhelmed by such didacticism. There is, however, some dramatisation, especially in the account of the creation of Adam and Eve, their nuptials, temptation, and repentance, and these are the portions of the poem in which the detailed resemblances to *Paradise Lost* are most striking.

We are now prepared to study Milton's own epic plan in its general literary and biographical relationship. It will be seen that the original dramatic structure still controls his handling of the material, but that the poet now has scope for the inclusion within its framework of whatever in the accumulation of lore and legend represented by Du Bartas is at all germane to this purpose. The mere outline of his plot might, as I have suggested, have served any author who undertook to treat this theme in its entirety with as strict a conformity as possible to the canons of epic unity. As a matter of fact no one else did so treat it, and Milton is well within the truth when he said he was writing—

Things unattempted yet in prose or rhyme.

He had arrived at this result in a natural way, by first planning a drama, then yielding to the dictates of the material as it grew to larger dimensions on his hands and making use of the throwback devices of ancient epic. If he had begun with an epic programme, the result might have been different. The poem might, indeed, have turned out a Christiad. Here is the outline, based on Milton's own arguments prefixed to the several books.

Book I

Satan, fallen leader of the rebel angels, rouses his followers in Hell and proposes to hold a council concerning an attack on newly created man.

Book II

The council is held. Satan voyages through chaos and arrives within sight of the new world.

Book III

God, sitting on His throne, sees Satan approaching earth and declares His own purposes toward man. The Son, now promoted to the first place after God in the hierarchy of being, offers himself as a satisfaction of divine justice. Satan, meanwhile, passing through the spheres which enclose the created world, stops to inquire the way of an angel in the sun, then proceeds to the terrestrial globe and alights on Mount Niphates.

Book IV

Satan overleaps the bounds of Paradise, sits in the form of a cormorant on the Tree of Life, and, listening to the discourse of Adam and Eve, learns of the prohibition which has been placed on them as the test of their obedience. The angelic guard is warned. Adam and Eve retire to rest. Satan in the form of a toad whispers temptation to the sleeping Eve but is driven thence by Gabriel.

Book V

In the morning of this second day, Eve relates her dream to Adam and is comforted. They pray and go forth to the pleasant labours of the garden. God sends the angel Raphael to warn them of approaching danger. He relates at Adam's request how the Archangel Lucifer, now called Satan, made jealous by the promotion of Christ, incited his followers to rebellion against God.

Book VI

Raphael tells of the three days' war in Heaven, the going forth of Christ against the rebel angels, their fall with horror and confusion to the place of punishment, and the Messiah's return in triumph to his Father.

Book VII

Raphael relates the six days' creation of the world, following the defeat of Satan.

Book VIII

Raphael answers Adam's questions regarding the structure of the universe and warns him to concern himself rather with his own being. Adam tells what he remembers of his own creation and recounts his first meeting and nuptials with Eve. Raphael warns him against passion and departs.

Book IX

Satan encounters Eve apart from Adam and persuades her to eat the apple. Adam "resolves through vehemence of love to perish with her" and eats also of the fruit. "They seek to cover their nakedness; then fall at variance and accusation of one another."

Book X

God sends the Son to pronounce judgment. Satan returns to Hell to boast of his success. Adam heavily bewails his fate, is reconciled to Eve, and puts her in mind of the promise made to them that her seed should be revenged on the serpent. The two repair to the place of judgment and implore God's mercy.

Book XI

The angel Michael is sent to dispossess them of Paradise. He reveals to Adam the things which shall happen to the flood.

Book XII

Michael continues his prophetic narrative, explaining by degrees who that seed of the woman shall be, His Incarnation, death, and Resurrection, and the state of the Church to His second coming, explaining also the programme whereby Adam and his descendants may recover lost Paradise within themselves. He leads them out of Paradise, "the fiery sword waving behind them, and the Cherubim taking their stations to guard the place."

Such then is the framework of the plot as Milton finally worked it out and as another poet might have done using the common body of traditional materials and employing an equal skill in proportioning and integrating them. The image of Milton's personality is to be found, if at all, in the varying response of his imagination to different elements in the story, in the emphasis which he gives to certain themes and motives, and in the human interpretation which he puts upon the whole.

We may begin by considering as a unit those passages in which he invites and analyses the sources of his inspiration and speaks explicitly of himself. These passages are a continuation of the autobiography which he had begun in the Latin poems and prose letters of his youth, and developed in the pamphlets, sonnets, and correspondence of his middle life. They are like a new assay at a type of self-portraiture in which he has by long practice become adept. The lineaments of this portrait are essentially the same, but there is a new depth in interpretation, a more complete confidence in execution. It is as if Milton, hitherto troubled by a weak desire for approbation from without, needed now no witness but all-judging Jove.

The Heavenly Muse is addressed in the opening lines of the poem with a serene though devout assurance. At first she is a creature half-mythological, dwelling like a goddess "on the secret top of Oreb or of Sinai" or in Sion or beside Siloa's brook, and thence to be invoked. As Milton proceeds, she becomes an experienced reality, the divine spirit itself, confined within no temple, but having her seat within the heart of man. She is at once the voice of Biblical revelation, which

> first taught the chosen seed,
> In the beginning how the heav'ns and earth
> Rose out of chaos;

and the creative power itself:

> thou from the first
> Wast present, and with mighty wings outspread
> Dove-like sat'st brooding on the vast abyss
> And mad'st it pregnant.

Milton's invocation is thus a lofty prayer for consecration to his task—

> what in me is dark
> Illumine, what is low raise and support.

His assurance of answer is the conviction that his purposes are themselves divine. The song which he is to sing is not merely an adventurous one—

> That with no middle flight intends to soar.

It is no less than a new apocalypse, the vision of "Eternal Providence" as it came to the blind John Milton, not suddenly, but as the gradually maturing fruit of a life lived wholly in His service.

Precisely this expression is not again to be found in *Paradise Lost* or indeed in Milton's poetry. The passage which I have already quoted from Book III, elevated as it is, is in a lower key. The poet is thinking not of his theme and purpose, but of himself. He relaxes for a moment to express his happy possession through the divine indulgence of the gifts of the imagination. "Day and the sweet approach of even or morn" are his by power of the inward eye. What need to regret his sight when he can—

> wander where the muses haunt
> Clear spring, or shady grove, or sunny hill.

Why, above all, repine at outward deprivation when the creative power is still at his command? It is interesting to note that the long excursion into the subject of blind bards in the *Second Defence* is here concentrated into a few lines:

> nor sometimes forget
> Those other two equalled with me in fate,
> So were I equalled with them in renown!
> Blind Thamyris and blind Maeonides,
> And Tiresias and Phineus, prophets old.

The need of clinging to such supports is past. The meditation remains with Milton as a delight. Even as he measures his uncertain against their certain fame, he is detached and calm.

The third invocation at the beginning of Book VII introduces

new material and suggests, to my reading, at least, the beginnings of a change. Milton's celestial patroness has led him into
the Heaven of Heavens, where he has "drawn ethereal air,"
her tempering; such exaltation cannot last. He prays for a safe
return to earth.

> Least from this flying steed unreined, (as once
> Bellerophon, though from a lower clime)
> Dismounted, on the Aleian field I fall
> Erroneous, there to wander and forlorn.

There is something more than rhetoric in this. Milton is weary
and afraid. He congratulates himself that his theme henceforth
is merely human. He remembers that he is fallen on evil days
and evil tongues. His imaginative world is no longer quite
impregnable, for he hears

> the barbarous dissonance
> Of Bacchus and his revellers.

He recalls not now Homer, renowned through Greece, but
Orpheus, singing to the woods and stones, until "the savage
clamour drowned both harp and voice." Milton's brooding
on the Orpheus myth dates from the time of "Lycidas." There
it was Edward King who was deserted by the Muse. Is it now
to be himself? The deep-lying fear, which has been in abeyance
since he began the poem, is admitted to consciousness but
immediately allayed. The power that Milton trusts is one with
whom there is no shadow of a turning. It is a meaning, not a
name, and the poet prays to it with confident hope that his
powers will suffice to carry him through the remainder of his task.

The final piece of conscious self-revelation occurs at the
opening of Book IX, when the theme changes from the subject
of creation to that of the temptation and fall of man. The poet
now fortifies himself by thoughts of his own wisdom in his
choice of theme. He congratulates himself that he has eschewed
wars and the tinsel trappings of romance. The human argument is

> Not less but more heroic than the wrath
> Of stern Achilles on his foe pursued
> Thrice fugitive about Troy wall;

and he himself is more sedulous by nature to indict—

> the better fortitude
> Of patience and heroic martyrdom,

or its reverse. His awareness of external annoyance and of the indifference of the world in which he lived is dead; he cares no longer, in the present, even for "fit audience though few." His fear is now that the age of such immortal achievement is past, that the northern countries do not permit a full flowering of the human genius, that he is himself too old. All this he maturely and rationally admits as heavily and perhaps fatally against him, though there is still the Heavenly Muse.

> Unless an age too late, or cold
> Climate, or years, damp my intended wing
> Depressed, and much they may, if all be mine,
> Not hers who brings it nightly to my ear.

We may note in these three passages a progressive maturing of Milton's thought of self, attended by a gradual recession of the tide of passion which had originally launched him on his theme. The poem itself reflects these changes. In the first four books, Milton is obviously carried forward by forces not his own. They represent the complete imaginative sublimation both of his ego emotions and of his sensuous desire. Later, art and meditation predominate. But all is Milton and demands interpretation as the record of his inner life.

Such interpretation must centre in the three protagonists of the drama of the fall: Satan, Adam, Eve. God is in the story as a kind of theory; Christ is the foil of Satan and the instrument of his defeat. The angels, good and bad, are minor vehicles of Miltonic personality and idea. The obvious judgment that Satan is the true "hero" of *Paradise Lost* was first expressed by Dryden. Blake went further in defining Milton's attitude when he asked the question why Milton wrote with freedom when he talked of Hell and the rebel angels, in chains when he talked of God and Heaven—and answered, "Because he was a true poet and of the devil's party without knowing it." But the deeper truth is that Milton is of all parties and of none. Satan is the representative of every power in him which battled against restriction. He is Milton defying the authority both of external circumstance and of his own reason. Christ *is* that reason—hateful, cold, relentless. There is no truce between the two and no real victory. Satan is triumphant but accurst; Christ, except in the passion of his obedience, is triumphant but joyless. The two represent the conflicts of a frustrated personality. They are essentially unmoral and unhuman, the upper and the nether millstones between which humanity is ground to dust. Adam, on the other hand, is man. He loves, he hates, he fears, he worships. If he is a mechanism he does not know it. He is Milton in his daily comings and goings, a plaything of the fates, requiring only to be left alone in order to be happy, but destined by his two-legged helplessness to be the interesting object of a cosmic experiment. Eve is Milton's extra rib. She is to him as he to the Gods. He knows her in the triune form of Mary, Katharine, Elizabeth. If she is of concern to the powers above, it is only as a means of testing his reactions.

The atmosphere of the opening scene is one of passion. We feel in every line the Milton we have learned to know, but it is difficult to resolve into simple elements the complex of emotions. The fierce joy with which he describes Satan's fall from Heaven suggests his own exultation in the punishment of Salmasius.

> Him the almighty power
> Hurled headlong flaming from th' ethereal sky,
> With hideous ruin and combustion, down
> To bottomless perdition, there to dwell
> In adamantine chains and penal fire,
> Who durst defy th' Omnipotent to arms.

We feel that Milton in writing these lines is participating in the wrath of the Almighty. A moment later, however, he is himself in Hell with Satan—

> for now the thought
> Both of lost happiness and lasting pain
> Torments him; round he throws his baleful eyes,
> That witnessed huge affliction and dismay,
> Mixed with obdurate pride and steadfast hate;
> At once, as far as angel's ken, he views
> The dismal situation waste and wild;
> A dungeon horrible, on all sides round,
> As one great furnace flamed; yet from those flames
> No light, but rather darkness visible
> Served only to discover sights of woe,
> Regions of sorrow, doleful shades, where peace
> And rest can never dwell, hope never comes,
> That comes to all; but torture without end
> Still urges, and a fiery deluge, fed
> With ever-burning sulphur unconsumed.

There is no accent of sadistic joy in this. The eloquence is wrought out of an agony that Milton himself has known, but never in his own person given rein to. These passages illustrate the impossibility of consistent autobiographical interpretation. In general, however, we may find in Satan the embodiment of Milton's will to power. Condemned by the limitations of his own nature to be a spectator where he would be an actor, a man of peace when he wants to wield the sword, a praiser of deeds which he would fain be doing, an exhorter of others to a leadership which he feels should be his own, he makes Satan the great commander—indomitable, independent, ruthless, self-controlled, inspiring. Words with him are backed by deeds. The responses which Milton himself could never get from men come to Satan without effort.

> Leader of those armies bright,
> Which but th' Omnipotent none could have foiled,
> If once they hear that voice, their liveliest pledge
> Of hope in fears and dangers, heard so oft
> In worst extremes, and on the perilous edge
> Of battle when it raged, in all assaults
> Their surest signal, they will soon resume
> New courage and revive.

The secret of Satan's personality is ambition, cherished and exploited without the sense of guilt. He must be first or perish, and his will if not his strength is adequate to the great emprise. Unlike Milton, he seeks no refuge from defeat.

> The mind is its own place, and in itself
> Can make a heav'n of hell, a hell of heav'n.
> What matter where, if I be still the same,
> And what I should be, all but less than he
> Whom thunder hath made greater?

If he cannot win the physical combat, he is yet incapable of yielding.

> . . . to bow and sue for grace
> With suppliant knee, and deify his power,
> Who from the terror of this arm so late
> Doubted his empire, that were low indeed,
> That were an ignominy and shame beneath
> This downfall.

His final weapon is "obdurate pride and steadfast hate"—
"the unconquerable will," "the study of revenge." The vision
of his rallied forces expands his spirit.

> He through the armèd files
> Darts his experienced eye, and soon traverse
> The whole battalion views; their order due,
> Their visages and stature as of gods;
> Their number last he sums. And now his heart
> Distends with pride, and hard'ning in his strength
> Glories.

Their loyalty moves in him a kind of love.

> . . . attention held them mute.
> Thrice he assayed, and thrice in spite of scorn,
> Tears, such as angels weep, burst forth.

But such satisfactions are only transitory. It is impossible for
Satan to rest in a delusion. This glorious army is after all
nothing, for there is nothing for it to do. Its utility, henceforth,
is that of an audience for Satan's own heroic deeds. His plan
is already formed when he summons the Infernal Council.
Beelzebub is his puppet; Moloch, Mammon, Belial set the stage
for his triumphant statesmanship and for the final demonstration of his right to lead. The proposal to attack God anew
through his creative universe demands a hero.

> . . . whom shall we send
> In search of this new world, whom shall we find
> Sufficient? who shall tempt with wand'ring feet
> The dark unbottomed infinite abyss?

In this question we have reached the objective of the whole
arranged debate. The triumph of Satan's pride is now assured.
With magnificent gesture, he seizes upon the mission for himself. It is a greater moment for his pride than that in which he
led the angelic hosts to battle, for now he casts aside his
instruments and acts alone for all. His reward is acquiescence
and acclaim.

> Towards him they bend
> With awful reverence prone; and as a god
> Extol him equal to the Highest in heav'n.

We have here the full imaginative realisation of Milton's deepest personal desire, the desire, namely, to act alone, though not without a cloud of witnesses, in the interests of a purpose of his own devising. He makes Satan disciplined, as he himself would be, but disciplined by no will other than his own. He makes him also, what he cannot be—lawless, unmoral, purely selfish. He makes him, finally, valiant and adventurous, defying the monsters, Sin and Death, exploring the unknown abyss, grappling with the elements as no Elizabethan seafarer ever grappled with them, winning finally the port, torn and weatherbeaten, but victorious. From this point on, Satan is less the vehicle of Milton's adolescent emotion. The poet had written this part of himself out and could now employ his skill in a more subtle if less glorious representation.

In Book IV, Satan is the victim of remorse of conscience—an emotion which John Milton knew only to bury beneath a snowdeep alp of self-righteousness; he is also the conscious and determined villain, reminding us of Shakespearian characters —Macbeth, Iago, Richard III. In the account of the war in Heaven he is the mere military leader, trusting solely to the fleshly arm, therefore alien to Milton's sympathies and destined to defeat. The poet's partisanship is with the loyal angels. In Book IX, Milton's skill and insight were never greater. Satan no longer exists as a personality at all. He is rather the voice of temptation—Eve's rationalisation of her desire to sin. He is finally disposed of as the grovelling serpent, a collapsed thing, the object of mere scorn.

Omitting for the moment a discussion of Milton's role as Christ, the next step in his self-revelation is to be sought in Adam. If Satan is Milton in mighty conflict with external authority and the inhibiting forces set up by his own reason, Adam is Milton sensuous and relaxed, dominating woman and yet swayed by her, pursuing happiness rather than power, failing through a weakness which he freely confesses and for which he sincerely reproaches himself, finally accepting the mixed lot of our humanity, and, chastened by experience, walking humbly henceforth with God.

In the opening scene in Paradise, Milton has portrayed the relationship of man and woman as reason, imagination, and fragments of experience have given it to him. Adam and Eve are the divinely gifted representatives of full humanity. They stand amidst the fresh created world.

Two of far nobler shape, erect and tall,
God-like erect, with native honour clad
In naked majesty, seemed lords of all,
And worthy seemed: for in their looks divine
The image of their glorious maker shone,
Truth, wisdom, sanctitude severe and pure,
Severe, but in true filial freedom placed,
Whence true authority in men; though both
Not equal, as their sex not equal, seemed;
For contemplation he and valour formed,
For softness she and sweet attractive grace;
He for God only, she for God in him.
His fair large front and eye sublime declared
Absolute rule; and hyacinthine locks
Round from his parted forelock manly hung
Clustering, but not beneath his shoulders broad:
She as a veil down to the slender waist
Her unadornèd golden tresses wore
Dishevelled, but in wanton ringlets waved,
As the vine curls her tendrils, which implied
Subjection, but required with gentle sway,
And by her yielded, by him best received,
Yielded with coy submission, modest pride,
And sweet, reluctant, amorous delay.

The sense of power which with Satan is defiant, mixed with hate, becomes in Adam serene, unquestioned, loving. Woman is man's true kingdom. To maintain its blessed peace requires but the harmonious co-operation of two wills. The story of the breaking of this harmony and of its partial restoration through the grace of God is the story of Milton's own domestic experience, as he himself analysed it from the sure though sobered contentment of his third marriage. He had been led in the divorce tracts to grapple with the marriage problem in the light of Scripture, and some of the basic thinking of *Paradise Lost* had been done at that time. Thus in *Tetrachordon* he writes his own exegesis of the first and second chapters of Genesis in such a way as to support his theory of marriage and divorce.

We may conclude, therefore, seeing orthodoxal expositors confess to our hands that by loneliness is not only meant the want of copulation : . . . and that it is a work more worthy the care and consolation of God to provide for the worthiest part of man, which is his mind . . . I say we may conclude that such a marriage, wherein the mind is so disgraced and vilified below the body's interest . . . is not of God's institution.

When Adam said "bone of my bone, flesh of my flesh," he spoke as Adam of "the shell and rind of matrimony." The soul of the relation is "conjugal love arising from a mutual fitness to the final causes of wedlock, help and society in religious, civil, and domestic conversation, which includes as an inferior end the fulfilling of natural desire and specifical increase."

When love finds itself utterly unmatched, the fleshly act indeed may continue but not holy, not pure, not beseeming the sacred bond of marriage.

By the time Milton wrote *Paradise Lost* he had found reason to think more genially of the marriage bed, but his philosophy remained unchanged, and it is his total experience which embodies itself in the poem, the Biblical symbol answering all his needs. Adam and Eve in innocence represent true marriage. Eve's sin breaks the spiritual bond. They attempt to prolong the relation of the flesh and their bed becomes, in the words of *Tetrachordon*, "a haunt of lust and malice mixed together, no love, no goodness, no loyalty." Their recovery is something for which in the divorce pamphlets no provision is made. It is achieved by the acceptance of limitation and by religious discipline under the tutelage of God.

The common opinion is that in accounting for the downfall of the well-ordered home (the true theme of *Paradise Lost*) Milton throws the major blame on Eve's perverseness. Emotionally he does so. Theoretically he does not. In the dialogue with Raphael in Book VIII he makes the situation clear, for Adam here confesses that reason, the god-like faculty in him, is not impregnable in his relationship to Eve—

> here passion first I felt,
> Commotion strange, in all enjoyments else
> Superior and unmoved, here only weak
> Against the charm of beauty's powerful glance.

The acknowledgment is no new one for Milton. It appears, though without real sense of danger, in one of the Italian sonnets, written in his university days.

In one sole part thou'lt find it [his heart] not so strong,
Where Love set his immedicable sting.

It is implicit even in the angry first divorce tract, when he admits that his choice of a beloved object may be wrong. In the lines which follow those just quoted from Book VIII, Adam rebels for a moment against the conditions of his creation.

> Or nature failed in me, and left some part
> Not proof enough such object to sustain,
> Or from my side subducting took perhaps
> More than enough; at least on her bestowed
> Too much of ornament, in outward show
> Elaborate, of inward less exact.
> For well I understand in the prime end
> Of nature her th' inferior, in the mind
> And inward faculties, which most excel.

The angel, with contracted brow, gives uncompromising answer.

> Accuse not nature, she hath done her part;
> Do thou but thine, and be not diffident
> Of wisdom; she deserts thee not, if thou
> Dismiss not her, when most thou need'st her nigh.

Having, then, formally shriven himself from the sin of pride, Milton is ready to turn loose the full passion of reproach on Eve. The account of her moral downfall and of the subsequent disruption of the paradise of love is, after the portrayal of the defiant Satan, the great achievement of his genius. Nothing could be more subtle than his knowledge of the female heart, or if not her heart, her behaviour. The analysis begins as early as Book IV where Eve is still free from sin or the suggestion of it. Her essential weakness is to be pride, as his is passion. The seeds of it are such innocent vanity as she displays at the moment of her creation, when, beholding her own image in the mirror of a pool, she pauses in narcissistic admiration.

>   I thither went
> With unexperienced thought, and laid me down
> On the green bank, to look into the clear
> Smooth lake, that to me seemed another sky.
> As I bent down to look, just opposite
> A shape within the wat'ry gleam appeared.

> Bending to look on me, I started back,
> It started back, but pleased I soon returned,
> Pleased it returned as soon with answering looks
> Of sympathy and love.

She is freed from danger by the voice of God, directing her gaze to the true object which his wisdom has provided for her.

> there I had fixed
> Mine eyes till now, and pined with vain desire,
> Had not a voice thus warned me, "What thou seest,
> What there thou seest, fair creature, is thyself;
> With thee it came and goes: but follow me,
> And I will bring thee where no shadow stays
> Thy coming, and thy soft embraces; he
> Whose image thou art, him thou shalt enjoy
> Inseparably thine, to him shalt bear
> Multitudes like thyself, and thence be called
> Mother of human race." What could I do,
> But follow straight, invisibly thus led?
> Till I espied thee, fair indeed and tall,
> Under a platan, yet methought less fair,
> Less winning soft, less amiably mild,
> Than that smooth wat'ry image; back I turned,
> Thou following criedst aloud, "Return fair Eve,
> Whom fliest thou? whom thou fliest, of him thou art,
> His flesh, his bone; to give thee being, I lent
> Out of my side to thee, nearest my heart,
> Substantial life, to have thee by my side
> Henceforth an individual solace dear:
> Part of my soul, I seek thee, and thee claim,
> My other half."

The first step in her alienation from Adam, represented by Milton, following the pattern of his inherited theology, as the result of Satan's malice, is her dream at the beginning of Book V. Psychologically it is the return of her primal instinct. Satan, in shape a toad, but with the voice of Adam, whispers temptation to her ear in sleep. He begins with flattery—

> heaven wakes with all his eyes,
> Whom to behold but thee, nature's desire?
> In whose sight all things joy, with ravishment
> Attracted by thy beauty still to gaze.

She rises in her dream and, missing Adam, gazes at the tree of interdicted knowledge and beholds beside it—

One shaped and winged like one of those from Heaven.

He eats and she, though horror-stricken, is fascinated by the promise—

> Taste this, and be henceforth among the gods
> Thyself a goddess.

At length under the compulsion not only of his words but of her own desire she also eats.

> Forthwith up to the clouds
> With him I flew, and underneath beheld
> The earth outstretched immense, a prospect wide
> And various.

The whole scene of the Fall is thus enacted in her fantasy. On waking, she turns to Adam with troubled mind and receives from him the gentle counsel of wisdom, dispelling guilt and restoring her to happy bondage. But the germ of sin is implanted in her heart.

Its effects are seen in her inability to remain contented with the normal ways of domestic life in Paradise. Neither she nor Adam sees the significance of her thought when in Book IX she proposes as a measure of household efficiency that she work for a day apart from Adam.

> Adam, well may we labour still to dress
> This garden, still to tend plant, herb and flower,
> Our pleasant task enjoined; but till more hands
> Aid us, the work under our labour grows,
> Luxurious by restraint; what we by day
> Lop overgrown, or prune, or prop, or bind,
> One night or two with wanton growth derides,
> Tending to wild. Thou therefore now advise
> Or hear what to my mind first thoughts present:
> Let us divide our labours; thou where choice
> Leads thee, or where most needs, whether to wind
> The woodbine round this arbour, or direct
> The clasping ivy where to climb; while I
> In yonder spring of roses intermixed
> With myrtle find what to redress till noon:

> For while so near each other thus all day
> Our task we choose, what wonder if so near
> Looks intervene and smiles, or object new
> Casual discourse draw on; which intermits
> Our day's work, brought to little, though begun
> Early, and the hour of supper comes unearned.

Adam's handling of this sweet rebellion is in Milton's eyes apparently all wisdom. He would assent to her proposal, innocent as it is and good, but that he dreads for her the nearness of the foe. His secret thought is that she is unworthy of the enjoyment of that moral freedom which is the portion of the mature human being. Eve feels the slight, and stubborn pride begins to take the place of love.

> Offspring of heaven and earth, and all earth's lord!
> That such an enemy we have, who seeks
> Our ruin, both by thee informed I learn,
> And from the parting angel overheard,
> As in a shady nook I stood behind,
> Just then returned at shut of evening flow'rs.
> But that thou shouldst my firmness therefore doubt
> To God or thee, because we have a foe
> May tempt it, I expected not to hear.
> His violence thou fear'st not, being such,
> As we, not capable of death or pain,
> Can either not receive, or can repel.
> His fraud is then thy fear, which plain infers
> Thy equal fear, that my firm faith and love
> Can by his fraud be shaken or seduced:
> Thoughts, which how found thy harbour in thy breast,
> Adam, misthought of her to thee so dear?

In the course of the contention she employs the very arguments of Milton's earlier defence of freedom.

> If this be our condition, thus to dwell
> In narrow circuit straitened by a foe,
> Subtle or violent, we not endued
> Single with like defence, wherever met,
> How are we happy, still in fear of harm?
> But harm precedes not sin: only our foe
> Tempting affronts us with his foul esteem
> Of our integrity: his foul esteem

> Sticks no dishonour on our front, but turns
> Foul on himself; then wherefore shunned or feared
> By us? who rather double honour gain
> From his surmise proved false, find peace within,
> Favour from heav'n, our witness, from the event.
> And what is faith, love, virtue unassayed
> Alone, without exterior help sustained?

Adam at length assents perforce—

> Go; for thy stay, not free, absents thee more.

He has followed exactly the programme of *Areopagitica*—"The rest as children and childish men may well be exhorted to abstain, but hindered forcibly they cannot be"—and apparently it has failed. To the ordinary judgment it is plain that Adam should have done one of two things. Either he should have accepted at once Eve's assumption of moral maturity, or he should have restrained her by brute authority. Is Milton at this late hour expressing doubt as to the validity of his own principles of procedure? No, for he has to deal with the inescapable fact of human weakness, and with the interference of an external power too strong and subtle for humanity to cope with. Had he acted otherwise Paradise would have been destroyed irrevocably. There might have been no sin but there would have remained no innocence. The situation must be accepted and the plan of God fulfilled.

The conscious fall of Eve is an elaborate repetition of her fall in sleep. Satan's arguments to her waking mind are eloquent and subtle. They induce in her a long series of self-deceiving thoughts, which undermine resistance. The secret of her weakness is envy of Adam's superiority. She resents her pupilage and yearns to "grow mature in knowledge" by the simple act of disobedience. But the final impulse to sin is purely physical.

> Meanwhile the hour of noon drew on, and waked
> An eager appetite, raised by the smell
> So savoury of that fruit.

Satan has achieved what is in all essentials a seduction. The result in Eve is an intense exhilaration, like that of drunkenness.

> satiate at length,
> And heightened as with wine, jocund and boon,
> Thus to herself she pleasingly began.

H

"O sov'reign, virtuous, precious of all trees
In Paradise, of operation blest
To sapience, hitherto obscured, infamed,
And thy fair fruit let hang, as to no end
Created; but henceforth my early care,
Not without song, each morning, and due praise
Shall tend thee, and the fertile burden ease
Of thy full branches offered free to all;
Till dieted by thee I grow mature
In knowledge, as the gods who all things know."

Sin blinds her to the sense of guilt which nevertheless is at
work within her.

heav'n is high,
High and remote to see from thence distinct
Each thing on earth; and other care perhaps
May have diverted from continual watch
Our great Forbidder, safe with all his spies
About him.

But if God is remote, Adam, His representative, is very near.
Loving confidence toward him is changed in her to fear, and
fear breeds jealousy. She debates her future course and decides
to make him the partaker of her lot.

But to Adam in what sort
Shall I appear? shall I to him make known
As yet my change, and give him to partake
Full happiness with me, or rather not,
But keep the odds of knowledge in my power
Without copartner? so to add what wants
In female sex, the more to draw his love,
And render me more equal, and perhaps,
A thing not undesirable, sometime
Superior; for inferior who is free?
This may be well: but what if God have seen,
And death ensue? then I shall be no more,
And Adam wedded to another Eve,
Shall live with her enjoying, I extinct:
A death to think. Confirmed then I resolve,
Adam shall share with me in bliss or woe:
So dear I love him, that with him all deaths
I could endure: without him live no life.

The fall of Adam is described in strict accord with Milton's conception of his hero's personality and his own. Unlike Eve, he comprehends the whole situation at a glance. His god-like reason plays him false not before but only after he has resolved to sin. As he sees Eve, her cheek flushed with distemper, and hears her insincere and erring speech, an immense wave of tragic passion overwhelms him. The vision of life without her presents itself and is dismissed. He feels the link of nature drawing him. His resolution is instantaneous and he delays action only long enough to fall into Eve's self-deceiving train of thought, with manly variations.

> Bold deed thou hast presumed, adventurous Eve,
> And peril great provoked, who thus hast dared
> Had it been only coveting to eye
> That sacred fruit, sacred to abstinence,
> Much more to taste it under ban to touch.
> But past who can recall, or done undo?
> Not God omnipotent, nor fate! Yet so
> Perhaps thou shalt not die; perhaps the fact
> Is not so heinous now, foretasted fruit,
> Profaned first by the serpent, by him first
> Made common and unhallowed ere our taste;
> Nor yet on him found deadly, he yet lives,
> Lives, as thou said'st, and gains to live as man
> Higher degree of life, inducement strong
> To us, as likely tasting to attain
> Proportional ascent, which cannot be
> But to be gods, or angels demi-gods.
> Nor can I think that God, creator wise,
> Though threat'ning, will in earnest so destroy
> Us his prime creatures, dignified so high,
> Set over all his works, which in our fall,
> For us created, needs with us must fail,
> Dependent made; so God shall uncreate,
> Be frustrate, do, undo, and labour lose—
> Not well conceived of God; who though his power
> Creation could repeat, yet would be loath
> Us to abolish, lest the adversary
> Triumph and say; "Fickle their state whom God
> Most favours, who can please him long? Me first
> He ruined, now mankind; whom will he next?"

> Matter of scorn, not to be given the foe.
> However I with thee have fixed my lot,
> Certain to undergo like doom; if death
> Consort with thee, death is to me as life;
> So forcible within my heart I feel
> The bond of nature draw me to my own,
> My own in thee, for what thou art is mine;
> Our state cannot be severed, we are one,.
> One flesh; to lose thee were to lose myself.

Eve salutes his decision as a "glorious trial of exceeding love," and offers him her blind intuitions as a guide to safety. The whole situation in Paradise is instantly reversed. Eve, under the spell of pride, has assumed the mastery; Adam, under that of romantic passion, has become the slave. His lower nature, symbolised by her, is in command, and lust, "the solace of their sin," replaces love. All theology aside, Milton is here describing the failure of a marriage and he is putting into it nothing that he has learned from books.

The scenes that follow may be, as Phillips's anecdote implies, a literal transcript of the development of Milton's relationship with Mary Powell after her return. But all the probabilities are against it. One doubts whether Milton ever openly indicted his partner with the devastating completeness of Adam's angry speech to Eve in Book X.

> Out of my sight, thou serpent! that name best
> Befits thee with him leagued, thyself as false
> And hateful!

And one feels sure, in spite of Phillips's anecdote, that human nature, or at least Powell nature, is incapable of such sincere and gratifying surrender as is represented in Eve's response.

> Forsake me not thus, Adam! witness heav'n
> What love sincere, and reverence in my heart
> I bear thee, and unwitting have offended,
> Unhappily deceived. Thy suppliant
> I beg, and clasp thy knees; bereave me not,
> Whereon I live, thy gentle looks, thy aid,
> Thy counsel in this uttermost distress,
> My only strength and stay: forlorn of thee,
> Whither shall I betake me, where subsist?
> While yet we live, scarce one short hour perhaps,

Between us two let there be peace, both joining,
As joined in injuries, one enmity
Against a foe by doom express assigned us,
That cruel serpent. On me exercise not
Thy hatred for this misery befall'n,
On me already lost, me than thyself
More miserable; both have sinned, but thou
Against God only, I against God and thee,
And to the place of judgment will return,
There with my cries importune heaven, that all
The sentence, from thy head removed, may light
On me, sole cause to thee of all this woe,
Me, me only, just object of his ire.

We are here rather in the world of Milton's compensatory
dreaming than in that of his experienced satisfaction. He has
realised in Adam the fulfilment of his thwarted desire for love,
as he realised in Satan the fulfilment of his passionate ambition.
The poem, from this point of view, is more deeply a revelation
of Milton's personality than anything in the recorded activities
of his life, more truly autobiographical than any direct expression of his thought or feeling in prose or verse.

It remains to consider the significance in relation to Milton's
personality as we know it of his handling of the other major
figures in the poem. Christ holds dialogue with God in Book III
in cold severity. He represents the power of reason and restraint
against the chaos of passion represented by Satan and the
sinning Adam. He is the instrument by which Milton judges
and rebukes the upsurging of his instincts. He is the theological
embodiment of Milton's philosophy of life, the product of
parental discipline imposed in youth and developed by life-
long devotion to the masters of wisdom and of truth. In
Paradise Lost, a work of impassioned imagination, the power of
Christ is only theoretical. In *Paradise Regained*, a work of
philosophic meditation, he is truly victor, not only over Satan,
but over Milton himself. It is in that poem, therefore, that we
must seek him.

The obedient angels call forth in Milton some emotion.
Raphael is the welcome counsellor and friend. He guides Adam
lovingly toward right thinking as a father might guide a child
or Milton himself a pupil. Adam's attitude of docile reverence
is something of which Milton himself was capable, and which

he had perhaps experienced in the days of his association with companionable tutors like Thomas Young. Michael is a sterner and more inspiring voice. He is the bearer of God's lesson to mankind as Milton understood it. Again, he is both the poet himself as a hortatory voice and the embodiment of such unquestioned authority as the child in him still craved. The glad obedience of the heavenly host represents an impulse which, as we have seen, Milton could himself occasionally give rein to. Valued, encouraged, praised, as he was in the early days of the Commonwealth, his instinct was for service. When opportunity for action was denied him he transferred his passion to the higher sphere. The sonnet on his blindness illustrates the processes of his imagination.

> thousands at his bidding speed
> And post o'er land and ocean without rest;
> They also serve who only stand and wait.

It is plainly false that Milton is only of the devil's party. Once freed from his spiritual foe of pride he is with equal sincerity among the loyal hosts of God.

Of all the angels, Abdiel, apostate from the ranks of Satan, is most completely representative of Milton in this phase of his personality. We have seen the poet building up in himself from childhood the ideal of the just man, isolated from his fellows, indifferent to their scorn, adhering to the lofty principles of his own nature, and dependent upon no reward save God's approval. So Abdiel, fearless in his righteousness, defies the multitude and appears before the throne to enjoy in fullest measure the perfect witness of all-judging Jove.

> So spake the Seraph Abdiel, faithful found
> Among the faithless, faithful only he:
> Among innumerable false, unmoved,
> Unshaken, unseduced, unterrified,
> His loyalty he kept, his love, his zeal;
> Nor number nor example with him wrought
> To swerve from truth, or change his constant mind,
> Though single. From amidst them forth he passed,
> Long way through hostile scorn, which he sustained
> Superior, nor of violence feared aught;
> And with retorted scorn his back he turned
> On those proud tow'rs to swift destruction doomed.

. . . gladly then he mixed
Among those friendly powers, who him received
With joy and acclamations loud, that one,
That of so many myriads fall'n yet one
Returned not lost. On to the sacred hill
They led him high applauded, and present
Before the seat supreme; from whence a voice
From midst a golden cloud, thus mild was heard:
"Servant of God, well done! Well hast thou fought
The better fight, who single hast maintained
Against revolted multitudes the cause
Of truth, in word mightier than they in arms;
And for the testimony of truth hast borne
Universal reproach, far worse to bear
Than violence: for this was all thy care,
To stand approved in sight of God, though worlds
Judged thee perverse."

With this illustration we may conclude the analysis of
Paradise Lost as an embodiment of the dissociated elements
which compose the extraordinary complex of Milton's personality. Of the poem as a record of his interests, of the evidence
it contains of his rich capacity to enjoy the world of beauty and
of knowledge, which remains his in spite of the loss of outward
sight, it is unnecessary to say much. His retentive memory holds
all that he has ever learned and felt, and in *Paradise Lost* he
pours forth with unexampled abundance the whole treasury
of his mind. His responsiveness to immediate sensation is, of
course, limited, but we can see him in the poem enjoying the
"sovran vital" warmth of the sun, or going forth into the
country to rejoice in its sweet sounds and smells. By way of
compensation his range of imagined sensation is limitless. It is
as if his faculties, long in bondage to reality, were at last
released. His imagination suffers no restraint as it portrays the
"darkness visible" of Hell, the ethereal splendours of the light
of Heaven, the wild tumult and confusion of Chaos, the rich
variety of created Nature. The full exploitation of this impulse
is largely confined to the first four books. His enthusiasm for
knowledge and ideas, on the other hand, remains a steady
flame throughout the poem. All history, all literature, all
science are laid under contribution. In a simile in Book I he

compresses the story of the Barbarian invasions of the Roman
Empire into a half dozen lines.

> A multitude like which the populous North
> Poured never from her frozen loins, to pass
> Rhene or the Danaw, when her barbarous sons
> Came like a deluge on the South, and spread
> Beneath Gibraltar to the Libyan sands.

In another he reviews the history of epic literature.

> . . . though all the giant brood
> Of Phlegra with th' heroic race were joined
> That fought at Thebes and Ilium, on each side
> Mixed with auxiliar gods; and what resounds
> In fable or romance of Uther's son,
> Begirt with British and Armoric knights;
> And all who since, baptized or infidel,
> Jousted in Aspramont or Montalban,
> Damasco, or Marocco, or Trebisond
> Or whom Biserta sent from Afric shore
> When Charlemain with all his peerage fell
> By Fontarabbia.

His knowledge of physics, chemistry, astronomy naturally
furnishes him abundance of material. There is a full discussion
of the Copernican versus the Ptolomaic hypothesis in Book
VIII. He alludes with precise knowledge to Galileo's telescope
and its revelations. He expounds the current theories of earth-
quakes and meteors. His deepest interest, however, is in
Biblical history, as a true revelation of the life of man on earth.
The eleventh and twelfth books contain an elaborate com-
mentary on the Old and New Testaments, written with such
grasp and insight as only a lifetime of study and meditation
could have produced. The incorporation of these materials
in *Paradise Lost* makes the poem a record not only of Milton's
personal conflicts but of his continued pursuit of the steadying
activities of the mind. Its composition had become a necessary
and an all-absorbing occupation, giving meaning and purpose
to an existence which without it would have been a mere
beating of the wind.

CHAPTER EIGHT

MILTON AGONISTES
1667–70

THE PUBLICATION OF *Paradise Lost* in 1667 was followed by
that of the two final master works, *Paradise Regained* and *Samson
Agonistes*, which appeared together in 1671. Ellwood's account
of the writing of *Paradise Regained* makes that work follow
promptly on the completion of *Paradise Lost* in 1665. Milton,
it will be recalled, gave him the manuscript shortly after his
return from Chalfont in the autumn of that year. Phillips says
that it was "begun, finished, and printed" after the *publication*
of its predecessor—that is, after September or November, 1667.
The two-year difference in chronology raises a question as to
the order of composition of *Paradise Regained* and *Samson*.
But Ellwood's statement is probably the more reliable, in which
case the drama can hardly have intervened between the two
closely related epics. The possibility that *Samson* belongs to a
still earlier period has been suggested. There is no external
evidence, and we shall proceed on the traditional assumption
that the two works belong to the same moment in Milton's life.
Obviously, they do not belong to the same inspiration, and this
fact gives us our present problem of analysis. Actually the two
works have a relationship beyond their nearness to each other
in point of time; they are, indeed, if our point of view is sound,
counterparts of each other, and taken together they complete
the pattern of Milton's poetical self-expression in a most
extraordinary way.

Paradise Regained, though it appears in Ellwood's anecdote as
an afterthought, is technically a continuation or amplification
of *Paradise Lost*. The theme of Christ's victory and triumph
over Satan was already touched on in the earlier epic. "Say
where and when their fight," asks Adam of his angelic monitor.

> To whom thus Michael: "Dream not of their fight,
> As of a duel, or the local wounds
> Of head or heel. Not therefore joins the Son
> Manhood to Godhead, with more strength to foil
> Thy enemy; nor so is overcome

> Satan, whose fall from Heaven, a deadlier bruise,
> Disabled not to give thee thy death's wound;
> Which he, who comes thy Saviour, shall recure,
> Not by destroying Satan, but his works
> In thee and in thy seed: nor can this be
> But by fulfilling that which thou didst want,
> Obedience to the law of God, imposed
> On penalty of death, and suffering death,
> The penalty to thy transgression due,
> And due to theirs which out of thine will grow."

Obedience to the law, as expressed in the temptation in the wilderness, with the consequent overthrow of Satan, is the subject treated in *Paradise Regained*. From the biographer's point of view, the poem expresses with fullness and precision a part of Milton's consciousness which is indeed represented in *Paradise Lost*, but only partially and in confused and wavering form. We have seen the poet in the earlier work depicting the cosmic strife of passion and right reason, and awarding to the latter, as his theology and his conviction bade him do, the palm of victory. That victory, however, is an inconclusive one. No defeat of Satan can outweigh the earlier manifestations of his triumphant will; no promise to Adam of a moral Paradise within can counterbalance the tragic ruin of his innocence. The conclusion of *Paradise Lost* is a contradiction of its beginning. In *Paradise Regained* the work of subjugating passion to reason is complete. Christ is victorious not by power, but by wisdom. Satan is defeated in a Socratic argument. His weapons of specious logic have proved valid against Eve; against Christ they are not so. The battle is thus transferred from the field of action to the forum of debate. Ideas, not personalities, are in conflict. Yet Milton as certainly identifies himself with his calm, philosophically triumphant Christ, as he had earlier identified himself with the rebellious Satan or the distraught and impassioned Adam, and the portrait is equally valid and important as a record of his inner life.

The key to this identification is the famous passage in Book I quoted earlier in this volume, in which Christ, on entering the desert, reviews His childhood and confirms Himself as the one appointed by God to be the protagonist of mankind in His struggle with the powers of darkness. The speech is an interesting dramatic adaptation to the personality of Jesus of the kind

of aspiration to which, as we know, Milton had repeatedly
dedicated his own life.

> . . . yet this not all
> To which my spirit aspired; victorious deeds
> Flamed in my heart, heroic acts; one while
> To rescue Israel from the Roman yoke,
> Then to subdue and quell o'er all the earth
> Brute violence and proud tyrannic pow'r,
> Till truth were freed, and equity restored:
> Yet held it more humane, more heavenly, first
> By winning words to conquer willing hearts,
> And make persuasion do the work of fear;
> At least to try, and teach the erring soul,
> Not wilfully misdoing, but unaware
> Misled; the stubborn only to subdue.

The analysis of temptation which follows the opening scenes
of the epic is in some degree a record of Milton's own conflicts,
generalised as the conflicts of mankind, and now represented
as resolved by truth. The bait of women is expressly excluded
from the scheme. Not Christ but Satan himself is made to
pronounce Milton's final word on the weakness which the poet
had made the cause of Adam's downfall.

> . . . for Beauty stands
> In the admiration only of weak minds
> Led captive. Cease to admire, and all her plumes
> Fall flat and shrink into a trivial toy,
> At every sudden slighting quite abashed.
> Therefore with manlier objects we must try
> His constancy, with such as have more show
> Of worth, of honour, glory, and popular praise;
> Rocks whereon greatest men have oftest wrecked;
> Or that which only seems to satisfy
> Lawful desires of nature, not beyond.

Milton will deal then, only with the less exciting infirmities of
humanity, and scope will be given to meditations for which in
Paradise Lost there was no place. The objects of appeal are
arranged in an ascending scale of value.

Setting aside the first temptation—"Command that out of
these stones there be made bread"—as without significance for
Milton personally, we have as the opening scene in the second

temptation—"the kingdoms of the world and the glory of them"—the offer of a luxurious Roman banquet, representative of all that the skill of man can do to enmesh the rational soul in gratification of the sense. In reading the passage we recall Milton's early adoption of the ascetic ideal as a part of his spiritual programme. But we remember also the occasional evidences of discriminating interest in food and drink.

> What neat repast shall feast us, light and choice,
> Of Attic taste, with wine.

The rich Satanic feast is proffered with the same arguments for self-indulgence that Milton had already employed in *Comus*.

> What doubts the Son of God to sit and eat?
> These are not fruits forbidden; no interdict
> Defends the touching of these viands pure;
> Their taste no knowledge works, at least of evil,
> But life preserves, destroys life's enemy,
> Hunger, with sweet restorative delight.

Christ rejects the offer, without reasoned answer, and Satan pronounces Him invincible in temperance. The temptation is on the lowest plane and does not seem to Milton worth long discussion. Yet the description of the banquet is the one richly coloured passage in *Paradise Regained*. The poet is for the moment back in the sensuous vein of certain portions of *Paradise Lost*. He brings to the account what he has read of the great feasts of the Romans and invests it in his richest poetic eloquence. It becomes, therefore, no mere sermon but a dramatic representation of one of the ways in which man has deviated from the path of wisdom, substituting false objects of desire for the true good.

The second step in the graded series of enticements is that of riches, but riches as a means to power. Here the argument of Satan is partly grounded on the historical situation. The Saviour's "high designs" are interpreted by His spiritual enemy as aiming at a temporal kingdom. The great acts which would bring Him power require "great means of enterprise." Christ is unknown, unfriended, low of birth. Wealth will give Him the throne of Judah as it had given this throne to Antipater and Herod. Christ's reply is a serene declaration of faith in spiritual as opposed to material values. Wealth, without virtue, wisdom, valour, is impotent to gain or keep dominion. Riches are the

"toil of fools," "the wise man's cumbrance if not snare,"
more apt—

> To slacken virtue, and abate her edge,
> Than prompt her to do aught may merit praise.

Both riches and realms are, then, to be rejected with an equal
aversion. The true king is he who reigns within himself, and
rules passions, desires, and fears. The highest leadership of
men is to guide them in the way of truth and release them
from the bondage of their passions.

> . . . this attracts the soul,
> Governs the inner man, the nobler part;
> That other o'er the body only reigns.

Here, again, we recognise the clear and authentic voice of
Milton. He had himself rejected the broad highway of gain,
offered him by his father's profession and chosen by his brother
Christopher. He had elected to be great by wisdom, to guide
nations by saving doctrine—

> and from error lead
> To know, and knowing, worship God aright.

Yet he did not remain untroubled by the thing his reason had
set aside as false, else he would not have chafed, as we know him
to have done, under the fear of poverty.

Of incidental interest in this passage as a final expression of
one of the great Miltonic themes is the description of the true
king as the wise and virtuous shepherd of his people.

> For therein stands the office of a king,
> His honour, virtue, merit, and chief praise,
> That for the public all the weight he bears.

The greatest rulers have attained their power through poverty
and self-sacrifice—Gideon and Jephtha among the Hebrews;
Quintius, Fabricius, Carius, Regulus among the Romans.

The offer of riches as a means to power is succeeded by that
of power as a means to glory. Satan's discourse is lacking in
conviction; Christ's reply is an eloquent and easy exposition
of Milton's developed thoughts on fame. What is glory but the
people's praise—

> And what the people but a herd confused,
> A miscellaneous rabble, who extol
> Things vulgar, and well weighed, scarce worth the praise?

To live dispraised by man may be the highest praise. This is the lot of "him who dares be singularly good"—the lot, then, of Abdiel, of Christ Himself, of Milton. The old Miltonic idea of fame in Heaven is here repeated in terms which carry us back to "Lycidas" and again call to our attention the fixity of Milton's rational principles and even of the imagery in which they are expressed.

> This is true glory and renown, when God,
> Looking on the Earth, with approbation marks
> The just man, and divulges him through Heaven
> To all his Angels, who with true applause
> Recount his praises.

The poet instances Job the Hebrew, Socrates the Greek, contrasting their glory with that of famous conquerors, and again revealing his hatred of the warrior type.

> What do these worthies,
> But rob, and spoil, burn, slaughter, and enslave
> Peaceable nations, neighbouring or remote,
> Made captive, yet deserving freedom more
> Than those their conquerors, who leave behind
> Nothing but ruin wheresoe'er they rove,
> And all the flourishing works of peace destroy.

Such thoughts had underlain the warning to the victorious Cromwell.

> Yet much remains
> To conquer still; peace hath her victories
> No less renowned than war.

The concept of true, as contrasted with false, fame represents Milton's means of escape from the dangers which lay for him in the undisciplined will to power and which had come near undoing him in his acceptance of the notoriety of the *First Defence*. It is the assured answer of his reason to the instinctive desires which he had in the first books of *Paradise Lost* embodied in Satan, who is accordingly represented in the dialogue as silenced "by the guilt of his own sin." Such a judgment on Satanic glory is, of course, implicit in *Paradise Lost*, but it is there weak against the poet's dramatisation of the passion itself. In *Paradise Regained* there is no dramatic passion, and it is Satan who is weak.

There is a momentary return of pity for the baffled tempter, revealing a genuine insight on Milton's part into sufferings not his own.

> . . . all hope is lost
> Of my reception into grace: what worse?
> For where no hope is left, is left no fear:
> . . . I would be at the worst, worst is my port,
> My harbour, and my ultimate repose,
> The end I would attain, my final good.

There is no accent of hypocrisy in this, or in the singularly beautiful lines which follow:

> . . . to that gentle brow
> Willingly I could fly, and hope thy reign,
> From that placid aspect and meek regard,
> Rather than aggravate my evil state,
> Would stand between me and thy Father's ire,
> Whose ire I dread more than the fire of Hell,
> A shelter, and a kind of shading cool
> Interposition, as a summer's cloud.

Gilbert Chesterton has spoken of the line in "Lycidas," "By the dear might of him that walked the waves," as the only place in Milton's poetry where Christ does walk. He might have made an exception of the quoted passage. The poet was evidently not incapable of Christian feeling, but it is seldom that he can surrender himself to it.

Failing of his effort to move Christ by argument alone, Satan presents "the kingdoms of the earth" visually before Him. The first vision is that of the rising military power of Parthia, the second that of the full-blown glory of imperial Rome. There is no new material in the essential temptation in either case or in Christ's replies. The Parthian armies are but "ostentation vain of fleshly arm"; Rome's grandeur and magnificence are but a mask of luxury and pride. Milton's descriptions show an extraordinary command over the detail of his historical reading; his ethical analysis represents the fruit of long and mature political reflection. We may note in his judgment of the Roman people a reaffirmation of his old conviction that virtue in the Commonwealth is the essential condition of true liberty.

> That people, victor once, now vile and base,
> Deservedly made vassal . . .
> Luxurious by their wealth, and greedier still,
> And from the daily scene effeminate.
> What wise and valiant man would seek to free
> These thus degenerate, by themselves enslaved,
> Or could of inward slaves make outward free?

Even so had England, ignoring his great warning, and preferring "bondage with ease to strenuous liberty," fallen beneath all hope of redemption.

The final vision—Athens in its day of intellectual supremacy—presents us with an object more plausible as an allurement to either Christ or Milton than any hitherto presented, and Satan's approach is far more subtle.

> Therefore let pass, as they are transitory,
> The kingdoms of this world; I shall no more
> Advise thee; gain them as thou canst, or not.
> And thou thyself seem'st otherwise inclined
> Than to a worldly crown, addicted more
> To contemplation and profound dispute;
> As by that early action may be judged,
> When, slipping from my mother's eye, thou went'st
> Alone into the Temple, there wast found
> Among the gravest rabbis, disputant
> On points and questions fitting Moses' chair,
> Teaching, not taught. The childhood shows the man,
> As morning shows the day. Be famous then
> By wisdom; as thy empire must extend,
> So let extend thy mind o'er all the world
> In knowledge.

Precisely such an invitation did the great humanistic tradition hold out to the most aspiring minds of the Renaissance, and Milton, from his childhood, had felt its force. It is not surprising, then, that in making Satan put the case for classical culture, he should equip him with the best of his own eloquence. If the description of Rome abounds in the rich ore of Milton's imagination, that of Greece exhibits a delicacy of workmanship which places it higher in the scale of poetic beauty.

> Look once more ere we leave this specular mount,
> Westward, much nearer by south-west; behold
> Where on the Ægean shore a city stands,

Built nobly, pure the air, and light the soil,
Athens, the eye of Greece, mother of arts
And eloquence, native to famous wits
Or hospitable, in her sweet recess,
City or suburban, studious walks and shades;
See there the olive grove of Academe,
Plato's retirement, where the Attic bird
Trills her thick-warbled notes the summer long;
There flow'ry hill Hymettus with the sound
Of bees' industrious murmur oft invites
To studious musing; there Ilissus rolls
His whispering stream.

The review of Grecian literature is condensed, systematic,
exact, and in it Satan shows himself to be a fine judge of values.

There thou shalt hear and learn the secret power
Of harmony, in tones and numbers hit
By voice or hand, and various-measured verse,
Aeolian charms and Dorian lyric odes,
And his who gave them breath, but higher sung,
Blind Melesigenes, thence Homer called,
Whose poem Phoebus challenged for his own.
Thence what the lofty grave Tragedians taught
In chorus or iambic, teachers best
Of moral prudence, with delight received,
In brief sententious precepts, while they treat
Of fate, and chance, and change in human life;
High actions and high passions best describing.
Thence to the famous Orators repair,
Those ancient, whose resistless eloquence
Wielded at will that fierce democraty,
Shook the Arsenal and fulmined over Greece,
To Macedon and Artaxerxes' throne.
To sage Philosophy next lend thine ear,
From heaven descended to the low-roofed house
Of Socrates; see there his tenement,
Whom, well inspired, the oracle pronounced
Wisest of men; from whose mouth issued forth
Mellifluous streams that watered all the schools
Of Academics old and new, with those
Surnamed Peripatetics, and the sect
Epicurean, and the Stoic severe.

What Satan here says of the poets is but a more carefully weighed rendering of the enthusiasm which Milton had expressed in his own person in Book VII of *Paradise Lost*. His judgment of the dramatists is identical with that of the Preface to *Samson Agonistes*. The characterisation of the orators has behind it the poet's acceptance of their achievement as the goal of his own endeavours in prose, for he, too, had tried to wield through words "a fierce democraty," and had, at least in *Areopagitica*, consciously sought to reproduce the eloquence of his ancient models. The account, finally, of the Greek philosophy is based not only on sound knowledge, but on devoted discipleship. Platonic thought, as we have seen, had been an all-powerful influence in shaping Milton's purposes in adolescence, and its basic principles remained central in the convictions of his maturity. If Satan praises Socrates, he is doing no more than Christ Himself, with a different emphasis, had already done. Stoicism also exerted an extraordinary fascination on Milton. Its metaphysics fell in with his pantheistic tendencies; its austere ethics were congenial to his temperament.

Satan, then, is pleading a cause which was, in one sense, already won. The difficulty, of course, is that Satan in offering the wisdom of the ancients offers it only on his own terms, as an instrument of ambition and without the corrective which the requirements of Milton's faith demanded. This corrective is supplied by Christ. His reply to Satan deserves careful analysis as containing the maturest expression of Milton's attitude toward an issue which had ever occupied the foreground of his thought. If the point of view seems partisan, it is only because here as elsewhere in *Paradise Regained* Milton has been obliged to divide his opinion against itself in order to give it a complete expression.

The central thesis of Christ's argument is identical with that of Raphael in his rebuke to Adam's curiosity in *Paradise Lost*. True wisdom is not to be sought by human means.

> . . . he who receives
> Light from above, from the Fountain of Light,
> No other doctrine needs, though granted true.

The Greek philosophers, representing the highest that man's intellect, unaided, can achieve, are after all but groping in the dark. Their teachings are at best—

> Conjectures, fancies, built on nothing firm.

Socrates, the wisest of them all, professed—

> To know this only, that he nothing knew.

Plato fell to fabling and "smooth conceits."

> The Stoic last in philosophic pride,
> By him called virtue; and his virtuous man,
> Wise, perfect in himself, and all possessing,
> Equal to God, oft shames not to prefer,
> As fearing God nor man, contemning all
> Wealth, pleasure, pain or torment, death and life,
> Which when he lists, he leaves, or boasts he can,
> For all his tedious talk is but vain boast,
> Or subtle shifts conviction to evade.

It is interesting to find Milton giving his chief attention to the refutation of the Stoic—sure proof that he was most attracted by it. Plato's fablings, once appealing as the ideal form of expression for philosophic truth, are easier for Milton to dismiss at this late stage of his development. Socrates remains for him the wisest of those who know, without true insight from above.

Denial of the validity of Greek thought is followed by an eloquent assertion of the claim of Hebrew literature. The hymns and psalms with which it is strewn are to all true taste more excellent than the poetry of Greece. The prophets are statesmen and orators divinely taught—

> and better teaching
> The solid rules of civil government
> In their majestic unaffected style,
> Than all the oratory of Greece and Rome.
> In them is plainest taught and easiest learnt,
> What makes a nation happy, and keeps it so,
> What ruins kingdoms, and lays cities flat;
> These only, with our Law, best form a king.

It is worth observing that Milton cannot bring himself to pronounce the arts of Greece quite valueless. He intimates that the Christ Himself is not unversed in them—

> Think not but that I know these things.

The Greek poets are confessed to express moral virtue—

> By light of nature not in all quite lost.

The ancient orators are

> statists indeed
> And lovers of their country, as may seem.

Milton thus saves himself from the full logic of his position. But the concession is a small one and we feel in the whole dialogue the deep and unreconciled breach between the two sides of the poet's experience, both of which he is compelled to assert, even though he makes use of the tongue of Satan to phrase an enthusiasm to which he cannot wholly give himself up.

This concludes Milton's interpretation of the second temptation. The poet has calmly surveyed the kingdoms of the earth and the glory of them. In themselves they are things indifferent and, when wisely used, capable of giving satisfaction; as substitute objects for spiritual good they are baits of Satan and to be condemned. Their hollowness is apparent to the eye of reason. Christ has proved Himself "superior and unmoved" by all that allures weak minds. He stands forth as the embodiment of right reason, the pattern and guide of human life. He is as Milton had willed to be in boyhood, and as, by a lifetime of self-discipline, according to the humanistic pattern, He had indeed become. But Milton's own victory is only of the mind— the mind which is its own place and can make a Heaven of Hell. The outward triumph of Christ, symbolised in the dramatic conclusion of the third temptation, has not been and will not be vouchsafed him. Satan, in the poem, baffled in all his arguments, goes about at last to try the way of violence. He snatches the Saviour up to a pinnacle of the temple and bids Him stand, if He can stand, or cast Himself down, "safely if Son of God." He plans to leave Christ no alternative but to tempt the Lord and in tempting disobey Him. For the pinnacle is a spire, where there is no standing. By divine grace, of which Satan in his fallen state knows nothing, a miracle is performed —unasked for, unanticipated, and involving no act of Christ in his own behalf. Satan's last attempt is foiled and he himself undergoes a second, an irrecoverable, fall. The scene, with all its implications, is one of the high moments of Milton's art, an English masterpiece of the baroque, analogous to great Italian painting.

> So saying, he caught him up, and, without wing
> Of hippogrif, bore through the air sublime,
> Over the wilderness and o'er the plain;

Till underneath them fair Jerusalem,
The Holy City, lifted high her towers,
And higher yet the glorious Temple reared
Her pile, far off appearing like a mount
Of alabaster, topt with golden spires:
There on the highest pinnacle he set
The Son of God, and added thus in scorn:
"There stand, if thou wilt stand; to stand upright
Will ask thee skill. I to thy Father's house
Have brought thee, and highest placed; highest is best.
Now show thy progeny; if not to stand,
Cast thyself down, safely, if Son of God;
For it is written, 'He will give command
Concerning thee to his Angels; in their hands
They shall uplift thee, lest at any time
Thou chance to dash thy foot against a stone.' "
To whom thus Jesus: "Also it is written,
'Tempt not the Lord thy God.' " He said, and stood:
But Satan, smitten with amazement, fell.

This brief but highly original treatment of the third temptation suggests the limits of our autobiographical interpretation of the poem. The poet loves the serenity of a victorious Christ, accepting the proof of His divinity as a matter of course, but the identification is an unstable one. *Effortless* victory over visible and invisible foes belongs for Milton to the realm of wish fulfilment. The contradictory drives of his own personality remain. The uninhibited projection of an inner world, still turbulent, could not or at least did not find a place in *Paradise Regained*. Milton needs a subject of identification different from either Christ or Satan. He found it in the Hebrew champion, Samson, blind among enemies and suffering from a deep sense of guilt, but struggling heroically and now granted a last opportunity to prove himself again God's chosen one.

The Milton which we see in *Samson Agonistes* is not, of course, unregenerate, not even psychologically unregenerate, but much in his nature that is suppressed or disguised or sublimated elsewhere in his work is here allowed to come to utterance. Samson is in a sense another Adam, but an Adam more completely abandoned to the warfare of the elements, more bitterly frustrated, more mature in suffering. The resolution of conflict, moreover, is on a different level from anything we have met elsewhere in Milton's work. There is no God from a machine. Samson accomplishes his restoration to favour by his own effort. He is dynamic even in bewailing his hard lot or confronting the image of his guilt. His final act, though felt to be divinely instigated, is yet an act of passion. Though the poem is religious, it is not right reason which triumphs, but the will of man. The purely human character of the materials, as Milton interpreted them, must have made this work uniquely satisfying. We shall see evidence that Milton consciously or unconsciously recognised the writing of it as having therapeutic value for himself.

It is important in this connection that the subject was not a new one in Milton's thought. In the list set down in the Trinity College manuscript shortly after his return from Italy, we find the titles of three plays dealing with various moments in the life of Samson: Samson Pursophorus or Hybristes, Samson Marrying or Ramath-Lechi, Dagonalia. The last would correspond in theme to the existing play. The story of Samson is more than once alluded to in the prose works in such a way as to show that it had become important for him as a symbol. In the *Reason of Church Government* the state and person of a king is likened to the mighty Nazarite Samson, "who being disciplined from his birth in the precepts and practices of temperance and sobriety, without the strong drink of injurious and excessive desires, grows up to a noble strength and perfection." More significantly, in a noble passage in *Areopagitica*, Milton for a moment visualises England under the image of Samson: "Methinks I see in my mind a noble and puissant nation rousing herself like a strong man after sleep and shaking her invincible locks." If Samson could stand for the state and person of a just monarch, he could also stand for England, free and potent. If he could stand for England, he could stand for Milton. In Samson's career as a champion of God's people he could see his own earlier heroic efforts in behalf of the good old cause. In the weakness which had betrayed him into the hands of a treacherous woman, he could read the causes of his own marriage disaster. The circumstances which surrounded his hero in blindness and captivity naturally associated themselves with the poet's immediate situation in the Restoration. The spiritual despair and the subsequent sense of God's favour represent an interpretaton of the Biblical personality in the light of his own deepest personal emotion.

Let us examine the drama somewhat carefully in order to see just how far Milton goes in stamping it with the impress of his own experience. In one sense Masson is right when he says that the poet has not strained the Biblical story of Samson's dying revenge for a personal purpose. Such transformation as he gives it is legitimate in art, is indeed the only condition on which an ancient motive can be rehandled with significance and power. Milton's use of the Samson story is parallel with Goethe's use of the legend of Faust.

The first scene shows Samson, blind and a captive, led forth by an attendant into the open air on the public holiday of the Philistines. The opening soliloquy is a meditation on his fate, rising gradually to a cry of woe as the full bitterness of his present situation, in contrast to his former happiness, comes home to him. There is nothing in Scripture to suggest the inwardness of Samson's thought. The simple folklore hero of the Bible tale is transformed at once into the spiritual image of his creator. Only the external circumstances remain, but of these not one is altered. Samson's mood as he comes on the stage is one of pure passivity and languor. He yields to the guiding hand which leads him on to a pleasant bank with choice of sun or shade. Escaped from the unwholesome prison draught, he feels a momentary relief in Heaven's breath—"Fresh blowing, pure and sweet, with day-spring born." So Milton, long in populous city pent, was wont to seek the country air; so, as Richardson reports, he used to sit in his garden to enjoy the sun.

But the thoughts which trouble him are not thus dissipated. There is "Ease to the body some, none to the mind." He reflects upon the superstitious Dagon worship of his enemies, to which cause he owes his day of rest. His mind revives the prophecy which attended his birth and early breeding—

> . . . ordered and prescribed
> As of a person separate to God,
> Designed for great exploits.

Clearly he stands in this as the counterpart of Milton's Christ, but his task of championship is cruder, and his endowment includes neither wisdom nor self-mastery. Milton himself stands somewhere between the two; he looks back on his early dreams with conflicting emotions. Has he, like Christ, fulfilled his spiritual destiny; or has he, like Samson, failed through weakness? The self-reproaches which Milton never allows himself to utter in his own person find free expression through the dramatic personality.

> Whom have I to complain of but myself?
> Who, this high gift of strength committed to me,
> In what part lodged, how easily bereft me,
> Under the seal of silence could not keep,
> But weakly to a woman must reveal it,
> O'ercome with importunity and tears?

Samson, like Adam, owes his fall to woman. His weakness is akin to that which Milton felt to be his own. But in the next lines the poet runs in haste away from the identification. Samson is not Adam, clear and strong in mind, but swayed to a wrong choice by passion. He is or has been rather the type of childish man, hence "liable to Fate by weakest subtleties," and acquiring self-knowledge only after the event. His mood prompts him to blame Providence as Adam had done, but he puts the thought aside and turns again to his present miseries—

> So many, and so huge, that each apart
> Would ask a life to wail.

The lines that follow are Milton's one untrammelled expression of rebellion at the fate which has deprived him of his sight. In his purely personal expressions in the sonnets, in *Paradise Lost*, in the *Second Defence*, there is always some consoling thought. Indeed, Milton allows himself the complaint only that he may show or lay hold upon his inward sources of happiness and strength. Here through the unreasoning voice of Samson he gives us the naked truth of his bitterest emotion.

> Blind among enemies, O worse than chains,
> Dungeon, or beggary, or decrepit age!

It is not the mere deprivation of objects of delight which affects him; it is more the sense of unwilling helplessness.

> Inferior to the vilest now become
> Of man or worm, the vilest here excel me;
> They creep, yet see; I, dark in light, exposed
> To daily fraud, contempt, abuse, and wrong.
> Within doors or without, still as a fool,
> In power of others, never in my own.

Surely we come close in this to Milton's own unchastened household morals. We recollect that his daughters attempted to cheat him in his marketings and that he did not in his dying hour forgive them.

But the poet stays only a moment on this weaker note. There is the grandeur of tragic feeling in what follows. It is the tone of Greek tragedy at its greatest, and the measure appropriately becomes irregular in imitation of the lyric parts of ancient drama.

> O dark, dark, dark, amid the blaze of noon,
> Irrecoverably dark, total eclipse
> Without all hope of day.

Samson invokes the light as Milton himself had done in *Paradise Lost*.

> O first-created Beam, and thou great Word,
> "Let there be light," and light was over all;

but without the sense of a compensatory irradiation of the spirit. The contrast is conscious and is pointed by the Chorus a few lines later.

> Thou art become, O worst imprisonment!
> The dungeon of thyself; thy soul,
> Which men enjoying sight oft without cause complain,
> Imprisoned now indeed,
> In real darkness of the body dwells,
> Shut up from outward light,
> To incorporate with gloomy night:
> For inward light, alas!
> Puts forth no visual beam.

Samson, then, is Milton as he might have been without the spiritual resources which he had built up within himself or, to put it differently, he is Milton in his moods of depression and vain rebelliousness.

The friendly company of Israelites, who make up the Chorus, approaches to console him. The question of his marriages is argued, and Samson defends, as coming from God, his choice of infidel women instead of those of his own tribe, but he returns to reproach himself for lack of manly firmness.

> The first I saw at Timna, and she pleased
> Me, not my parents, that I sought to wed
> The daughter of an Infidel. They knew not

That what I motioned was of God; I knew
From intimate impulse, and therefore urged
The marriage on, that by occasion hence
I might begin Israel's deliverance,
The work to which I was divinely called.
She proving false, the next I took to wife
O that I never had! fond wish too late!
Was in the vale of Sorec, Dalila,
That specious monster, my accomplished snare.
I thought it lawful from my former act,
And the same end, still watching to oppress
Israel's oppressors. Of what now I suffer
She was not the prime cause, but I myself,
Who, vanquished with a peal of words—O weakness!—
Gave up my fort of silence to a woman.

Samson's ethical discernment is now clear. Accepting the idea
of his own shortcomings, he yet refuses to accept responsibility
for the present servitude of Israel.

That fault I take not on me, but transfer
On Israel's governors, and heads of tribes,
Who, seeing those great acts which God had done
Singly by me against their conquerors,
Acknowledged not, or not at all considered,
Deliverance offered. I, on the other side,
Used no ambition to commend my deeds;
The deeds themselves, though mute, spoke loud the doer.
But they persisted deaf, and would not seem
To count them things worth notice.

In this passage we are again very close to Milton. The failure
of the Israelites to maintain the freedom which has been won
for them is obviously parallel to the return of the English
through their own perverseness into slavery. The more personal
thought that he himself has been an instrument of God's
proposed deliverance is also Milton's, though he never, except
here in dramatic form, allows it to come so frankly to expression.
Certainly he had liked to fancy himself a single-handed
champion, rushing unarmed into the combat; bearing glorious
witness to the truth, and failing of his mission only because the
leaders of his nation had failed to recognise him as one whom
God had raised by special favour to be their guide. The case

for autobiographical interpretation of Samson's words is made
the clearer by the absence of any such conception in the Bible
story. Milton has carried over into the interpretation of the
simple Israelite his own messianic conviction, making him
generalise, as Christ Himself had generalised, on the fate of
corrupt nations fallen and the ingratitude of the common herd
toward those who toil to free them from their bonds.

> But what more oft in nations grown corrupt,
> And by their vices brought to servitude,
> Than to love bondage more than liberty,
> Bondage with ease than strenuous liberty;
> And to despise, or envy, or suspect,
> Whom God hath of his special favour raised
> As their deliverer? If he aught begin,
> How frequent to desert him, and at last
> To heap ingratitude on worthiest deeds.

Out of such thoughts there comes to Samson something of a
renewal of faith. God's work goes on, though his is done. The
Chorus responds to his conviction and asserts against vain
reasoning the justice of God's ways with men. The whole
episode thus becomes evidence of Samson's spiritual strength,
and constitutes a first step in the final proving of his faith.
The visit of Manoa makes this theme still clearer. We may,
without too much straining, consider the dialogue as an
imaginary one between Milton and his parent. Manoa laments
the miserable change which has come upon his son. His deep
disappointment takes the form of a complaint against God's
providence.

> Oh, wherefore did God grant me my request,
> And as a blessing with such pomp adorned?
> Why are his gifts desirable, to tempt
> Our earnest prayers, then, giv'n with solemn hand
> As graces, draw a scorpion's tail behind?
> For this did the Angel twice descend? for this
> Ordained thy nurture holy, as of a plant
> Select and sacred, glorious for a while,
> The miracle of men; then in an hour
> Ensnared, assaulted, overcome, led bound,
> Thy foes' derision, captive, poor and blind,
> Into a dungeon thrust to work with slaves?

> Alas! methinks whom God hath chosen once
> To worthiest deeds, if he through frailty err,
> He should not so o'erwhelm, and as a thrall
> Subject him to so foul indignities,
> Be it but for honour's sake of former deeds.

Samson's reply is a new analysis of his weakness in the past, a more complete acknowledgment of the part this weakness has played in the present triumph of the Philistine god, and a more convinced assertion that, though the strife with him hath end, Jehovah will bring upon Dagon—

> Such a discomfit, as shall quite despoil him
> Of all these boasted trophies won on me,
> And with confusion blank his worshippers.

In all this Samson is doing what Milton never did but what it was in his heart to do. The drama thus becomes his unconscious confessional. His clear self-knowledge raises him above the timid parent and makes him proof against his anxiety and overzeal. Manoa, like the Chorus, feels for a moment the uplifting force of Samson's faith, but he misguidedly endeavours to cheer him with plans for submission and escape. The result is a renunciation of all hope of personal happiness, and a final expression of spiritual desolation. It is no longer the outward fact of blindness which engages him, but the inner agony which is working like a poison in his heart. The utterance relieves him and prepares him for the recovery of energy and purpose. In the choric comment with which this scene closes, Milton philosophises on the wretched state of man. The opening lines contain the record of his fruitless endeavour to achieve serenity through the human wisdom of the ancients.

> Many are the sayings of the wise,
> In ancient and in modern books enrolled,
> Extolling patience as the truest fortitude;
> And to the bearing well of all calamities,
> All chances incident to man's frail life,
> Consolatories writ
> With studied argument, and much persuasion sought,
> Lenient of grief and anxious thought:
> But with the afflicted in his pangs their sound
> Little prevails, or rather seems a tune
> Harsh and of dissonant mood from his complaint,

> Unless he feels within
> Some source of consolation from above,
> Secret refreshings, that repair his strength,
> And fainting spirits uphold.

In the remainder of the passage he turns his thought again to the baffling problem of God's uneven dealings with His creatures.

> God of our fathers, what is Man!
> That thou towards him with hand so various,
> Or might I say contrarious,
> Temper'st thy providence through his short course,
> Not evenly, as thou rul'st
> The angelic orders and inferior creatures mute,
> Irrational and brute?
> Nor do I name of men the common rout,
> That wandering loose about
> Grow up and perish, as the summer fly,
> Heads without name no more remembered,
> But such as thou hast solemnly elected,
> With gifts and graces eminently adorned
> To some great work, thy glory,
> And people's safety, which in part they effect:
> Yet toward these, thus dignified, thou oft,
> Amidst their highth of noon,
> Changest thy countenance and thy hand, with no regard
> Of highest favours past
> From thee on them, or them to thee of service.
>   Nor only dost degrade them, or remit
> To life obscured, which were a fair dismission,
> But throw'st them lower than thou didst exalt them high,
> Unseemly falls in human eye,
> Too grievous for the trespass or omission;
> Oft leav'st them to the hostile sword
> Of heathen and profane, their carcasses
> To dogs and fowls a prey, or else captived:
> Or to the unjust tribunals, under change of times,
> And condemnation of the ingrateful multitude.
> If these they scape, perhaps in poverty
> With sickness and disease thou bow'st them down,
> Painful diseases and deformed,
> In crude old age;

> Though not disordinate, yet causeless suff'ring
> The punishment of dissolute days, in fine,
> Just or unjust, alike seem miserable,
> For oft alike both come to evil end.

We may note the gradual narrowing of these generalisations to the poet's individual case. The phrases—"unjust tribunals under change of times," "their carcasses to dogs and fowls a prey"—suggest the fate which had come upon Milton's friends, but which he had himself escaped. Disease and poverty are the worst misfortunes on which he himself had fallen. He goes so far as almost to specify the rheumatic ills from which we know him to have suffered—

> Painful diseases and deformed,
> In crude old age.

The thought that such afflictions, ordinarily the fruit of dissipation, have come to him in spite of a life of exemplary temperance makes his sense of injustice the more acute. We recollect how ardently he had maintained the idea that his blindness was not a punishment for sin but a special mark of the divine favour. It was more difficult to rationalise the gout, and besides, the energy for such compensatory thought was failing.

What Milton yearns for is such restoration of his powers as might come with new opportunities to prove them. Events now unexpectedly bring such opportunity to Samson. He is visited by Dalila and shows himself no longer subject to her wiles. The exhibition of firmness before this particular temptation supplements the ordered triumphs of *Paradise Regained*, where Satan, it will be remembered, rejected the bait of sex as a possible mode of attracting Christ. It is characteristic of Milton that he cannot represent his hero as victorious over his "accomplished snare" save by making him harsh and hostile. She dreams for him, with apparent sincerity, a picture of domestic ease, to be attained through her affection and assistance.

> Though sight be lost,
> Life yet hath many solaces, enjoyed
> Where other senses want not their delights,
> At home, in leisure and domestic ease,
> Exempt from many a care and chance to which
> Eyesight exposes daily men abroad.

I to the Lords will intercede, not doubting
Their favourable ear, that I may fetch thee
From forth this loathsome prison-house, to abide
With me, where my redoubled love and care,
With nursing diligence, to me glad office,
May ever tend about thee to old age.

It is just such tenderness that Samson, knowing himself, most
fears. His distrust is too deep-rooted and he minces no words in
his reply.

I know thy trains,
Though dearly to my cost, thy gins, and toils.
Thy fair enchanted cup and warbling charms
No more on me have power, their force is nulled;
So much of adder's wisdom I have learnt,
To fence my ear against thy sorceries.
If in my flower of youth and strength, when all men
Loved, honoured, feared me, thou alone could hate me,
Thy husband, slight me, sell me, and forgo me;
How would'st thou use me now, blind, and thereby
Deceivable, in most things as a child
Helpless, thence easily contemned, and scorned,
And last neglected? How would'st thou insult,
When I must live uxorious to thy will
In perfect thraldom.

There is new light here on Milton's attitude toward women.
His two successful marriages have done nothing to wipe away
the memory of his earlier experience, and no wonder when the
living daughters are with him to perpetuate it. The Chorus,
as usual, generalises and points the moral. It is Milton's harshest
expression of the doctrine of male domination, already formulated in its milder form in *Paradise Lost*. There is a strange
perversity of thought in the suggestion that the man is better
proved by his sternness in quelling domestic rebellion than
amid the expanding affection of a happy clime.

Favoured of Heav'n who finds
One virtuous, rarely found,
That in domestic good combines:
Happy that house! his way to peace is smooth;
But virtue which breaks through all opposition,
And all temptation can remove,
Most shines and most is acceptable above.

Therefore God's universal law
Gave to the man despotic power
Over his female in due awe,
Nor from that right to part an hour,
Smile she or lour:
So shall he least confusion draw
On his whole life, not swayed
By female usurpation, nor dismayed.

The verbal quelling of Harapha, the boaster, is easy after this more subtle victory. It is as if Milton were face to face with a new Salmasius and, confident of his powers, asks only for the opportunity to exhibit them in battle. In the command to appear at the feast of the Philistines such an opportunity draws near. Without understanding why, Samson feels "some rousing motions" in him. His day of despondency is over, and he goes forth to action, with the renewed sense of God's guidance, though without expectation or desire of personal happiness or continuance. The literal parallels of biographical incident end at this point. The consummation vouchsafed to Samson was destined, as Milton well knew, to be denied to him. The drama becomes, then, in its central incident a last imaginative gratification of the poet's will to power.

The mingled mood of acquiescence and of exultation at the close is the fruit of Milton's successful transference of his emotions to the person of his dramatic hero. When the messenger has told the story of Samson's death, the Chorus interprets it as a fulfilment of God's purposes in him.

O dearly-bought revenge, yet glorious!
Living or dying, thou hast fulfilled
The work for which thou wast foretold
To Israel.

The triumph is the more complete because of its unexpectedness.

But he, though blind of sight,
Despised, and thought extinguished quite,
With inward eyes illuminated,
His fiery virtue roused
From under ashes into sudden flame,

. . . . . .

> So Virtue, given for lost,
> Depressed and overthrown, . . .
> Revives, reflourishes, then vigorous most
> When most unactive deemed.

The deed of Samson, though it has involved his death, is without taint of sin: he lies among his slain—

> . . . self-killed
> Not willingly, but tangled in the fold
> Of dire Necessity, whose law in death conjoined
> Thee with thy slaughtered foes.

Neither the spirit nor the reception of the act is Christian. If Milton had accepted for himself the lot of those who only stand and wait, he had done so against his nature. His imagination envisages another kind of ending to his career: death on the field of action amid the applause of multitudes. It is Manoa, the father, who pronounces Samson's fitting elegy.

> Come, come, no time for lamentation now,
> Nor much more cause: Samson hath quit himself
> Like Samson, and heroicly hath finish'd
> A life heroic, on his enemies
> Fully revenged, hath left them years of mourning,
> And lamentation to the sons of Caphtor
> Through all Philistian bounds. To Israel
> Honour hath left and freedom, let but them
> Find courage to lay hold on this occasion;
> To himself and father's house eternal fame;
> And, which is best and happiest yet, all this,
> With God not parted from him, as was feared,
> But favouring and assisting to the end.
> Nothing is here for tears, nothing to wail
> Or knock the breast; no weakness, no contempt,
> Dispraise, or blame; nothing but well and fair,
> And what may quiet us in a death so noble.

The drama closes on the note of faith. Samson's story has shown again the sureness of God's purposes, the justice of His ways to men. What, we may ask, has the writing of it done for Milton and how has it left him for the three or four or five years he still had to live? Discussing this question many years ago, I pointed out the importance which Milton attaches to the

I

CA-
THARSIS

Aristotelian formula of catharsis or emotional purgation as the effect of tragedy, and the richness of his interpretation of this brilliant and suggestive idea. He quotes an abbreviation of the definition of tragedy on his title page: "Tragedy is the imitation of a serious action . . . through pity and fear effecting a purgation of such emotions." He elaborates the "homœopathic" theory of Mintorno in the prefatory statement: "Nor is nature wanting in her own effects to make good his assertion, for so, in physic, things of melancholic hue and quality are used against melancholy, sour against sour, salt to remove salt humours." Finally, he alludes to the doctrine, both directly and by implication, in the play. Obviously, the matter was of much concern to him. The reason for this concern is, I believe, the exceptional intensity of his experience, in this the most personal of his works, of the liberating effect of art.

In considering Milton's deliberate interpretation of the principle, we must observe, first of all, that, by representing a clearly marked triumph of the human will over its own weakness, and by the substitution of Providence for blind fate as the power which overrules the action, *Samson Agonistes* provides material for a different understanding of catharsis from that contemplated by Aristotle, an understanding which falls in with the first part of Milton's description—that tragedy is the gravest, moralest, and most profitable of poetic forms—rather than with the last—that it transforms painful emotions into pleasurable. On a superficial view we might, indeed, be tempted to regard the purgation, as Milton actually worked it out, as a purely ethical and religious process, the result of a consciously didactic purpose by which our faith is strengthened and our sympathy with Samson's pain swallowed up in our exultation in his triumph. It is the function of Manoa's last speech and of the final chorus to emphasise this idea.

> All is best, though we oft doubt,
> What the unsearchable dispose
> Of highest wisdom brings about,
> And ever best found in the close.

To some critics such expressions have seemed an adequate critical formula for the poem, and a mark of the failure of *Samson Agonistes* to embody the genuinely tragic motive of the unsuccessful struggle of man with fate. Such a judgment fails to take account of the actuality of the tragic impression which the drama must leave upon every reader who comes to it unhampered by definitions and comparisons. The pain of the earlier scenes is something which cannot be so easily displaced. Sealed as it is with the hero's death, it outlives all consolation, as the tragic suffering of Hamlet outlives the accomplishment of his purpose, the choric benediction of Horatio, and the restoration of a wholesome commonwealth by Fortinbras. The pronouncement "All is best" is of scarcely more avail than the identical formulæ which bring Greek plays to their conclusion and from which this one is derived. The consolation which is offered of "What can quiet us in a death so noble" is not enough. Samson should have gone on from one glad triumph to another and emerged unscathed. Outward circumstance, the treacheries of others, and his own conspiring fault have brought him low, and have constrained him to wear, however gloriously, the crown of martyrdom. Here surely is tragedy enough. Though Providence is proclaimed, its ways are dark, and its face, at times, is hardly to be distinguished from the countenance of Fate herself. The secret is that there remains an irreducible element in the midst of Milton's faith—a sense as keen as Shakespeare's of the reality of suffering which neither the assurance of God's special favours to himself nor his resolute insistence on the final triumph of his righteousness can blot out. The antique strain in Milton's experience and thought stands side by side with the Christian, and the two alternate or combine in their domination of his artistic moods. It is in vain that he repudiates stoicism as a futile refuge and a false philosophy; he is betrayed by the vehemence of his declarations against it, and he instinctively adopts its weapons.

These considerations return us to catharsis in its psychological and æsthetic sense. Milton's effort to demonstrate in his drama the truth of Aristotle's pronouncement is obviously part and parcel of a thorough-going conscious classicism, which extends far beyond such matters as the ordering of the incidents and the employment of ancient devices like the messenger. It is shown in a more philosophic and intrinsic way in the subtle turns which the poet gives to the interpretation of his theme in order to bring it more nearly into conformity with the spirit of ancient tragedy. Professor Baum counts it a major defect of *Samson Agonistes* that the hero's tragic fault is undignified and sub-heroic. But observe the means which Milton takes to dignify it. He associates it with the most dignified of all tragic faults—

rebellious pride. Intoxicated by success, Samson forgets
to refer his victories to their source, and so becomes, in Milton's
interpretation, an instance of classical hybris. Like Shakespeare's Mark Antony he "struts to his destruction."

> Fearless of danger, like a petty God
> I walked about, admired of all and dreaded
> On hostile ground, none daring my affront.
> Then, swoll'n with pride, into the snare I fell
> Of fair fallacious looks, venereal trains.

This is somewhat forced, one must confess, and Milton appears
to be aware of it. Witness the shading he is compelled to give
to the idea in the following:

> But I God's counsel have not kept, his holy secret
> Presumptuously have published, impiously,
> *Weakly at least, and shamefully*; a sin
> That Gentiles in their parables condemn
> To their Abyss and horrid pains confined.

The cloak of Prometheus and Tantalus evidently refuses to fit
the less majestic Hebrew Titan. The conception of hybris and
Ate applies more perfectly to the Philistines and is accordingly
invoked in the triumphant semi-chorus beginning in line 1669.

> While their hearts were jocund and sublime,
> Drunk with idolatry, drunk with wine,
> And fat regorged of bulls and goats,
> Chaunting their idol, and preferring
> Before our living Dread who dwells
> In Silo his bright sanctuary:
> Among them he a spirit of frenzy sent,
> Who hurt their minds,
> And urged them on with mad desire
> To call in haste for their destroyer;
> They, only set on sport and play,
> Unweetingly importuned
> Their own destruction to come speedy upon them.
> So fond are mortal men,
> Fallen into wrath divine,
> As their own ruin on themselves to invite,
> Insensate left, or to sense reprobate,
> And with blindness internal struck.

Both passages, however, are illustrative of the degree to which Milton had grasped the central motive of Greek tragedy and the pains he was at to bring his own material under the ethical, religious, and artistic formulæ afforded by it.

But the profounder aspect of his relation to his ancient models is his ability to appropriate the inner agony of Greek tragedy in its darkest moments, and it is in so doing that he must have felt within himself the reality of the Aristotelian purgation and the need of it. The question of the means whereby affliction may be soothed is one which had always interested him, and his works contain numerous suggestive utterances on the subject. It is prominent in the discussion of the case of Samson. Thus, in the passage already quoted, he makes the Chorus tell how useless for the sufferer in his pangs are those wise consolations of philosophy, "writ with studied argument, lenient of grief and anxious thought." It is only, they affirm, by "secret refreshings from above" that the afflicted wretch can be restored. But such refreshings are obviously not always to be commanded. To prepare for their benign influence the mind must first be emptied of its pent-up bitterness, and for such a process tragedy, in the Aristotelian conception, supplies the means. So, one would suppose, might Milton have thought and felt. And if such was his experience, it is not surprising that he should have dwelt with such insistence on the rationale of the process in his prose Preface. Pity, fear, and like passions are in their raw state dangerous and painful. They may be tempered and reduced to just measure by the pleasurable intensity of art.

Very significant is the use of the medical analogy in an outstanding passage in the play itself. Samson has just expressed his indifference to the efforts proposed in his behalf and his expectation of an early death. Manoa's reply—

> Believe not these suggestions, which proceed
> From anguish of the mind, and humours black,
> That mingle with thy fancy,

wrings from him the most unmitigated expression of his spiritual woe.

> O that torment should not be confined
> To the body's wounds and sores,
> With maladies innumerable
> In heart, head, breast, and reins;

But must secret passage find
To the inmost mind,
There exercise all his fierce accidents,
And on her purest spirits prey,
As on entrails, joints, and limbs,
With answerable pains, but more intense,
Though void of corporal sense.
My griefs not only pain me
As a lingering disease,
But, finding no redress, ferment and rage,
Nor less than wounds immedicable
Rankle, and fester, and gangrene,
To black mortification.
Thoughts, my tormentors, armed with deadly stings,
Mangle my apprehensive tenderest parts,
Exasperate, exulcerate, and raise
Dire inflammation, which no cooling herb
Or medcinal liquor can assuage,
Nor breath of vernal air from snowy Alp.
Sleep hath forsook and given me o'er
To death's benumbing opium as my only cure.
Thence faintings, swoonings of despair,
And sense of Heav'n's desertion.

The idea which Milton here develops with somewhat shocking explicitness is obviously the same as that which underlies his conception of catharsis—the idea, namely, that the passions operate in precisely the manner of bodily poisons, which, when they find no outlet, rage destructively within. Samson is given over to pity and fear, and there is no apparent prospect of relief, no cooling herb or medicinal liquor to purify the "black mortification" of his thoughts. It is quite clear, then, that Milton intends to suggest an Aristotelian diagnosis of Samson's tragic state, parallel to the more obvious religious interpretation which I have previously expounded. But if he partly identified himself with his hero, then such a diagnosis would serve also to that extent to describe his own. As, however, he draws a sharp distinction on the religious side between Samson's spiritual darkness and his own illumination by an inner light, so here he must have been conscious of a difference in the manner of their deliverance from the morbid introspection to which they are equally subject. The intensity of Samson's pain lasts only so long as he remains inactive. His lyric elaboration of his inward woe is immediately followed by the unexpected visits of his foes. His attention is thus distracted from his suffering to a series of situations which confront him and he finally loses himself in glorious though disastrous action.

Milton himself is enrolled perforce among those "whom patience finally must crown." But he has in his possession a recourse without which the way of patience is at times too hard. The purgation which the untutored champion of Israel must find in deeds is available to the man of culture through the activity of the mind and spirit. It offers itself to Milton in a dual form, corresponding to his twofold inheritance from the Reformation and the Renaissance. As the play draws to an end the two motives are subtly balanced and as nearly reconciled as, perhaps, it is within the power of human skill to reconcile them. The champion's final deed and the triumph of God's uncontrollable intent promote in us a sense of exultation and confirm our faith, but the greatness of his suffering and the pathos of his death produce a different effect, making possible the serene dismission of the close.

> His servants he, with new acquist
> Of true experience from this great event,
> With peace and consolation hath dismissed,
> And calm of mind, all passion spent.

These are Milton's last words written under the inspiration of the Heavenly Muse. They suggest a finality of artistic and personal achievement which would have been lacking at the conclusion of his other works.

CHAPTER NINE

FAIR DISMISSION

1670–4

THE FINAL FLARE-UP OF creative energy in *Samson Agonistes*, whether it came immediately on the completion of *Paradise Regained* or after an interval of one or more years, occurs in a period of increasing relaxation in Milton's life. His great tasks were finished; his poetic plans fulfilled with a satisfying completeness. What was left to do, if he were to present his true account and depart unchidden, must have seemed less pressing. Actually, there was an unexpected amount of achievement, not all of it by any means of a routine character, and though the record is one of relative placidity, the display of personality is as Miltonic as ever. The tone and temper of these years impresses us as artistically coherent with the total portrait of a designed career.

Taking, then, the year 1670, four before his death, as the moment in which we are to attempt to envisage Milton in his last phase, we may look first at his immediate personal environment and his routine of life. He is sixty-one years old and in fair health. He lives in a settled home in a familiar neighbourhood, with his wife of thirty, one female servant, and perhaps a man. The house is quiet and well kept. There are plenty of visitors and some literary helpers. The poet's days are still spent in dictating and being read to, in meditating and walking abroad, in singing and playing the organ, in conversation and in exercise. The detail of this picture is filled in by the contemporary biographers. Except for Phillips, who remembered vividly the impressions of his early life, their intimate information is pretty much confined to the period of the great poems and the years that followed. John Aubrey knew Milton personally, but only after about 1650. He was, however, inquisitive of gossip and he ran about after the poet's death interviewing various informants, notably the widow. His fragmentary notes of what he was told bring us closer to Milton than Wood's reprocessing of them in his formal biography. Jonathan Richardson collected fewer facts, but he had a journalistic gift similar to Boswell's and his anecdotes about Milton in old age are unforgettable. The mysterious writer, finally, of the biography found among Wood's papers knew Milton as an understanding friend and speaks with unimpeachable authority of certain aspects of his personality. I quote from the testimony of these witnesses without attempting to make an exact chronological assignment of the information which they give about Milton's daily life. What is said specifically of poetic composition may be true also of other literary work. The writers were naturally most interested in circumstances having a bearing on his art.

The Anonymous Biographer

He rendered his studies and various works more easy and pleasant by allotting them their several portions of the day. Of these the time friendly to the muses fell to his poetry; and he waking early (as is the use of temperate men) had commonly a good stock of verses ready against his amanuensis came, which, if it happened to be later than ordinary, he would complain, saying "he wanted to be milked." The evenings he likewise spent in reading some choice poets, by way of refreshment after the day's toil, and to store his fancy against the morning.

Edward Phillips

All the time of writing his *Paradise Lost*, his vein began at the autumnal equinoctial, and ceased at the vernal, (or thereabouts, I believe about May).

John Aubrey

He was very healthy, and free from all diseases, only toward his later end he was visited with the gout, spring and fall; he would be cheerful even in his gout fits and sing.

He was an early riser, *scil.* at 4 o'clock *mane*, yea, after he lost his sight. He had a man read to him. The first thing he read was the Hebrew Bible, and that was at 4 h. *mane* $\frac{1}{2}$ h—. Then he contemplated. At 7 his man came to him again, and then read to him and wrote till dinner; the writing was as much as the reading. . . . After dinner he used to walk three or four hours at a time (he always had a garden where he lived): went to bed about 9. Temperate man, rarely drank between meals. Extreme pleasant in his conversation, and at dinner, supper, etc., but satirical.

He had a delicate, tuneable voice, and had good skill. . . . He had an organ in his house; he played on that most.

Jonathan Richardson

Other stories I have heard concerning the posture he was usually in when he dictated, that he sat leaning backward obliquely in an easy chair, with his leg flung over the elbow of it, that he frequently composed lying in bed in a morning ('twas winter sure then). I have been well informed, that when he could not sleep, but lay awake whole nights, he tried; not one verse could he make; at other times flowed "easy his unpremeditated verse," with a certain *impetus* and *aestro*, as himself seemed to believe. I have also been told he would dictate many, perhaps 40 lines as it were in a breath, and then reduce them to half the number. After he was blind he used a swing for exercise.

Music he loved extremely and understood well. 'Tis said that he composed but nothing of that has been brought down to us. He diverted himself with performing which they say he did well on the organ and base viol. And this was a great relief to him after he lost his sight. . . . Temperance was with him a favourite virtue. . . . Milton was not nice, but took what was set before him. All kinds of strong liquors he hated.

Other gleanings are that "he made his nephews songsters," that he could himself bear a part in vocal music, that he wore a sword with a silver hilt while he had his sight and was skilled in using it. "He was of a moderate stature and well proportioned, light brown (auburn) hair, and handsomest features." His latest visitor, a Dr. Wright, quoted by Richardson, found him in a small house, "up one pair of stairs, sitting in an elbow chair, black clothes, and neat enough, pale but not cadaverous, his hands and fingers gouty and with chalkstones." Among the pleasantries which were remembered of him was the remark on hearing a lady sing finely: "Now I swear this lady is handsome." Dryden remembered that he pronounced the letter "r" very hard, "a certain sign of a satirical wit," and Richardson tells the story of his amusing himself at the expense of a "very honest silly fellow" who was a zealous and constant follower of one of the nonconforming sects.

When he came from the meeting his master would frequently ask him what he had heard and divert himself with ridiculing their fooleries, or, it may be, the poor fellow's understanding; both one and 'tother probably. However, this was so grievous to the good creature that he left his service upon it.

The net impression of all this is clear enough. Milton was living patiently and on the whole enjoyably after his retirement.

The harsher strain in him was in abeyance; he had great charm and was capable both of affection and geniality but sometimes showed himself lacking in the milk of human kindness. He is not at all like an embittered and self-reproaching Samson, blind among enemies, but resembles rather a retired general or statesman who has known the excitement of triumph and defeat and is resigned to let things take their course while he winds up his commitments, courts relief from boredom with women and servants, and talks with persons interested in what he has done and known. The lines of this picture deepen when we look further at his personal environment in its latest aspect and record the remaining achievements of his career.

The "ungrateful daughters" Milton had by Mary Powell are off the scene, pursuing the trade of lace-making and perhaps communicating oftener with the Powell family than with the Miltons. The factional warfare is open and undisguised but relatively harmless, now that there is separate residence and a divorce of mutual responsibility. Milton's implacability may not actually be as great as it seems, and a tactful friend of both parties might conceivably have brought them together. There is good reason for thinking that the youngest daughter, Deborah, was less alienated from her father than the others; it is possible, indeed, to think of her as relatively uninjured by the broken family situation and of maintaining an affectionate relationship with her father till his death. Aubrey says that "he taught her Latin and she was his amanuensis." If this is true, it must have been after Milton had tried and failed to use his other daughters, and probably after the period of *Paradise Lost*, for Deborah was only eight years old in 1660. Of more importance than this statement are the various scraps of evidence tending to show that Deborah was on good terms with Milton's widow and that she retained warm memories of her father. Unlike the other daughters, she received from Mrs. Milton as administratrix of the estate not only the £100 which the law had apportioned to her, but "several goods of the said John Milton deceased," including, as we happen to know, his private seal. When "discovered" and visited by Addison and others in the eighteenth century, she spoke of her father with reverence and fondness. The story told by Richardson of her discrimination in the matter of the portraits which were shown her sounds authentic and is in substance confirmed by George Vertue. "The picture in crayons I have of him [i.e. the Faithorne drawing]," says Richardson, "was shown her after several others, or which were pretended to be his. When these were shown, and she was asked if she could recollect, if she had ever seen such a face *No, No*; but when this was produced, in a transport, '*Tis my father*, '*Tis my dear father, I see him, 'tis him*, and then she put her hands to several parts of her face, '*Tis the very man! here, here*."

In confirming the story that Milton employed his daughters in reading languages which they did not understand, she appears to have borne no resentment. She quoted his caustic remark that "one tongue was enough for a woman," and re-peated verses from Homer, Ovid, and particularly Euripides. Masson infers from Phillips that Deborah was "sent out" with Anne and Mary to learn the craft of lace-making or em-broidery, and he assumes that none of the daughters was in Milton's household after 1670. She may, however, have remained longer than the others under his roof. We know only that she was in Ireland at the time of his death, in the capacity of a companion to a lady named Merian and was there married to Abraham Clarke, a weaver or silk merchant.

At least two other members of the poet's family continued to be in more or less intimate relationship with him after his third marriage—namely his brother Christopher and Edward Phillips. Both took a certain amount of responsibility and were apparently relied on in practical matters. Whether Milton liked or approved of them is another matter. Our chief evidence of the part played by Christopher in Milton's later life is to be found in the will proceeding initiated by the widow with his help immediately after the poet's death. The court record of these proceedings, from which quotation has already been made, takes us inside the Milton household in a most remark-able way. Here is the memorandum of the verbal will itself, dated November 23rd, 1674, and signed by the servant, Elizabeth Fisher:

MEMORANDUM, that John Milton, late of the parish of St. Giles Cripplegate in the County of Middlesex, Gentle-man, deceased, at several times before his death, and in particular on or about the twentieth day of July, in the year of our Lord God, 1674, being of perfect mind and memory, declared his Will and intent as to the disposal of his estate after his death, in these words following, or of like effect:

"The portion due to me from Mr. Powell, my former wife's father, I leave to the unkind children I had by her, having received no part of it; but my meaning is, they shall have no other benefit of my estate than the said portion, and what I have besides done for them; they having been very undutiful to me. All the residue of my estate I leave to the disposal of Elizabeth, my loving wife." Which words, or to the same effect, were spoken in the presence of Christopher Milton.

X (Mark of) Elizabeth Fisher.

This document was exhibited to the Prerogative Court in an allegation of Elizabeth Milton against Mary, Anne, and Deborah on December 2nd. Depositions of Christopher Milton, Elizabeth Fisher, and her sister, Mary, were taken on December 5th and 15th respectively, and these witnesses were cross-examined, according to a set of interrogatories drawn up in the interest of the daughters. These allegations, interrogatories, depositions, and cross-examinations are preserved. Among the more significant questions to be asked are the following:

3. *Item*, Upon what occasion did the deceased declare the said Will? Was not the deceased in perfect health at the same time? Do you not think that the deceased, if he declared any such Will, declared it in a present passion, or some angry humour against some or one of his children by his former (first) wife?

4. *Item*, Ask each witness, whether the parties ministrant were not and are not great frequenters of the Church, and good livers; and what cause of displeasure had the deceased against them?

5. *Item*, Ask Mr. (Christopher) Milton and each other witness whether the deceased's Will, if any such was made, was not that the deceased's wife should have £1,000, and the children of the said Christopher Milton the residue; and whether she hath not promised him that they should have it if she prevailed in this cause? Whether the said Mr. Milton hath not since the deceased's death confessed so much, or some part thereof?

6. *Item*, Ask each witness whether what is left to the ministrants by the said Will is not reputed a very bad or altogether desperate debt?

7. *Item*, Ask the said Mr. Milton whether he did not get the said Will drawn up and inform the writer to what effect he should draw it? And did he not enquire of the other witnesses what they would or could depose? And whether he hath not solicited this Cause and payed fees to the Proctor about it?

8. *Item*, Ask each witness what fortune the deceased did in his lifetime bestow on the ministrants? And whether the said Anne Milton is not lame and almost helpless?

The testimony of Milton's maidservant has already been quoted in part as suggestive of family tension at the time of Milton's third marriage. A further item from her statement may refer to a still earlier period. To the fourth interrogation, "what cause of displeasure had the deceased against them," she answers, quoting a former servant, "that all his said children did combine together and counsel his maidservant to cheat him (the deceased) in her marketings, and that his said children had made away some of his books and would have sold the rest to the dunghill woman, or he the said deceased spoke words to the self-same effect and purpose." Presumably Elizabeth Milton took over the marketings, and Milton, as we learn from Phillips, later negotiated the sale of his own library. It was only the memory of such injuries that remained to implement the case against the daughters' heritage.

What the facts were we cannot tell, nor can we be certain that the obviously partisan testimony of the maidservant fairly represented Milton's words and attitude. What does come out of the proceedings is a convicting picture of the atmosphere of the Milton home and of the relationship of Christopher with his brother and his brother's wife, when he himself is a busy solicitor and the poet a man composed in his retirement, but not well and perhaps already aware that he had not many years to live. Christopher Milton in his deposition of December 5th gives the following circumstantial account of what must have been his last visit to the poet:

That on or about the twentieth day of July, 1674, the day certain he now remembreth not, this deponent being a practicer in the law and a Bencher in the Inner Temple, but living in vacations at Ipswich, did usually at the end of the Term visit John Milton, his this deponent's brother, the testator articulate, deceased, before his going home; and so at the end of midsummer term last past, he this deponent went to visit his said brother and then found him in his chamber within his own house, situate on Bunhill within the parish of St. Giles, Cripplegate, London; and at that time, he the said testator, being not well, (and this deponent being then going into the country,) in a serious manner, with an intent, (as he believes,) that what he then spoke should be his Will, if he died before his this deponent's coming the next time to London, declared his Will in these very words as near as this deponent can now call to mind. Viz., "Brother, the portion due to me from Mr. Powell, my former (first) wife's father, I leave to the unkind children I had by her; but I have received no part of it, and my Will and meaning is, they shall have no other benefit of my estate than the said portion and what I have besides done for them, they having been very undutiful to me. And all the residue of my estate I leave to the disposal of Elizabeth, my loving wife." She, the said Elizabeth, his the deceased's wife, and Elizabeth Fisher, his the deceased's then maidservant, was at the same time going up and down the room, but whether she then heard the said deceased so declare his will as above or not, he knoweth not.

Replying to the interrogations, Christopher recalled that his visit was in the morning before the departure of the Ipswich coach, "which goeth not out of town till noon or thereabouts," that the poet "complained but without passion" of his children's unkindness toward him, giving no particulars, that he had in former times heard him complain that they "were careless of him being blind and made nothing of deserting him." Regarding the issue of his own interest in the disposition of the estate, he made the following important declaration:

That since this respondent's coming to London this Michaelmas term last past, this respondent's sister, the party now producent in this cause, told this respondent that the deceased his brother did after his this respondent's going into the country in Trinity vacation last summer (say) that if she should have any overplus above a £1,000 come to her hands of his the deceased's estate, she should give the same to this respondent's children; but the deceased himself did not declare any such thing to this respondent at the time of his declaring his Will, the time above deposed of.

It is not clear whether this conversation took place before or after the poet's death on November 8th. But on November 23rd or thereabouts Christopher drew up the memorandum of Milton's words of the previous July and read them over to Elizabeth, who remembered and set her mark to them. He also waited on the widow at Dr. Exton's chambers about the suit and lent her two crowns. There is nothing more about Christopher's activity in the matter of the will and no further detail concerning the July visit. The testimony of Elizabeth and Mary Fisher, however, enables us to reconstruct two other domestic scenes, apparently subsequent to the one we have just described. Mary deposes that she was well acquainted with John Milton for about a year before his death and that about two months since (i.e. in October, but she was doubtful about the date) she being present in the kitchen, where Milton and his wife were having dinner, heard him among other discourse speak to his said wife and utter these words:

"Make much of me as long as I live, for thou knowest I have given thee all when I die at thy disposal;" there being then present in the said kitchen this deponent's sister and *contest*, namely Elizabeth Fisher. And the said deceased was at that time of perfect mind and memory, and talked and discoursed sensibly and well, and was very merry, and seemed to be in good health of body.

Elizabeth in turn reports another mealtime conversation of the same tenor, occurring on a Sunday afternoon about July, 1674.

Elizabeth Milton the party producent having provided something for the deceased's dinner which he very well liked, he the said deceased then spoke to his said wife these or the like words as near as this deponent can remember, viz. "God have mercy, Betty, I see thou wilt perform according to thy promise in providing me such dishes as I think fit whilst I live, and when I die thou knowest that I have left thee all," there being nobody present in the said chamber with the said deceased and his wife but this deponent; And the said testator at that time was of perfect mind and memory and talked and discoursed sensibly and well, but was then indisposed in his body by reason of the distemper of the gout, which he had then upon him.

In her cross-examination Elizabeth Fisher added that Milton was at that time "very merry and not in any passion or angry humours, neither at that time spoke anything against any of his children." She recalled, however, hearing him declare on later occasions that "he had made provision for his children in his lifetime and had spent the greater part of his estate in providing for them and that he was resolved he would do no more for them living or dying . . . and likewise that there was £1,000 left in Mr. Powell's hands [i.e. the unpaid dowry] to be disposed among his children hereafter."

It will occasion no surprise that this will did not stand in court, particularly in view of Christopher Milton's admission of his own expectations from the estate and the role he obviously played in instigating the proceedings. Why, it might well have been asked, did he, a lawyer, not draw up a written will for Milton, a scrivener's son, to sign and Elizabeth to witness if Milton's intentions on the occasion of his last visit were so clear. The answer could be that Milton's decision was a sudden one precipitated by the conversation itself. Drawing a will was hardly a matter to be accomplished while waiting for an Ipswich coach unless there was great urgency, as apparently there was not. It would be ungracious to observe that Christopher had not yet learned of John's intention regarding the residue of the estate above £1,000. In any case, we have evidence of friendliness between the brothers, dutifulness at least on Christopher's part, and confidence at least on Milton's. As for the conclusion to be drawn regarding the poet's feeling toward his children in its latest phase, some allowance must be made for partisanship and even for self-interest in the testimony. Yet the brother, the widow, and the loyal servant sound like honest people, and their consensus is not lightly to be dismissed.

Milton felt convinced that his daughters, or at least the two older ones, had made a poor return for their nurture by deserting him at the time of his greatest helplessness, and he was ready to act on his conviction of their ingratitude, even to the point of preferring Christopher's children to his own blood. If his feelings toward Deborah were somewhat warmer than this, he nevertheless did not except her from a treatment he considered just. In another and perhaps more charitable view (but it comes to about the same thing), he was simply taking the only remaining means he had of recovering a bad debt.

We are reminded that the business side of marriage was more explicit then than now and that Milton came of a collecting family. But our study of Milton's earlier reaction to his first marriage has taught us to look beyond these rationalisations. Is he not still compensating for the great frustration? Is it not, in spite of Katharine and Betty and *Paradise Lost* and *Samson*, still necessary for him to prove himself firm against the dangers of woman to which he once and only once succumbed?

Turning now to a less intimate but still domestic aspect of Milton's personal relationship, we may consider what satisfaction, if any, he still had in the society or the achievements of his nephews and former pupils, the Phillips boys. Edward's biography gives evidence of continued intimacy with his uncle during the composition of *Paradise Lost*. He had the perusal of the poem, as he tells us, from the very beginning in parcels of ten, twenty, or thirty verses at a time. The copy, being written by whatever hand came next, was sometimes deficient in spelling and punctuation, and Phillips corrected it. He wrote a few of the late entries in the Commonplace Book and corrected the printer's copy of Book I of *Paradise Lost*. Edward was loyal enough to Milton personally, but if the poet ever expected that either he or his brother would maintain a devotion to the principles which he had instilled in them, he was sadly mistaken. Edward's addition to Baker's chronicle in 1660 is already a compromise with Royalism. His revision of 1665 contains a character of Charles I which one feels sure he did not read to the author of *Eikonoklastes* and the *Tenure of Kings and Magistrates*.

He was the best of husbands, and (perchance) the best of men. His general insight in arts and sciences, both liberal and mechanical, was wonderful; nor was any prince better instructed in the principles of government. In effect he was too good a man to be a happy prince; and rather betrayed by his own tenderness than subdued by the force of his adversaries. The rebellion was in itself barbarous; but the formalities of proceeding against him, by arraignment, trial, sentence, and execution filled all Christendom with indignation and horror; and his blood yet cries aloud for vengeance upon the promoters, as well as the instruments of that execrable murder.

In later years Edward may, in spite of politics, have been more closely associated with his uncle than the biography indicates. His *Theatrum Poetarum*, an index of the poets of all countries and ages, contains materials that seem to reflect Milton's ideas; his English dictionaries may well have been begun under the poet's instruction, and his Latin lexicons are confusedly built on the data accumulated from the *Thesaurus Linguae Latinae* which Milton had in preparation. As his uncle's literary executor, Edward Phillips published and later translated into English the Letters of State. His biographical memoir, which shows intimate knowledge of the poet's later as well as his earlier years, is the work of a man who has largely sunk his own personality in a stronger one and who lives in the shadow and memory of greatness which he feels but cannot comprehend. .

The younger nephew, John, whom the poet had, in all essential respects, adopted as a son, was more brilliant and more wayward. There are symptoms in him of rebellion against the discipline which had been imposed on him. He left his uncle's house after writing the pamphlet in defence of Milton in 1652, and we find him even before the Restoration pandering to the Sons of Belial by collaborating in a licentious publication, *Sportive Art*. His *Satyr Against Hypocrites*, written in 1655 and re-published in 1661 under the title, *The Religion of the Hypocritical Presbyterians*, is a witty and hard-hitting performance which Milton may or may not have found tolerable. It describes first a Puritan church service, then a christening, then a mid-week meeting in the home of a parishioner. The heroine of the second scene is a midwife who talks like Chaucer's Wife of Bath; in the last the religious conversation becomes so warm as to lead to an assignation between the parson and his hostess. The year before Milton's death Phillips published a travesty of Virgil in which Harrison, Bradshaw, and Vane appear in Hell. The Preface suggests that pedagogues may cavil at the subject "for affronting their classic author." It is not possible to agree with Miss Darbishire that John Phillips is the author of the anonymous life of Milton found among the papers of Anthony Wood. All in all, his career was such as to bring home to the poet the central lesson of his lifetime; ordinary human clay is incapable of retaining worthy form, no matter how skilfully it may be moulded. That he, of all people, should have become the foster-parent of a Restoration hack may well have seemed to him a last indignity of fate.

He did not live long enough to see the unworthiness of another pupil or assistant, Daniel Skinner, who attempted to publish his State Letters and the treatise *Of Christian Doctrine*, but gave the project up when it threatened to interfere with his advancement. The story adds to the Miltonic drama and serves to illustrate again the precariousness of his life purposes, and his sad liability to error of judgment regarding persons— which made those purposes still more precarious. Skinner was the ambitious son of a trade-fallen merchant in Mark Lane. He must have presented himself or been presented to Milton fresh from Trinity College, a mere boy, in the last year of the poet's life. How much they worked together we do not know. Skinner made an entry or two in the Commonplace Book and recopied the State Letters and the first part of the Christian Doctrine, whether at Milton's orders or on his own initiative after his master's death. Edward Phillips, it will be remembered, also had access to the papers and later published a version of the letters. He could hardly have countenanced a parallel enterprise had he been able to prevent it. Nor would he willingly have handed over the great theological treatise which he knew to be his uncle's lifetime work. Milton, on the other hand, may have entrusted these documents to his latest amanuensis or invited him to make and keep copies, thinking that he would be more likely to issue them than Phillips. At any rate, Skinner possessed and proceeded to try to market the somewhat scandalous works. Meanwhile he had become a protégé of Samuel Pepys, who had apparently enjoyed the favours of his sister and after his wife's death was to make her the mistress of his household. There is extant a letter of Skinner to Pepys asking for help and referring to the love he bore for Mary and one from Pepys to the secretary, Sir Leoline Jenkins, recommending him. Skinner was duly given a post with the English Ambassador to the United Provinces. His arrangement for the publication of *De Doctrina* was discovered. Pepys wrote a warning to him; Skinner recalled the MS. from the printer and sent it to his father to be delivered to the secretary as evidence of good behaviour. We have enough of Skinner's correspondence to show his selfishness. One wonders whether Milton himself perceived it and what hopes, if any, he built on this young man. The chances are that he had long since digested the schoolmaster's as well as the father's disillusionment and expected little of anyone who presented himself to learn or serve.

The data regarding Milton's late relationships with maturer friends is scanty but suggestive. It is interesting that two of his acquaintances were book-dealers: George Thomason, whose wife's death he celebrated; the other, Millington, in whose house he lodged for a time in Little Britain and who, according to Richardson, might be seen leading him about the street, arm in arm. The physician Paget, who stood close to Milton from at least as early as 1663, was evidently a man of parts. He was associated with the leaders of the new scientific movement, having collaborated with Glisson in his pioneering work on rickets, and the sale catalogue of his library gives an indication of wide interests. Milton's own works in prose and poetry are listed there and, more remarkably, a large collection of the heretical writings of Socinus. Like Thomason, Paget collected the pamphlet literature of the day, specialising apparently in Quaker controversy. One doubts his being a sectarian, but assumes that he had, like Milton, a curious interest in these matters.

There were still other cultivated persons who shared Milton's acquaintance on one level or another of intellectual interest, and some of them, though the data is less abundant, were perhaps as close to him as any that have been mentioned. We have already seen his tendency to cultivate by correspondence the acquaintance of worthy admirers at home and abroad. Such friendships continued to mean much to him. Aubrey reports that "he was visited much by the learned, more than he did desire." The foreigners who came in the earlier period to England "chiefly to see O. Protector and Mr. J. Milton" and would see the house and chamber where he was born, probably continued their visits to some extent after his retirement. A great name does not lose its attractive power with the downfall of outward greatness. There survived a few men with whom he had been associated in public life, notably Andrew Marvell, of whose devotion there can be no doubt. The best record of their intimacy is Marvell's commendatory poem, prefixed to the second edition of *Paradise Lost*. Both here and, as we shall see, in his prose writing, Marvell took up the cudgels for Milton and helped prepare for the security of his reputation in the next age. The celebrated and well-attested visit of Dryden was a meeting rather of competitors than of friends, but it appears to have been an occasion on which matters of deep interest were discussed, and Milton evidently treated his young visitor without sullenness. There is an indulgent humour in the blind poet's reply to the request for permission to write a rhymed version of *Paradise Lost*. "It seems you have a mind to tag my points and you have my leave to tag 'em."

Such, then, is the older Milton, as we see him in the contemporary record. How he actually apportioned his time after the completion of the poems we only partly know. Composition, as he practised it, had been a great resource, filling with accomplishment hours which would otherwise have been vacant. When the last work left his hands, he could only fall back on routine tasks or find some new object of thought or become increasingly a sitter in the sun. The publication of a second edition of the Minor Poems in 1673 and of *Paradise Lost* in 1674 suggests one form of occupation not unconnected with the deeper satisfactions of the past. His wife reports that he attended no church, but that his meditation was a continuous prayer. If the prayer no longer moved harmonious numbers, it could at least return him to contemplation of his own created work, as God rested on the seventh day.

The evidence that Milton did actually dally with his poetry after its publication is decisive. There is minor revision in both cases, some of it certainly not the work of a "corrector of the press." It is a reasonable conjecture that the good and simple Betty helped by reading to him out of his own works, though Phillips and others may have done so too. The division of *Paradise Lost* into twelve books instead of ten could easily have been accomplished from memory, but one tell-tale text correction shows that somebody was working closely with him. The poet had early adopted a little trick in emphasis by alternative spellings of the personal pronouns, "he," "me," "we," and "she." He doubled the vowel when they bore an accent in the verse. Now this was something no printer could be consistent in, and Milton's blindness made it all but impossible to secure adherence to his intention without assistance. The number of obvious errors suggests that he had no trustworthy proofreader instructed to make this kind of correction. The following alteration in one of Satan's boastful utterances in Book II suggests that a careless reader (aut Betty aut diabolus) missed the slight emphasis on the pronoun (important both for meaning and for rhythm) and was asked to write an extra "e" in the margin.

> But I should ill become this throne, O Peers,
> And this imperial sov'ranty, . . .
>   . . . if aught proposed
> And judged of public moment in the shape
> Of difficulty or danger could deter
> Me from attempting.

"*Mee* from attempting," said the poet, with or without asperity. It is equally possible to prove Milton's hand in the textual correction of the *Poems*, but some and perhaps all of the author's changes were made before his loss of sight. There was, on the other hand, mischievous work in the printing office, and the poet either passed over or had no opportunity to check on a few compositor's errors and some deliberate though minor alterations.

To this edition Milton added the college verses on the English language, the early poem on the Fair Infant, and the poems (Sonnets, Psalm Paraphrases, etc.) written between 1645 and 1660. He had a decision to make (or it was made for him by the stationer) regarding the poems in praise of the hero-villains of the great rebellion. The sonnets on Vane, Cromwell, and Fairfax were withheld, to be published only after the events of 1688 had made it possible to remember Puritans with admiration. The trail of Milton's helpers with these affairs of publication is to be followed in the amanuensis entries in the Trinity College manuscript. It is clear there, for example, that Milton, after his blindness but not necessarily after 1660, had supervised the preparation of copy for the printer which actually contained the dangerous poems. Fragments of this copy were kept along with the original drafts, headed: "These sonnets to follow the ten in the printed book." It is impossible to know specifically what went on in the poet's workshop at the time of publication; but we may reasonably infer from his habits and interests that his dealings with the printer were direct.

Other evidences of literary and editorial activity connected with works long since completed are the publications of the *History of Britain* in 1670, the *Artis Logicae* in 1672, and the *Familiar Letters* in 1674. There is at least the probability that a more difficult and time-consuming occupation was afforded by the vast manuscript of the treatise *Of Christian Doctrine*. The facts, beyond what have been given, are these. Milton began in his early teaching days the collecting and arranging of Biblical quotations toward a comprehensive system of divinity based directly and exclusively on Scripture and therefore valid for all truly Protestant sects. The magnitude and importance of the undertaking could not have seemed less than the writing of an epic poem worthy to take its place with the greatest creations of the past. By 1660 or a few years later the manuscript stood complete in the hand of one Jeremie Picard, a trained amanuensis. It already bore signs of second and third thoughts in the interlinear and marginal corrections. Milton may have been planning on immediate publication when the disturbance of the Restoration intervened, or he may have expected to keep the work under revision for a longer period, perhaps to his death. He was aware that it contained objectionable doctrine, objectionable even to the main body of English Puritans, and dangerously so to the ruling authority of the Restoration. He would naturally have felt a responsibility for the exactness of the statements on disputed points which did not resolve itself as easily as in the doctrinal parts of *Paradise Lost*, where the magic of poetry somewhat disguised the issues.

At any rate, Milton went on working with the document, using a succession of amanuenses after Picard was no longer in his employ. The half-indecipherable scrawls filled the margins of Picard's manuscript when in the 1670s the young Daniel Skinner entered Milton's employ. Did the poet set him to work on the project of finally preparing *Christian Doctrine* for the press? Apparently, yes, for he has recopied the first part of the manuscript and some difficult later passages in a fair hand. The possibility exists that Skinner stole the manuscript from among Milton's papers at his death. We have spoken of his attempt to have it brought out by Elzevir. But the chances are that he was commissioned, for better or for worse, to arrange for publication. Milton could hardly have borne the thought of consigning this second fruit of a laborious lifetime to oblivion. Contrary to the opinion of some scholars, there is nothing in the stages of the *Christian Doctrine* text to show any important development of Milton's thought after the period of *Paradise Lost*. The changes are a matter of amplification and exactness. What interests us here is the continuity of his purposes, the skill and the resolution which enabled him to work at a task like this or the Latin dictionary, requiring minute reference, under the conditions of his later life.

More surprising than any of these evidences of the persistence of Milton's purposes is his return in this eleventh hour of his career to his old role of publicist. He does so, to be sure, in but two brief pamphlets composed in 1673 and 1674, one of them a translation, the other of no particular originality of idea, but both demonstrating that he had in no sense withdrawn himself from the outer world, or at least that he was capable of returning to such interests after a long period of apparent unconcern —demonstrating also that his basic principles were unchanged. To estimate the significance of this episode, as belonging to the last phase of Milton's life, and illuminating his personality and conviction after the great downfall of his cause, we must examine the public situation which engaged their author's attention and to which he thought he could contribute. We must remember first that for years it had not been safe for him to express himself. He was known as an unrepentant traitor who richly merited a punishment which somehow he had escaped. He was "that villain Milton," famous to be sure and perhaps an ornament to learning, but acceptable to no loyal person as a guide to political thought or action. By the late '70s, his position was a good deal better.

The son of Charles I was no longer embraced as a saviour of his people by a torn and weary nation. The inevitable reaction against reaction had taken place, and a language something like that of the good old cause—the same but not the same—was again beginning to be heard. Specifically, the old issue of toleration was again open and acute. The form of this issue, of course, was new. The Cavalier Parliament in restoring the Anglican Establishment had forced the Puritan ministers to choose between conformity and expulsion. A large majority of them had conformed. The two thousand who did not became legatees of the cause of religious liberty. Charles II meanwhile had secretly allied himself with Louis XIV and was moving toward the restoration of Roman Catholicism to its old predominance in England. As a step in this procedure, he issued in 1672 a "declaration of indulgence" suspending both the old laws penalising Catholics and the more recent provisions of the Clarendon Code which were aimed at the Nonconformists. This act aroused a storm of opposition in the newly elected Parliament, and Charles was forced to withdraw it. Parliament then passed the Test Act excluding all Dissenters, Catholic and Protestant alike, from public office. This made it impossible for Charles to retain his closest counsellors or for his brother James to continue in his place as Lord High Admiral, and so allayed the fear of Catholic domination. It left the Puritans in the same hard case as before.

Milton's pamphlet, which appeared with many others in 1673, bears the title *Of True Religion, Heresy, Toleration, and the Growth of Popery*. Its avowed purpose is to lend a hand to the efforts of those who, alarmed at the late increase of popery, are exhorting the public to beware "the growth of this Romish weed." Milton is in a sense back where he was at the time of the first ecclesiastical pamphlets. There is a new motion of reformation—defensive now primarily, since the feared reaction is not actually in power, but soon to take on the character of a more thorough-going return to the Protestantism of a purer tradition. The public is again malleable, and other champions are already in the field. The gifts of a special enlightenment and broader purposes are Milton's as before, but he does not feel the need of vaunting them. Experience has sobered and humanised him. Sacrifice and devotion have purified his relation to the cause, but the cause itself is what it was, and Milton is more, rather than less, sincerely one with it. If he earlier in any degree assumed the virtue of impersonal devotion to the public good, surely now, when all is done, he has it. Masson calls the pamphlet a "rather tame one," contrasting it, of course, with the agitated pleas for religious liberty written in the last days of the Commonwealth. Actually, it represents Milton's maturest thought on the great problem which had first brought him into public controversy. We recall his sense of being especially equipped by his studies to deal with the distinction between ecclesiastical and civil rights. His studies have been perfected by experience. He speaks now as an expert, and this, for better or for worse, is his final word. If the statement is plain, its plainness is calculated, and sorts with the doctrine of Gospel simplicity which Milton is inculcating, sorts also with his own progress away from the arrogance of learning, which was the temptation of his youth.

I will not now enter the labyrinth of councils and fathers, an entangled wood, which the papist loves to fight in, not with hope of victory, but to obscure the shame of an open overthrow, which yet in that kind of combat many heretofore, and one of late, hath eminently given them. And such

There is no man so wicked but at sometimes his conscience
will wring him with thoughts of another world, and the peril
of his soul; the trouble and melancholy, which he conceives of
true repentance and amendment, he endures not, but inclines
rather to some carnal superstition, which may pacify and lull
his conscience with some more pleasing doctrine. None more
ready and officious to offer herself than the Romish, and
opens wide her office, with all her faculties, to receive him;
easy confession, easy absolution, pardons, indulgences,
masses for him both quick and dead, Agnus Deis, relics,
and the like: and he, instead of "working out his salvation
with fear and trembling," straight thinks in his heart,
(like another kind of fool than he in the Psalms,) to bribe
God as a corrupt judge; and by his proctor, some priest, or
friar, to buy out his peace with money, which he cannot
with his repentance. For God, when men sin outrageously,
and will not be admonished, gives over chastising them,
perhaps by pestilence, fire, sword, or famine, which may all
turn to their good, and takes up his severest punishments,
hardness, besottedness of heart, and idolatry, to their final
perdition. Idolatry brought the heathen to heinous transgressions, Rom. ii. And heinous transgressions ofttimes bring
the slight professors of true religion to gross idolatry: 1 Thes.
ii. 12, "For this cause God shall send them strong delusion,
that they should believe a lie, that they all might be damned
who believe not the truth, but had pleasure in unrighteous-
ness." And Isaiah xliv. 18, speaking of idolaters, "They have
not known nor understood, for he hath shut their eyes that
they cannot see, and their hearts that they cannot understand."
Let us therefore, using this last means, last here spoken of,
but first to be done, amend our lives with all speed; lest
through impenitency we run into that stupidly which we now
seek all means so warily to avoid, the worst of superstitions,
and the heaviest of all God's judgments—popery.

This is Milton's final word to England—actually the last
written by his pen and the essence of his doctrine: *Love virtue, she
alone is free.*—And safe. The historical conditioning so conspicuous in this latest statement is nothing new. Milton is and
has always been Protestant of Protestants, Puritan of Puritans.
The Romish Church yawns like the pit of Hell for those who prefer "bondage with ease to strenuous liberty." Its blandishments

are those of Comus and "wind into the easy heart of man"
to his destruction. It is, indeed, the instrument of God's
dealing with the unregenerate. To those who endeavour
repentance with sincere intent God gives his umpire
Conscience—

>   whom if they will hear,
> Light after light well us'd they shall attain,
> And to the end persisting, safe arrive.

Those who neglect repeated warnings fall at last on God's
harshest punishment, the blindness which goeth before
destruction.

> This my long sufferance and my day of grace
> They who neglect and scorn, shall never taste;
> But hard be hard'nd, blind be blinded more,
> That they may stumble on, and deeper fall.

What they stumble on into is the Roman Church if that happens
to be easily available. It is this that the men of the Reformation
meant when they called the Pope Antichrist and what Englishmen meant when they thanked God for the discovery of the
Gunpowder Plot.

Milton had grown up in the tradition of this particular
symbolism, and it is always in the background of his mind.
Current politics have accented its employment in this pamphlet.
It is, however, implicit also in *Samson Agonistes*, the idolatrous
Philistines playing the role of Romanists. Their vices have
multiplied to the point of unregeneracy, and God has afflicted
them with a strong delusion. Their spiritual blindness is like
the hybris of the Greeks, and Milton is well aware of the
coincidence of these parallel interpretations of the ways of
God to man.

> While their hearts were jocund and sublime,
> Drunk with idolatry, drunk with wine,
> And fat regorg'd of bulls and goats,
> Chaunting their idol, and preferring
> Before our living Dread who dwells
> In Silo his bright Sanctuary:
> Among them he a spirit of frenzy sent,
> Who hurt their minds,
> And urg'd them on with mad desire
> To call in haste for their destroyer.

Samson's inner illumination, which Milton contrasts with this, is that of the Protestant Englishman who is chastened by God's warning and amends his life betimes. We have, then, in this pamphlet a last reiteration of Miltonic doctrine, carefully calculated with reference to the issue of the moment and the public mood, aiming at the many rather than the few, but parallel in content and purpose to the great masterpieces of poetic art. Milton has forsworn passion and said farewell to the eloquence which attended it, but his convictions are unchanged; his intellect and techniques are unimpaired; and his hopefulness is perhaps greater than at any time since the heyday of the Commonwealth. It is, indeed, a fair dismission.

Milton's death took place at the end of a busy and, from all evidence, a happy year. He had sat his last summer in the sun and felt the premonitory damps of winter in the London air. The gout from which he suffered spring and autumn, "struck in." "He died with . . . so little pain or emotion that the time of his expiring was not perceived by those in the room." The last sentence is from the unknown biographer, who stood close to Milton in his later years. Was he perhaps among those who watched as he lay dying? Edward Phillips gives no such detail and perhaps lacked the sentiment which would cause him to record it. Of the funeral he writes, speaking of course as an eyewitness: "He had a very decent interment according to his quality, in the Church of St. Giles, Cripplegate, being attended from his house to the church by several gentlemen then in town, his principal well-wishers and admirers." Wood adds that he was buried in the chancel in his father's grave; sexton-minded Aubrey says "the upper end of the chancel at the right hand, the stone being now [1681] removed in the raising of the floor." "I guess Jo. Speed and he lie together." Thus the biographers in mortuary chorus. The exact location of Milton's remains was inquired into in 1790; a coffin believed to be his was opened; and for a few days a poet's bones, with vestiges of auburn hair (Alas, poor Yorick!), were exhibited to the curious at a shilling or two a head. There was a clandestine sale of relics, until outraged decency compelled the closing of the grave. Cromwell on his pikestaff, recently photographed from a private collection for the Press, suffered a no more scandalous indignity.

CHAPTER TEN

FIT AUDIENCE

THE SURVIVAL OF MILTON in his poetry and prose, in the story of his deeds, and in the rumour of his personality is logically very much a part of his biography. A book, he said in *Areopagitica*, a good book, "is the precious life blood of a master spirit, embalmed and treasured up on purpose to a life beyond life." He intended his books to be such treasures and to contain in themselves the "potency of life" which came from him. Better than children they continued him, and the tale of his days could not be ended until they themselves were dead. It is not, moreover, merely his intellect which lives. We recall that in his early thought the book and the whole man were one. He who would write a heroic poem must be himself a true poem. Milton wrote himself into work as few poets or publicists have ever done. These thoughts about the products of the human spirit, his spirit in special, animate and give personal significance to his meditations upon fame. "Fame is the spur," and true fame is God's final judgment on each deed. But the heavenly and intangible reward is not enough. Its visible earthly counterpart is the approval of chosen individuals, the elect of God, "with gifts and graces eminently adorned," in aftertimes. And this is the immortality for which Milton hoped.

Recent writers have commented on the little stir which Milton's existence created in his own lifetime. Their point is made against David Masson, who tended to take Milton's words at their face value, though he knew that the facts were often inflated by him. We have already described the immediate reception of the early poems and the controversial tracts and given some evidence of the personal notoriety of Milton in his retirement. It is a matter of judgment whether we say that he was at the time of his death famous or obscure or something between the two. But certainly the meed of public acceptance with full understanding was small from his or any standpoint. He had enough experience of friendship to know what such acceptance could be like. He invited posterity to continue to accord him, as one or two had done, the name of a just man, a prophet, and a poet, with all that these words imply. He asked that posterity's judgment, in each of the roles, be made with knowledge and discrimination under God. How posterity has responded to this appeal it is now our business to inquire.

Actually, the story of Milton's posthumous fame and influence begins with the late contacts we have given some account of in the preceding chapter. He associated, after his active career was over, with younger contemporaries who accommodated themselves to the new age, and their voices were a factor in moulding later opinion. The number of such associates is, as we have seen, not inconsiderable. Edward Phillips, for example, wrote Milton's name in large enough characters in his *Theatrum Poetarum*, a dictionary of writers intended for the use of the European republic of letters. It is doubtful if Milton would have found his place there had the work not been written by a loyal acquaintance. Dryden's visit and request of Milton were reported and a striking bit of the conversation on this or some other occasion was given by Dryden himself in *Preface to the Fables*.

Milton was the poetical son of Spenser, and Mr. Waller of Fairfax, for we have our lineal descents and clans as well as other families. Spenser more than once insinuates that the soul of Chaucer was transfused with his body and that he was begotten by him two hundred years after his decease. Milton has acknowledged to me that Spenser was his original.

The famous epigram canonizing Milton once and for all among the world's epic poets appeared under the portrait in the folio edition of 1688.

> Three poets, in three distant ages born,
> Greece, Italy, and England did adorn.
> The first in loftiness of thought surpassed,
> The next in majesty, in both the last:
> The force of Nature could no farther go;
> To make a third she joined the other two.

Andrew Marvell's warmer and richer, if less sophisticated feeling about Milton marks him as the chief of the surviving partisans who constituted the really fit among Milton's earliest audience. His understanding is officially delivered to posterity in the poem prefixed to the *Paradise Lost* of 1674. To how many individuals it was conveyed by word of mouth we can only

K

guess. The leading ideas are such as could have arisen only in
a fellow poet deeply in sympathy with the subject of his praise,
yet independent and impersonal in his judgment. He speaks
(dramatically, to be sure, but knowing Marvell, we may
believe sincerely) of fearing lest Milton's purposes in writing
Paradise Lost should prove un-Christian and indeed vindictive.

> . . . the argument
> Held me a while misdoubting his intent
> That he would ruin (for I saw him strong)
> The sacred truths to fable and old song
> (So Samson groped the temple's post in spite,
> The world o'er whelming to revenge his sight).

Reassured of the poet's pious aim, he questioned his capacity
to realise it

> . . . in fields
> O'er which lame Faith leads understanding blind,

thinking he might "perplex the things he would explain."
Such thoughts are those of a reverent and subtle mind confronted with the phenomenon of Milton's personality and
genius and already sensitive to a critical and indeed a moral
issue which has been the theme of much later comment.
The doubts of Milton's allegiance to good and of the validity
of his technique in dealing with the realm of spirit—these
doubts are at length submerged in a kind of approval which
would surely have been more acceptable to Milton than Dryden's metallic praise. We must recall that they were intended
for his ear.

> The majesty which through thy work doth reign
> Draws the devout, deterring the profane . . .
> Where couldst thou words of such a compass find?
> Whence furnish such a vast expanse of mind?
> Just Heaven, thee like Tiresias to requite,
> Rewards with prophecy thy loss of sight.

Here was praise of the man in his essential work, a pronouncement on the truth of his own conception of his inspiration and
of himself. It was the truest commendation with which Milton
could have been delivered to the conditioned judgment of the
new age. And to point the challenge Marvell presents satirical

compliments to John Dryden in terms which further reflect
intimacy with the Miltonic viewpoint.

> Well mightst thou scorn thy readers to allure
> With tinkling rime, of thy own sense secure;
> While the Town-Bayes writes all the while and spells,
> And like a pack-horse, tires without his bells.

A year before the publication of the dedicating poem,
Marvell had championed Milton more explicitly if less exaltedly
in the second part of his prose satire against Samuel Parker,
Bishop of Oxford. Parker, whose passing but eager intimacy
with Milton we have already mentioned, answering the first
part of the *Rehearsal Transposed* in 1673, made a point of the
friendship of Marvell with the king-killing Milton and quoted
passages from *Areopagitica* as a sort of *reductio ad absurdum* of
Marvell's plea for toleration. An anonymous pamphlet of the
same year, believed by Marvell also to be Parker's, elaborated
the story of Milton's political and religious misdeeds with a
knowledge more intimate than any of his earlier enemies had
ever shown, referring to no less than ten of the prose works
as well as to *Paradise Lost*. It quotes, for example, the invocation
to light at the beginning of the third book with the comment:
"No doubt but the thoughts of this vital Lamp lighted a
Christmas Candle in his brain." Marvell denies that Milton
had any hand in his work, declaring that he had by chance not
seen him for two years before and had carefully avoided visiting
him while he was engaged in writing the satire. As to Milton's
errors—"it was his misfortune, living in a tumultuous time,
to be tossed on the wrong side. . . . At his Majesty's happy
return, J. M. did partake . . . of his Regal clemency and has
ever since expiated himself in a retired silence." What conversations Parker had with Milton when he "haunted his
house day by day" Milton himself is "too generous to remember." "But he never having in the least provoked you, to
traduce him . . . as a School-Master . . . and to lay at last my
simple book to his charge . . . it is inhumanely and inhospitably
done." There is earnest partisanship and identification in this,
and the issues which lie behind the personalities are the great
old ones to which Milton was even then giving renewed attention. Marvell was, indeed, fit audience, but he was also a
contemporary and a friend.

As for the Restoration generally, we have some evidence other than Dryden of disinterested admiration of Milton on æsthetic grounds. Richardson's story of Sir John Denham's enthusiasm for *Paradise Lost*, "wet from the press," may or may not be true, but it stands for the undoubted fact that the wits, in spite of politics, were already aware that the publication of Milton's epic was a major event in literary history. The actual circulation of the early editions of *Paradise Lost* is a matter of interest in this connection: 1,300 copies of the first by 1669, at least as many more of others by 1688. This is by no means failure.

The Revolution of 1688 nevertheless constitutes the great turning point in Milton's political, personal, and literary popularity. The extent to which his writings actually played a part in the ideology of this event is a subject too intricate for detailed analysis in this book. He belongs, of course, with the so-called Classical Republicans and animated the heroic movement which, in the words of the best scholar on this subject, Zera Fink, "died on the scaffold with Algernon Sydney in 1673." Its ideas to a certain extent survived to be incorporated in Whig thought in the eighteenth century and transmitted to the founding fathers of American democracy; and since America, rather than England, was the immediate heir of the Puritan Revolution, the eighteenth-century fortunes of Milton's political ideas are most significantly followed on this side of the water. Scanty as the record is, it deserves an attention which has not been accorded it by American historians.

His influence begins with his friends and fellow travellers in the good old cause: Roger Williams, the younger John Winthrop, Reverend John Clarke of Newport, John Oxenbridge, to mention only his actual acquaintances. In the person of Williams, Milton was truly present in America. Their programmes of reform were similar, and there was nothing in Williams's behaviour that Milton would not have approved. Williams, we know, commended Milton's writings to his friends. Increase Mather was a bird of other feather, but his library contained the two defences of the English people. To these volumes Cotton Mather added *Eikonoklastes*, and he freely quotes *Paradise Lost* in his *Magnalia*. Passing by Colonial and later knowledge of Milton's poetry in America as being chiefly an echo of English interest, we may note the growing acceptance of his political philosophy and the occasional evidence of his being influential in helping formulate the

American idea. Direct transmission of his thought to the intellect of New England was promoted by the liberty-loving Thomas Hollis, an enthusiastic devotee of Milton, who supplied the Harvard College Library with works on government, including Milton's, and commended their revolutionary principles by republican inscriptions: "Felicity is Freedom, and Freedom is Magnanimity." "Floreat libertas, pereat tyrannis." Hollis wrote of his gift in 1766 to the Reverend Jonathan Mayhew with the exhortation: "Men of New England, brethren, use them for yourselves and for others, and God bless you." To Mayhew personally he had previously sent copies of *Eikonoklastes* and of the complete prose. The arguments of this "morning gun of the Revolution" in *Unlimited Submission and Non-Resistance to Higher Powers* have been shown to be in part derived from *Tenure* and the defences. Another correspondent of Hollis's was the Reverend Andrew Eliot, who wrote that he was never wearied of reading Milton's *Defence of the English People*. From these and other men there was dissemination of Miltonian ideas in the New England pulpit. Here, then, is the fulfilment in a degree of Milton's hope of a life beyond life. We recall the warning in *Areopagitica* that books are "as lively and as vigorously productive as the fabulous dragon's teeth; and being sown up and down, may chance to spring up armed men."

The enlightened propagandist for human liberty, implementing his arguments with Milton's, was fit audience to the extent of his comprehension and his scope. But no politically minded person could, as such, rightly interpret to himself and others the full Miltonic message. Jefferson, philosophical reformer classically trained, might have been the fittest of American readers, but he could not, with his rationalism, accept Milton in Miltonic terms, and actually refers to him less frequently than we might have expected. The audience must after all be like-minded, though not equal-minded, with the poet-prophet. They must be poet-prophets themselves after their kind, receptive humanists, and culturally Christian. Only in traditional and Hellenic England and among the more visionary *élite* could one expect to find persons attuned to a deep and full understanding of the human phenomenon that was Milton. When the firsthand knowledge was no longer available, such persons must depend largely on the written record. Their reactions, however, were inevitably conditioned by the ideals and interests of the age. We have, therefore, to record the fortunes of Miltonic scholarship as well as of Miltonic appreciation and to see both against the changing cultural history of three centuries. The treatment of Milton is, indeed, one of the touchstones of these changes. The story is more complicated than has ever been told, and only its broadest features can here be touched on.

The growth of Milton's fame and popularity among Englishmen after the Revolution of 1688 is evidenced by the publication of edition after edition of *Paradise Lost*, five already before 1700, and by the chorus of praise from poets and critics, which gains continuously in volume. Dryden, of course, more than anyone else had set the ball rolling. Aside from the changes in political values, which, as we have seen, had already affected Milton favourably before his death, the return of the normal moral sobriety of Puritan-hearted England to social and literary esteem did most for his status as a poet. Both his devotion and his morality were acceptable. *Christian Doctrine* being unpublished, few realised the Arian tendencies in his theology, while his Arminianism did no violence to prevailing Anglican belief and has usually passed unnoticed, even by persons of Calvinistic background. The doctrine of married love, as expressed in the fourth book of *Paradise Lost*, fell in with the reaction against Restoration cynicism, and sentimentalism found a fair field for satisfaction in the primal romance which is after all so nearly Milton's central theme. There is a report that ladies' fans having the loves of Adam and Eve painted on them were popular in eighteenth-century drawing-rooms.

These correspondences, valid as far as they go, come far short of establishing a perfect doctrinal sympathy between Milton and the eighteenth century. What, for example, has become of his Platonism and of the analysis of the degradation of love in Adam and Eve after the Fall? What also of the rapport between man and angel, of the Hebraic yearning of the soul for God? What, finally, of the inward paradise and Adam's discovery of how it is to be won? To the subtler overtones of Milton's high spiritual requiem the Augustan Age remained a clod. There were, however, other cultural values in his work and other causes (some of them not wholly extraneous to the poetic essence as he conceived it) of the high valuation that was put on it.

Dryden's comments are already suggestive of these interests. England needed a major poet for veneration, and those of the remoter past did not quite do. Fader Chaucer was quaint and old; Spenser deviated too far from the norm of classicism, depended too much on the half-feudal politics of his own time, was really more outmoded than his predecessor. Milton, linked in filial piety with both Spenser and Chaucer, yet taking the ancients more strictly as his models and employing a theme universal but redolent of living issues—Milton, for all his Puritan conditioning, was available for canonisation by the highest critical authority of the new age. Dryden speaks as a fellow poet when he ranks him above Homer and Virgil. In the cooler element of critical prose he has many reservations, but at least he pays him the tribute of serious discussion. He calls him, with Spenser, "the nearest in English to Virgil and Horace," but found Milton, who "has endeavoured everywhere to express Homer," lacking in certain Augustan qualities of style which Spenser had derived from Virgil. Again Dryden denies Milton's *Paradise Lost* the title of a true epic: Milton's "event is not prosperous, like that of all other epic works; his heavenly machines are many, and his human persons are but two." His thoughts are elevated and his words sounding, but he sometimes runs into a "flat of Scripture" and goes beyond moderation in his coinage of new words. He wrote blank verse, not for the high reasons he alleges, but because rhyme was not his talent. (Later Dryden himself uses Milton's argument about the "modern bondage" in justifying his own liberties with the couplet.)

All this in the mouth of the father of English literary criticism and at the beginning of a period of renewed lucubration on all the well-worn issues launched Milton on a career among the luminati. The verdict that *Paradise Lost* did not conform to the rules of epic prompted a sturdy defence among Milton devotees who were themselves classicists. Addison's famous series of papers on Milton in the *Spectator*, though it had much to say of the beauties of *Paradise Lost* and of its pure morality, undertook mainly to justify it as an epic. These papers, appearing first on successive Saturdays, then as a separate publication in 1719, became at once a standard piece of Milton criticism. They confirmed the already rising popularity of *Paradise Lost* in England and prompted a study and translation of the poem on the Continent. Addison was a good and sensitive reader of

Milton, but much of what he says seems either obvious or irrelevant. The issues, as we see them to-day, are not exactly those to which Addison addresses himself. In one paper he says that the "fable" is that of a tragedy rather than an epic, that some of his incidents have not probability enough for epic, that his allusions to heathen fables "sin against the canon of unity." One can readily imagine Milton's answering him—out of Aristotle, Scripture, the practice of many old famous poets, the God-given light of reason itself.

No such full Miltonic answer to neo-classic reservations was forthcoming before the end of the eighteenth century, though the tendency to exalt imagination and emotion in poetry above "correctness" made increasing way for a more exalted praise. Milton had invented a new type of poem, the "divine epic," superior to Homer and Virgil. His genius was above the rules. The poet himself would have accepted this, of course, but it was not exactly what he meant. It required a riper romanticism to emphasise the essential qualities of imagination and emotion in his poetry. The new interest in Nature and appreciation of its grander aspects, the taste for colour and romance, developing humanitarian sentiment, and finally the rising religious fervour of the late eighteenth century were all favourable to Milton in contrast to the dominant poetic school of Pope. Finally, political revolution again put his personality and career in question, resulting in a new complex of opinion which even the present has not sufficiently resolved. Samuel Johnson in *Lives of the Poets* reflects in his summary judgment the already traditional glorification of *Paradise Lost*, "a poem which, considered with respect to design, may claim the first place, and with respect to performance, the second among the productions of the human mind," but he loathed Milton's politics and disparages his character at every point.

Meanwhile literary scholarship, a relatively new craft, had begun the erudite accumulation which has since grown to mountainous height. Milton invited this, no doubt, and, being of the scholar breed himself, might have been indulgent toward some, though by no means all, of the effort expended in his behalf. He might, for example, have thought the expository editing of Hume (1695), Patterson, Newton, Todd, Verity, and others supererogatory for persons decently literate. He would surely have laughed at Richard Bentley's attempts to restore the text on the assumption that some editor, taking advantage of a poet's blindness, had corrupted it. The assumption was perhaps in Bentley's real thought a fiction, designed to clear him from the odium of traducing Milton. He was, however, bold enough to perpetuate some of his worst offences without insisting on the idea of an interloper.

> They hand in hand, with wandering steps and slow
> Through Eden took their solitary way.

So Milton in the *textus receptus*. Bentley rewrites the lines to bring them into conformity with literary decorum. The pair was not solitary for they had each other. Their steps were not wandering for Providence was their guide. Hence—

> They hand in hand with social steps their way
> Through Eden took with Heavenly comfort cheered.

Such an emendation is worth many pages of analysis as evidence of literary obliquity. It may serve for the moment to conclude our account of the diversions of men of intellect and knowledge upon the corpus of Milton's work. The reader should, however, be reminded that Bentley did make one or two sound corrections of the text and that some of his exceptions to Milton's taste or artistry have been interestingly defended by the super-subtle modernist, William Empson.

We turn again to the poet-followers, a line which in the eighteenth century seemed destined to stretch out unto the crack of doom. Milton's style replaced that of Spenser as the traditional mode of utterance in English verse. It affected various individuals variously. The couplet writers, who were out of the dominant older tradition, but had temporarily taken the lead in literary fashion, were influenced only by certain externals of imagery and diction, most happily in burlesque. Thus the familiar epic monument of *Paradise Lost* is sparklingly reflected in Pope's *Rape of the Lock*, along with epic Homer and epic Virgil. The artificialities of poetic diction which infected most kinds of eighteenth-century verse have also a Miltonic reference. But here the chief transmitter was not a rhymester, but the first of the great blank verse imitators, James Thomson. A monumental study has been written by Raymond Havens on the Miltonic imitators, listing and examining literally hundreds of English works which wear their lineage in their faces. There is no point in reasoning long about them. Each writer was to the extent of his gifts and insight an admirer, but few give evidence of an acceptance of anything besides the obviously Miltonic in mood or language, imagery or idea. Thomson writes of man and nature with a noble seriousness. *The Seasons*, though not avowedly so, is more truly a Miltonic imitation than the *Castle of Indolence* is Spenserian. In the argument to *Spring*, Thomson says he will describe the season "as it affects the various parts of nature, ascending from the lower to the higher"—the Miltonic scale of being—and that he will conclude with a dissuasion from the wild and irregular passion of love, opposed to that of a pure and happy kind. The theme, then, is the same. He abounds in Miltonic phrase—"the illimitable void," "the grand aetherial bow," "lifts the light clouds sublime"—and sometimes converts a whole Miltonic passage.

> Prime cheerer, light!
> Of all material beings first, and best!
> Efflux divine.

This is nothing, really—mere poetical paraphrase—but Thomson is also capable of reproducing an authentic if minor Miltonic harmony in a not too servile way. The poetry of the closing lines of *Spring* would not have been but for Adam and Eve, yet it belongs distinctly to the later age and is quite Thomson's own as well.

> The Seasons thus,
> As ceaseless round a jarring world they roll
> Still find them happy; and consenting Spring
> Sheds her own rosy garland on their heads
> Till evening comes at last, serene and mild;
> When after the long vernal day of life,
> Enamoured more, as more remembrance swells
> With many a proof of recollected love,
> Together down they sink.

From Thomson to Cowper, from Cowper to Wordsworth, from Wordsworth to Tennyson and his Victorian succession, the story is much the same. The broad full river flows, but sometimes seems to sleep. Eliot and others have thought the Miltonic influence injurious. He is *vox et praeterea nihil*, victim of a "dissociation of sensibility," which began in English poetry with him. That is as it may be. But these continuators have been the most faithful and in many ways the best of the

If, as seems probable, the poet had glaucoma, psychic trauma may have been a cause, as well as an accompaniment, of his disease. Primary glaucoma is described as "initial retinal edema which gradually leads to irreversible atrophic changes in the nerve tissue, manifested in the late stages by peripheral contraction of the field or ring scotomas."[1] It is "not a local disease of the eyes but seems more probably the ocular manifestation of some constitutional disturbance still unknown."[2] The governing mechanism of intraocular pressure is the autonomic nervous system, interacting through the hypothalamus with the higher cerebral centres. This system is vulnerable to psychic disturbance, and such disturbance, prolonged but reversible, can eventually give rise to irreversible organic disease.

The study of this subject is new, and it is not surprising that medical opinion on Milton should hitherto have made little reference to it. Only one of the authorities cited by Miss Eleanor Brown suggests a psychogenic factor in his loss of sight.[3] This is Dr. William H. Wilmer, who finds that most of the symptoms described in the famous letter are characteristic of chronic simple glaucoma and lists as possible contributing causes: (1) temperament, (2) gout, (3) excessive use of the eyes, (4) nervous strain connected with his wife's leaving, etc., (5) age compatible with glaucoma. In the light of this opinion, students of Milton will await with interest the continuation of such investigations as those reported by Dr. David O. Harrington, "Ocular Manifestations of Psychosomatic Disorders";[4] Dr. Mark J. Schoenberg, "The Role of States of Anxiety in the Pathogenesis of Glaucoma";[5] and Helen L. Hibbeler, *Personality Patterns of White Adults with Primary Glaucoma.*[6]

The last named study, using the Minnesota Multiphasic Personality Inventory in testing twenty-seven glaucoma patients, reports a marked personality deviation in two-thirds of the cases, as compared with 5 per cent. of a normative group. No single pattern was common to all, but tendencies toward hypochondria, depression, and hysteria predominated in the

---

[1] *American Journal of Ophthalmology*, 30, 804.
[2] Duke Elder, *Textbook of Ophthalmology*, 3, 3,356.
[3] *Milton's Blindness*, New York, Columbia University Press, 1934, p. 38.
[4] *Journal of the American Medical Association*, 133, 669-74.
[5] *Archive of Ophthalmology*, 23, 96-103.
[6] Summarised; *American Journal of Ophthalmology*, 30, 181-6.

males. Where, as in a third of the cases, other members of the family had eye trouble, the degree of personality disorder was greater. The writer mentions the importance of suggestion from or identification with a loved person in the choice of a site for physical handicap. Milton's mother, according to Aubrey, had very weak eyesight and used glasses presently after thirty.

In this connection, we may recall the seriousness with which Milton's age took the idea that such afflictions were a punishment for sin. The poet's own words suggest a characteristic searching of the conscience on this point: "I am not aware of any recent or remote crime which by its atrocity can have drawn down this calamity exclusively on my head." We may see in the vehemence of his repudiation of the thought a measure of its real danger to him, and it may be that an unconscious acceptance of the intimations of the culture should be added to the factors mentioned by Dr. Wilmer as contributing to his disease. Milton's identification of himself with the blind bards of antiquity, his elaboration of the idea, "God took away outward sight to give inward vision," as a counterformula, and the final transfer of the sense of guilt to Samson should be studied as correlative parts of a single process, unique in its details with Milton but belonging to a general pattern familiar in psychological inquiry.

use of Milton's very phraseology to claim his own emancipation from the shackles of regularity.

> When this verse was first dictated to me, I considered a monotonous cadence, like that used by Milton and Shakespeare and all writers of English Blank Verse, derived from the modern bondage of Rhyming, to be a necessary and indispensable part of a verse. But I soon found that in the mouth of a true orator such monotony was not only awkward but as much a bondage as rhyme itself. I therefore have produced a variety in every line, both of cadence and number of syllables.

Blake enters the Miltonic realm of ideas and images in the earliest prophetic books, *Tiriel*, *The Book of Thel*, and *The French Revolution*. There is, however, nothing explicit until we come to *The Marriage of Heaven and Hell*, composed about 1793. The fundamental ideas of this work are at once Miltonic and anti-Miltonic. Blake deals mystically with the problem of unity and duality, recalling Milton's pantheism and his admission of the inseparability of good and evil.

> Without contraries there is no progression. Attraction and repulsion, Reason and Energy, Love and Hate are necessary to Human existence. From these contraries spring what the religious call Good and Evil. Good is the passive that obeys Reason, Evil is the active springing from Energy. Good is Heaven, Evil is Hell . . . Energy is the only life and is from the Body; and Reason is the bound and outward circumference of Energy. Energy is Eternal Delight.

The direct challenge to official Miltonic doctrine lies in his reversal of the roles of reason and desire as hero and villain in the cosmic struggle, which is also the struggle of the individual.

> Those who restrain desire do so because theirs is weak enough to be restrained; and the restrainer or reason usurps its place and governs the unwilling.
>
> And by being restrain'd, it by degrees becomes passive, till it is only the shadow of desire.
>
> The history of this is written in Paradise Lost, and the Governor or Reason is called Messiah.

Blake gets into terrific difficulties with this hypothesis, since he does not really wish to exalt desire above reason but to restore the ruins of creation by reuniting them. Hence his famous comment on Milton is in the nature of a paradox or partial truth which demands correction.

> The reason Milton wrote in fetters when he wrote of Angels and God, and at liberty when of Devils and Hell, is because he was a true poet and of the Devil's party without knowing it.

Milton, to fulfil Blake's requirement, must obviously be of both parties, as indeed he was. But Blake was in the current of reaction against the dominant rationalism of his age and felt it his mission to redress the balance. He sees clearly enough that Milton is at war with himself, as men are generally, and he champions the coursers against the charioteer. This is a new, an analytic approach. It is destined to have a history. Milton of the Christian Renaissance has at length encountered the romantic revolution, and he is found to have anticipated it—blindly.

The full weight of Blake's emotional and ideological reaction to Milton and what he was conceived to stand for can be understood only by the arduous process of interpreting the vast sequence of the Prophetic Books. The reader with time and brains to spare is referred to S. Foster Damon's volume, *William Blake, His Philosophy and Symbols*. It must suffice here to comment on the poem *Milton*, composed by Blake after his quarrel with Hayley in 1802. Professor Damon thus explains the relationship of the poem to Blake's recent painful experience:

> Blake had been pondering the whole situation, which some time before had begun to resolve its problems in a new poem. Hayley was not an accident: he was typical. It was just such poetasters as he who got the applause of the world and prevented the real artists from winning their due; and thus kept the world immersed in bad taste. But what was the cause of the Hayleys? Had they always been in power? No: there had been the days of Elizabeth, a time which would be the glory of England forever, a time of peace, of wealth spiritual and material, a time of great poets. What had happened since then? Blake saw the black cloud of Puritanism spreading over Europe, ruining the cathedrals and abbeys, closing the theatres, preaching the deadly duties

of warring upon our neighbours. It had blotted out the glories of the Renaissance, it had scorned and suppressed all beauty, had reduced religion to a system of ethics enforced by law, had turned all but a very few into fools or hypocrites, and had dealt the old spirit of "merry England" a blow from which it had never recovered. Outwardly, Puritanism had involved England in a series of wars such as would have been impossible under the pacifistic policy of Elizabeth; internally, it had brutalised the people with a cruel system of impossible ideals. Chief among these were the conceptions of absolute chastity for the unmarried, and perfect fidelity for the married. And who was responsible for Puritanism? The answer must have been unexpected even to Blake: it was his beloved Milton!

For though Milton "was a true Poet, and of the Devil's party," he was led astray by the mad logic of his times. He had supported Cromwell's schemes for making England moral by force of armed law; he had celebrated Virtue and taught that Lust was Sin; and he had reduced his Deities to Abstractions. Being the greatest man of his time, he was therefore its greatest sinner; all the more so, since his pernicious errors still were spreading.

The poem describes how Milton, "unhappy though in Heaven," perceiving his errors, returns to earth to redeem his "Sinful Emanation," i.e. his three wives and three daughters, with whom, because of his false religion, he had failed to be at one. He enters the body of Blake himself in an attempt to revise his doctrines and is united in his brain with Los, the poetic spirit. A personification of the truth which Milton has rejected, Ololon, "a virgin of twelve years," herself the immortal counterpart of the imperfect and erroneous Sixfold Emanation, descends from Eternity, like Christ becoming flesh. Her meeting with Milton-Blake symbolizes the solution of his errors. Satan opposes but in vain. The poet, now made whole, unites with God and becomes Jesus himself, "clothed with Ololon as with a garment."

Blake is the first and greatest transvaluer of Miltonic values; he is not by any means the last. It has, indeed, been so much the fashion in the nineteenth and twentieth centuries to find Milton of the Devil's party without knowing it, that a return to anything like acceptance of his official doctrine seems almost paradoxical. Such a return, in so far as it is part of an effort to see Milton clearly in his cultural pattern, is a valuable corrective of romantic and revolutionary eccentricity. It does not quite give the poet the fit audience for which he asked—a more daring and imaginative Marvell, a saner and less rebellious Blake. And the time has indeed gone by when such an audience is at all conceivable.

Poetically, Meredith's sonnet "Lucifer in Starlight," which accepts the ethical order of *Paradise Lost* but is silent regarding any providential order, salvages as much as can be salvaged by the modern mind of Milton's cosmic thought. And even this expression is palpably Victorian. T. S. Eliot, speaking as one who has kept watch over the destinies of English poetry, believes that contemporary writers may now safely study Milton's verse, as they could not a few decades ago when the "Chinese wall" which he erected was still unbroken. This is doubtless so. But such study will hardly commend itself or bear important fruit without a warmer attitude toward the Miltonic personality and ideal than any of the moderns exhibit.

The truth is that Milton, despite the wish so often voiced that he might be living at this hour, is truly of the past. We may perhaps see him objectively, to use a phrase of Professor Griersou's, as a great soul in a great and troubled age. But we must judge him humanly in error and capable only of misleading if he leads at all. He was not really free himself and without being so he could not enfranchise others. To say this is not to deny that some portion of the world's majesty is available through him as through no other poet. Nor is it to declare meaningless the strength of his personality and the virtue of his intent. Mankind is still baffled by its weaknesses, but it is still resolved against its own destruction. Milton's essentially tragic struggle, by making humanity better understand its own resources, has helped give sinew to this resolve.

POSTSCRIPT

LOOKING BACK ON WHAT is written in Chapters Five and Six regarding the physical and moral crisis of Milton's middle life, I feel that I cannot leave the subject without a reference to the bearing on it of recent research in psychosomatic medicine.

INDEX

INDEX